Jami

**The Book of Joseph and Zuleikhá**

Jami

**The Book of Joseph and Zuleikhá**

ISBN/EAN: 9783337424527

Printed in Europe, USA, Canada, Australia, Japan

Cover: Foto ©Lupo / pixelio.de

More available books at **www.hansebooks.com**

کتابِ
یوسف و زلیخا

# THE BOOK

OF

# JOSEPH AND ZULEIKHÁ

BY

MULLÁNÁ ABDULRAHMÁN JÁMÍ.

*HISTORICAL ROMANTIC PERSIAN POEM.*

TRANSLATED INTO ENGLISH VERSE BY

ALEXANDER ROGERS,

LATE BOMBAY CIVIL SERVICE; EDITOR OF THE "BUSTÁN"; TRANSLATOR OF
"PERSIAN PLAYS", "REINEKE FUCHS", ETC.

LONDON:
DAVID NUTT, 270, 271, STRAND.
1892.

# ERRATA.

Page 11, line 10 from bottom, *for* "heav'n" *read* "heaven".

Page 46, line 7, *for* "making" *read* "waking".

Page 168, line 10 from bottom, *change to*
"Wool on his silver body be not worn."

Page 193, line 12 from top, *change to*
"Her eye of blood a fountain would disclose."

# PREFACE.

THE poet Nasr-ul din Abdúlrahmán, called Jámi, from having been born in the town of Jám in Khorasán, was one of the most celebrated and prolific of Persian poets. Of his writings, the poem of *Yusuf and Zuleikha*, the latter commonly known as the wife of Potiphar, into whose house Joseph was sold as a slave in Egypt, is the most widely known and most appreciated in the Eastern world, especially among Mussulmans. Joseph is esteemed by them a type of manly beauty and virtue. Whereas the Jewish Scriptures in the Old Testament mention little in connection with him and Potiphar's wife but the fact of the temptation of the former, his resistance to it, and his consequent imprisonment, this poem enters into the details of the manner in which the latter became acquainted with Joseph in three dreams, in the last of which he informed her, rather prematurely, that he was Vazír of Egypt. As her health was suffering from her unrequited longing for Joseph, her father sends an embassy to Egypt to the Vazír to inform him of Zuleikha's state of mind, and obtains his consent to her marriage with him. The Vazír meets her on the road, and there Zuleikha, looking through a hole made by her nurse in the tent, finds, to her despair, that he is not Joseph. She is, however, received with all honour in Egypt. The poet then leads the reader to Canaan, and, after brief references to Adam and the patriarchs, relates the early history of Joseph, the hatred of his brothers to him on account of the dreams foretelling his future superiority over them, their putting him into a well, and finally selling him into slavery. When he is put up for sale in the market, Zuleikha sees and recognizes him, and, doubling other people's offers, obliges the Vazír to purchase him. Then commences the account of her long and vain pursuit of him, until her nurse persuades her to allow her to build a palace in which wherever Joseph might look—on the walls, on the roofs, or on the floors—he might see himself pictured with Zuleikha in his arms. The palace completed, she leads him into it, and urges their union with every blandishment. He is on the point of yielding, when he sees something behind a curtain, which she informs him is the idol to which she is in the habit of praying, and which she has concealed behind a curtain that it may not see what she is doing. Horrified at this, he feels the position in which he has placed himself, and tries to escape ; but Zuleikha overtakes him at the entrance, and tears his vest down behind. As he goes out, the Vazír meets him and leads him back to Zuleikha, who imagines he has betrayed her, and at once makes a counter-accusation against him, on which the Vazír, notwithstanding his denial of the charge, sends him to prison. Then a miraculous event is introduced, in which a child of two years of age is made to point out to the Vazír that, if Joseph is innocent, his vest will be found to have been torn from behind; but, if he is guilty, it will have been torn in front. Put to this test, Joseph's innocence is established, and he is released. One or two episodes are now introduced, which do not interfere with the main thread of the story. Zuleikha persuades the Vazír to imprison Joseph again, to hide the disgrace she has been brought to; and she still feeds her futile flame for him by visiting him secretly in prison by night, and looking by day at the walls that confine him. Then follow the interpretation by Joseph of the dreams of two of his fellow-prisoners, and its accomplishment by the death of one and the restoration of the other to favour. The king of Egypt dreams his two dreams of the seven fat and seven lean kine, and the seven fat and lean sheaves of corn. Joseph is sent for to interpret them; and, Zuleikha having admitted her guilt, he is restored to honour, and entrusted with the government of the land. The Vazír dies, and Zuleikha, being left in poverty, pines away for Joseph's love, and loses her beauty and her eyesight. She builds a reed-hut by the way-side, that she may hear him passing by, and at last gains admittance into his presence, and tells him who she is. He is moved with compassion, and, at her request, prays that her youth and beauty may be restored. This miracle takes place, and she again pleads for union with him. He consents to this on being directly inspired by the angel Gabriel. The marriage happily takes place, and the pair are blessed with offspring. Finally, Joseph dies, and Zuleikha also, after tearing out her own eyes in grief. The poem winds up with a diatribe against the fickleness of fortune, a homily addressed to the poet's son, and the winding up of the book with praise to God for its accomplishment, in which the date of its completion is given as in the Hijri year 898, or A.D. 1492.

Before the actual tale is commenced, a great deal of the preliminary writing common to Oriental poets has to be waded through. This has all been translated, with the exception of a few couplets in praise of Sultan Hussein, one of Jámi's patrons, as it not only contains some beautiful passages, but shows the child-like faith of the best type of Moslems, their real piety, and their devotedness to their religion. For this reason it will quite repay perusal.

It has not been a light task for the translator to put into rhyme over 7,000 couplets, whilst adhering to the literal meaning of the original. The attention paid to the latter point will, he trusts, prove a sufficient excuse for any want of smoothness the critic may find in the former. The partial translations into English that he has seen were far too free to be of use to students in studying the Persian, and Rosenzweig's edition, printed in 1824, in addition to being inaccurate in many instances, is in German, and therefore inaccessible to many in England, and more in India. The latter is, however, entitled to the present translator's warm acknowledgments for assistance in the elucidation of many obscure passages.

The text made use of in this translation is the lithographed edition of Naval Kishor, published at Lakhnáo, the Persian notes in the margin of which have been found of much use. The transliteration of Persian words in the notes has been carried out on the Hunterian system, but the sounds of the "ye" and "váo" are those used in Persia—that is, "ee" and "oo", and not "é" and "o", as in India.

To those who have enabled the translator to bring out this work, which has been one of love for him, by their kind subscriptions for copies, he tenders his grateful thanks, and trusts they will not be disappointed.

THE TRANSLATOR.

# YUSUF AND ZULEIKHÁ.

# YUSUF AND ZULEIKHA.

 GOD! the rosebud of my hope unclose,
Show from th' eternal garden me a rose;
With smiles from that bud's lip my garden
    fill:
Into my brain that rose's scent distil.
Of restless trouble in this resting-place
Make me to know Thy own abiding grace.
With thoughts of gratitude full fill my mind;
Grant to Thy praise my tongue may be inclined.
Good days (1) with wisdom's guidance give to me;
Bestow in realm of speech the victory.
Of virtue full Thou didst a heart bestow:
That heart's wealth may my tongue both weigh and know.
My nature's musk-bag (2) it was Thou didst shred;
From Kâf to Kâf (3) make me musk-perfume shed.
With verse a sweet tongue may my reed be found,
And may my book shed amber perfume round.
The word's accomplishment I cannot find, (4)
'Naught of the book but name is left behind;
And in this tavern, with its tales so sweet,
Of that fair air no echo do I meet.
My comrades drank the wine, and they are gone;
They left the taverns empty, and are gone!
And ripened by this vain feast none I see,
A cup of that wine on whose hand may be.

Of wine and of cupbearer's bowl bereft,
For me but sorrow there is nothing left.
Come, Jámi, bashfulness now lay aside;
Whate'er thou hast, or clear or dregs, provide. (4)

## The Opening of the Book in the One-Name.

The amulet of souls, to Him I cry,
On tongues whose praises as swords' lustre lie, (5)
For from His Name the tongue its object gains, (6)
And dew from fountain of His grace obtains.
Through Whom to wisdom do themselves declare
A thousand subtle points fine as a hair.
For that hair's sake the tongue a comb is made,
The teeth in order as the comb's teeth laid.
The Highest God, eternal wisdom, hail!
Strength to the weak to give Who dost not fail;
To heaven's host (7) with stars Who givest light,
The earth with men as stars Who makest bright;
Of elements upon the four walls based,
Of the revolving sphere the vault hast placed;
The musk-bag on the rosebud's navel bound,
Round beauteous rose-bush rosy jewels wound;
For brides of spring Who hast fine raiment wrought,
The cypress on the stream its stature taught,
Who dost the lofty wind with grandeur crown,
And him himself who fancies castest down,—
To drunkards of the cup dost pardon give,
And back to Grace old hypocrites receive;
Their friend the night who watchful pass away,
His comrade who in labour spends the day,—
Of ocean of Whose Grace the spring-cloud born
Gives water to both jessamine and thorn;
The autumn wind from Whose mine's bounty-store
Rich scatters gold upon the meadow's floor,—

Who with His sweets the good man's palate fills
Poison in bitter-tongued one's joy distils.
His own existence is the brilliant sun,
Whence for each separate atom light is won.
From sun and moon His face should He e'er hide,
Their ball to non-existence would subside.
He is, and gave us being in His Grace,
Our non-existence did with life replace.
By hundred paths of fancy or of sense
From deepest earth up to the heav'n immense,
Should men ascend, or hurry down with speed, (8)
The least from His command are they not freed.
His essence from all "How" and "Why" is free,
Far freer than or low or high may be. (8)
From His divinity are "How" and "Why",
Before His majesty low are the high.
Before Him wisdom aye perplexed remains,
Nor search upon His road a footing gains. (9)
Towards us should He not advance in Grace,
Each moment farther are we from His face.
When of His majesty the ringing cry,
In the eternal palace echoes high,
At their own folly are the angels vexed,
And at its own distraction heaven's perplexed.
'Twere better we, a handful steeped in lust,
Should from lust's mirror wipe away the rust,
Of our own being should forgetful be,
And henceforth sink of silence on the knee.

## THE SETTING FORTH IN ORDER OF THE PROOFS OF THE REAL EXISTENCE OF THE MOST HIGH, AND TAKING DELIGHT IN REFLECTING THEREON.

O heart, how long 'neath this inconstant sphere
Wilt thou with dust play, as do children here?

Thou 'rt that audacious bird brought up with care,
Beyond this sphere who dost thy nest prepare.
Why to this nest art thou becoming strange?
Like base owl why dost in this desert range?
Shake from thy feathers off this earthly leav'n,
And soar up to the battlement of heav'n.
See, the blue fringes (10) in the dance are whirled,
The mantles shedding light throughout the world,
Revolving all by night as well as day,
Intent to seize of victory the way,
With its own motion each advancing still,
Dancing as ball struck by the mace of will,
One (11) from the West turns tow'rds the Eastern mark;—
One in the West will overwhelm his bark;
To day's assembly one gives heat and light,
Whilst one illuminates the throng of night.
One (12) to his word the form of fortune lends,
Whilst (12) of good luck the rope another rends.
All on the road press forward with such zest,
That from their movement they will never rest.
Not wearied out by labour of their way,
For foot no rest, in loins no pain have they.
Who knows to what affair such energy they lend,
Or towards whom their faces all they bend?
Each (13) moment though some new form they assume,
Painters (13) to be would none of them presume.
In doubt's hand how long wilt thou place the rein?
"This is my God" (14) to each repeat again.
Like God's friend, (15) strike of certainty the door:
"I love not those that set," (16) cry more and more.
Toward one face above thy face inclined,
Doubt and suspicion banish from thy mind.
Behold and name One only; but One own:
Desire, and read, and seek for One alone.
Tow'rds Him a road from ev'ry atom lies
His being's evidence each multiplies.

The hearts of all wise men a writing bear:
"Pictures to paint a Painter must be there."
On tablets though a thousand forms they write,
Without a scribe is not one *Aleph* right,
And no brick in this desert can one find
Without a model of a perfect kind.
Upon each brick the finger's pen has writ,
That hand of some wise man has fashioned it.
This word inscribed upon each bricklet's face,
Of the Brick-maker's self thou hast the trace. (17)
Creation manifest to all mankind,
To the Creator how turns not thy mind?
Turn to the Worker, seen His work, thy face,
And in the work itself the Worker trace.
In that last moment whence no man can fly,
Thy case may only with that Worker lie.
Bend upon Him the look of thy desire;
For blest end of thy case to Him aspire.

### Lifting up of the Hand in Prayer for Aid to the Needy.

O God, from this existence we were free;
Terror of non-existence none had we.
Through Thee from naught to being we arose;—
Thou water and clay's fetters didst impose;
From impotency's weakness didst Thou save,
And us in place of folly wisdom gave.
A book, too, hast Thou sent where all is plain
What we should do, from what we should abstain.
Together good and bad did we confound,—
Failing at times, at times transgressed all bound,
The path of Thy commands did not pursue,
Our footsteps slipped in what we should not do.
Constant in favour's way dost Thou abide;
Salvation's light from us Thou didst not hide.

Though in Thy grace Thou hidest not the light,
What better, since we strive not, is our plight?
At our own want of earnestness we sigh:
Give us Thy grace, that we our best may try.
Both are submerged, the ignorant and wise:
What between ignorance and wisdom lies?
With evil purpose that lust would impose,
The way of good deeds to us do not close,
But in our sighing, in our narrow strait,
To mercy's road, oh! open us a gate—
Be tow'rds Thy temple on that road our guide,
And to the true faith bear us by Thy side.

### The Reservation of Supplication to the Ruler for Aid to Companions and Associates.

I am that bird for whom thy grain is spread,
And whose enchantment is the charm I dread.
For my concerns dost thou arrange before,—
Thou openest for me of grace the door.
My service to approve the favour thine,
In trust to worship is the honour mine.
On thy path *Surma*-rubbed (18) my forehead lies;
Thou hast rubbed *Surma* on my longing eyes.
Loos'ning my tongue thy praises to express, (19)
Thy name's love on my heart didst Thou impress.
A morsel mild and luscious to the taste
Within my mouth Thou from my tongue hast placed
One to the teeth that never causes strain,
Nor the throat swallowing feels any pain.
In thanks for this my words with sweetness bless;
Sweeten my acts and save from bitterness.
To evil words turn not my tongue for me;
Let not my tongue become my misery.

If in my pen a word of evil lies,
Question of " how " and " wherefore" whence may rise,
Draw through my evil word a pardoning pen ;
Cast me, like seed, not into strife again.
I am as grass in Thy reliance reared,
Of mud and water by Thy own hand cleared :
Through ill desire my head turns every way,
My foot still clinging to Thy street in clay.
That clay (20) that to my foot in thy street clings
Excels the rose (20) of Thee no scent that brings.
As this grove's bud grant me a single heart,
And as the tulip but one scar impart.
Upon this road a single heart is gain,—
To have a double heart can be but vain.
The single kernelled *pastah* (21) teeth do not oppress,
As they the almonds do two kernels that possess.
A hundred grains the ear bears in its breast ;
For grain its head is by the knife (22) oppressed.
Buds from the thorn that single grow up strong
From a thousand prickles do not suffer wrong—
Beyond all limit though my sins be found,
Far more than these will aye Thy grace abound.
Two hundred harvests though my fault should be,
But one sigh's lightning burns them up for me.
Though of my sins a hundred books full lie,
Thou mayest wash them from my tearful eye.
For each rose-cheek that tinged my eye with red,
My blood is now from ev'ry eyelash shed.
That face's image wash I from my eye,
And thus upon my face blood tears must lie.
Towards disgrace though much my look has striv'n,
In my affair great glory tears have giv'n.
My own two eyes are rivers of regret,
Enough of honour till the Judgment yet.
That from this commerce (23) profit I may gain,
Bear to the Prophet of my song the strain.

## THE PRAISE OF THE LORD OF CREATED THINGS, THE CHIEF OF BEINGS, THE BLESSING OF ALLAH BE ON HIM AND HIS DESCENDANTS, WITH PEACE.

He who with pen Mohammad's name has named,
Girdle and collar of its "*Mim*" (24) has framed.
The word erased from non-existence' board,
A ring for "*mulk*" and "*malak*" (25) would afford.
Can wisdom with all knowledge know what's hid
In that so secret "*Há*"? (26) Now God forbid!
In this six-sided sphere through it is manifest
Th' eight-sided grove of gardens (27) eight possessed.
With the *Dál's* (28) anklet when his foot he decked,
Did he the Faithful 'neath his feet subject.
In being's Council Hall, ah! what a name!
No other one has e'er excelled its fame.
Should my tongue chant one letter of the whole,
With pleasure would be filled my heart and soul.
Since such the name, what must its bearer be?
Far more illustrious than all is he.
The race of Adam in the earth are famed;
Most noble he of all who great are named.
God him the chief of every ruler made,
The headship of all prophets on him laid.
On being's road when Adam first did pace,
He spoke with love of his morn-bright'ning face.
Had he the road not, generous, open made,
When on the Mount (29) had Noah's ark been stayed?
God's friend obtained from him the balmy air
Which made the fire (30) for him a garden fair.
Messiah of his coming gave the tidings bright,
And Moses (31) from his torch, too, looked for light.
From Canaan's realm a slave with money bought,
In Egypt to high place was Joseph brought.

When Sáleh (32) from the vale his camel drew,
The *Muhmil* (33) brought to mind, both happy grew.
A graceful cypress of faith's garden he,
A pheasant from the grove of purity,
The heav'ns are based upon his stature tall ;
Life to dead bones his lip will aye recall.
The cloud above him is the *Chutter's* (34) shade,
As golden dome the sun above his head.
His signal dart (35) when on the round moon's face
He struck with finger of miraculous grace ;
Its "*Mim*" (35) asunder as two "*Nuns*" (35) was laid,
Forty was by his thumb two fifties made.
The pen since he himself held in his hand,
To split the moon his finger wrote command.
He did not write, yet with his reed in haste
Both Pentateuch and Gospel (36) were defaced.
His graceful cypress shadow never knew,
Yet did his grateful shade the world renew.
His dignity above all shadow lies,
And in his shadow are both earth and skies.
His body's essence of pure spirit made,
On earth none ever saw his spirit's shade.
Both earth and heav'n him with their shade supply,
And yet beneath his fort as shadows lie.
Wounded his lip by stone from foemen's hand, (37)
Their backs were broken with a little sand.
Though their crude eyes were blinded by the same,
As bright with *Surma* Islam's eye became.
His mouth, that box of gems of pearly hue
With blood into a box of coral grew.
Resembling a *dinár* in mildness wise,
The stone proved him, as gold the touchstone tries.
When by that stone as touchstone proved was he,
There was no coin of greater purity.
To build the wall of faith was aye his aim ;
And his four friends (38) in it four gates became.

Who in religion's road has suffered pain,
Who for each ill a med'cine did not gain?
Soul's med'cine, Jámi, be their pain to thee!
His heart by their grief ever nourished be!

## The Ascent of the Asylum of Prophecy, on whom and his Family be the Blessing of Allah and Peace.

The preface to good fortune's morn, one night,
Than blessing more the day that renders bright,—
The "Night of Pow'r" (39) an image of its might,
The full-moon night a charter of its light;
Its jet-black tresses even Huris (40) slight;
Its forehead's white star is a light on light.
The Zephyr combed its locks of spikenard hue,
Its air made droplets of the tears of dew.
With fixed stars' nail the planets' sphere that whirled
Had closed ill-fortune's gates against the world.
The wolf and sheep had both together slept,
And company the deer and lion kept.
The lip as smiling morn was with delight;
The day of trouble fled away all night.
Before that night the lamp (41) that men beheld,
By men in honour worthy to be held,
Since fortune by his foes from him was kept,
In Ummcháni's (42) house of wealth he slept.
To rest a pillow on the ground he laid,
A cradle for that tender life the earth he made.
His heart awake, his eye in sleep so sweet
As fortune's eye in dream might never meet.
Sudden the mighty Námus (43) entered in,
More quick in movement than this peacock green. (44)
"Arise," he rubbed him with his wing, and said:
"Thy dream to-night has thee to fortune led.

Out of this sleeping-place thy baggage bear,
Lively who hast earth's fortune in thy care—
Thy road to heaven I have now prepared
To bring Burák, (45) the lightning-paced, have cared."
Wind-like upon the face of earth he scours,
Like the blessed *Humá* (46) in the air he tow'rs.
With philosophic wisdom he moves round the heav'n,
To him to mete earth as geometer is giv'n.
Upon his reins none lays his hand as yet,
And in his stirrup no foot has been set.
From idols as the heart away that flies,
The scar of trouble never saw his thighs.
Did he a stable want wherein to feed,
The heav'ns were busy to supply his need.
His tender back from saddle's pain is free;
And pain from none his saddle's back may see.
Religion's lord when from this fortune's place
He tow'rds the narrow saddle moved with grace,
Of holy ones in heav'n the voice was raised:
"Who made his slave ascend His name be praised!" (47)
From Mecca whilst Burak in lightning pace
Struck with his hoof *dirams* (48) on the Aksa's (48) face.
A half or less than half a moment stayed,
A door-ring with his hoof's round cup he made. (49)
In that mosque chief of prophets (50) he became,
Leader in rank of former ones of fame.
As thence he mounted tow'rds the heav'n blue
The moon a halo round about him threw;
Then slavery's brand upon its brow it laid,
And in this wise his name more perfect made.
Then higher rising still, upon the head
Of Mercury (51) the choicest gifts he shed.
Thence as he rose to Zuhrah (52) further on,
The border of his truth she seized upon.
To wash his foot with this rose-water pure,
Did the fourth heaven bring him out an ewer. (53)

To the fifth heaven when his steed attained,
Mars kissed its hoof and profit thence obtained,
From his red lip on Jove (54) then pearls he shed,
And filled his hand (54) full of the gems he spread.
When his shoes rubbed upon the seventh sphere,
Were Saturn's (55) difficulties all made clear.
Thence on the *Sidrah's* (56) branch would he alight,
And Gabriel's wing was weary with its flight.
To the eighth heaven as he then moved on,
Through him the fixed star's eye more brightly shone.
The Pleiads and the Daughters of the Bier (57)
In verse and prose ring out his praises here.
Glad at his face's light, the Eagle, (58) too,
Like to the moth, around him circling flew.
With joy at his fair cypress-form as well
Down at his feet the Lyre (59) as shadow fell.
In pleasing thought to the Atlas (60) sphere he flew,
Himself down at his feet then Atlas threw.
To aid, *Saráfíl*, (61) from his ambush sprung,
A room of green (62) as litter round him flung.
And when the green had honour from him known,
Quickly there took him from its hand the Throne. (63)
Left with this sphere his body as a rag, (64)
To robeless nothingness he raised his flag.
His draughtsman from the board he saved with force: (65)
Beyond the narrow space he leapt his horse.
From this low vestibule they bore his clay
Upon that lofty shrine his hand to lay.
He found a place from all space that was freed,
To body not forbid, nor soul indeed.
Of fate antiquity washed off the rust; (66)
The possible by need aside was thrust. (66)
But he remained free from constraint of all, (67)
Free both of what is great and what is small.
He saw what was beyond the bounds of sight.
Ask me no farther of what took place that night.

No question is there there of "how?" "how long?"
Hold back from what is one or more thy tongue.
There words unspoken by a voice he heard,
Mystery on mystery, secret word on word.
Nor tongue nor palate is of it aware,
Nor speech nor explanation is there there.
The soul's ear had but wind to understand;
To reach its sense the heart was short of hand.
Too narrow for it wisdom's clothes became,
And in its desert learning's steed grew lame.
Too high for sight or hearing to attain,
From speaking of it must the tongue refrain.
Place no foot, Jámi, thou beyond thy bound;
Withdraw from this soul-wearing ocean's round.
Words in this martyrs' place speak none at all:
Place seals upon thy words, for God knows all.

## THE CLOTHING ONESELF WITH HUMILITY, AND BEGGING FOR INTERCESSION.

By absence the world's weary soul is torn:
To us, God's prophet, be thy mercy borne!
On both worlds to have mercy is't not Thine?
Why dost thou careless sit of those that pine? (68)
O moist, fresh tulip, from the dust arise!
How long, Narcissus, shall sleep hold thy eyes?
Thy head from out the shroud of *Yaman* (69) raise;
Thy face is as of life the morning rays—
Turn into day for us this doleful night,
And with thy countenance our day make bright.
An amber-scented robe around thee wind,
And on thy head a camphored turban bind.
Let from thy head fall down thy waving hair;
Round thy fair cypress' foot a shade prepare.
Of *Taï'f's* (70) skins make for thy foot a shoe,
And of our souls' ropes latchets for it, too.

Experienced men are carpets in thy street,
And would as carpets kiss thy blessèd feet.
From chamber to the holy plain thy foot be led;
Of those who kiss thy road stand on the head.
Assist thou those who low before thee lie;
To those who give their hearts with love reply.
Though in crimes' ocean we immersed are all,
Dry-lipped in dust upon thy road we fall.
'Tis well Thou art the cloud of grace, and why?
That sometimes on the thirsty thou mayst cast an eye.
Blessed we when we approach thee through thy dust,
And thy streets' dust into our eye have thrust.
Towards thy mosque we bow in grateful prayer,
And to thy lamp as moths our souls repair.
Bold wandering among thy groves we went;
Cage-like, our heart in many holes was rent.
Out of their cloud, from eyes that never slept,
On thy grove's holy threshold tears we wept.
The dust we swept at times from off that plain,
Or gathered thorns and rubbish thence again.
With that light blackness to our eyes impart,
With this we lay a plaster on our heart.
Towards Thy pulpit then we took our way,
From off our face in gold its foot to lay. (71)
From Thy *Mehrab*, (72) we sought our aim in prayer,
And with our eye's blood washed Thy threshold there.
We stood upright at ev'ry pillar's base,
And as the righteous prayed Thee for Thy grace.
With happy hearts, though scarred with Thy desire,
We set the candles with our hearts on fire.
Our bodies though dust of that holy plain,
Thank God, our souls may ever there remain.
Helpless am I through breath of self-conceit;
Look on my feebleness and pardon mete.
Should like Thy favour nothing us befriend,
Naught could we bring to a successful end.

Ill fate will throw us off our proper way ;
For God's sake hear us when to God we pray,
Assurance of our life that He bestow,
And we in things of Faith may firmness know.
Of Judgment when the dread shall rise at last,
He fire upon our honour may not cast,
But give, though we have strayed from right indeed,
Command to thee for us to intercede ;
Thy people's ball, with bowed head as a mace,
Thou mayest bring to mediation's place ;
That Jámi's business, through thy favour meet,
The scoff of others, may be made complete.


SEEKING A BLESSING BY RECITING THE NAME OF
KHÁJAH UBEIDULLAH IHRAR, (73) THE SAINT
AND HIS OWN SPIRITUAL GUIDE.

Best preface to the book of wretched men,
The ink that flows off from our master's pen.
None of the painters could a picture limn,
On great men's tablet wonderful, like him.
In royal garb when poverty there comes,
Through Ubeidullah's management it comes.
Mark of true poverty on whom is seen,
He lordship's tunic draws his feet between.
Of his own will he poverty who knows,
His *khirkah* (74) on his form to tunic (74) grows.
In his eyes is the world a simple field ;
He loves the produce only it should yield.
The grain, contemptible in mortal's eyes,
Comes to his net straight down from Paradise,
And in a thousand fields the seed he sows
Will give food as to Paradise he goes.
Seed in this field he scatters far and wide,
In the next world his granaries to provide.

What's a dust handful on the road to him,
To whom a pinch of dust the world would seem?
The dust-pinch on the road (75) that he may see,
Whence on his skirt defilement can it be?
Be it the Kaiser or Faghfour (76) of Chín,
Both equally his ears of grain will glean.
Wherever upon tillage he is bent,
Just like his cattle, he is aye content.
And if his gracious favour should allow,
Heaven and earth's bulls would together plough. (77)
His bounteous grace the harvest-corn to tread
From Taurus down the heavenly Bull has led.
Behold the heav'n with bright stars sprinkled o'er,
As sieves of grain out of His harvest store.
Shouldst to His husbandry thou not say nay,
'Twould be as if "Great Spirit!" thou shouldst say. (78)
Compound or simple though the earth may be,
All is embraced within His clemency.
Grass from His bounty profit gains at length,
And tow'rds perfection reaches in His strength.
Can this that mighty spirit's value raise?
And of it aught but blame can be this praise?
Higher than thought the place for him to dwell,
Beyond the faculty of tongue to tell.
His heart a sea of Allah's mysteries:
One drop alone 'twixt full and new moon (79) lies.
And when tumultuously swells the sea,
How can a mere drop's motion patent be?
When an observer sits with fast-closed eye,
Both worlds forgets his heart's eye by-and-bye.
Yet sees he One, by no one who is bound,
And thus in trivial straits is never found. (80)
Above both and below His face is shown:
In small as well as great Him must we own.
In His existence one oneself blots out,
And looks on being two with eye of doubt.

Should in the sea a drop to nothing turn,
How can its presence one again discern?
Ah! happy those upon his dust who lie,
Heart and soul to his saddle-straps that tie!
All in his capital are prosp'rous made;—
All in his light are blotted from his shade.
Oh! from the world may not his shade take flight;—
Of him deprived day's eye is void of light.
The years of angel-natured nobles free,
May they than heaven's circlings longer be.
Those of his sons especially of name, (82)
Who of his virtues great enjoy the fame,
In this begilded and rust-coloured sphere,
Their grace and generosity appear!
May this world be the mirror of their aim,
Their feet in this light win a martyr's fame!


TO SET FORTH THAT EVERY ONE FROM BEAUTY
AND LOVE IS A BIRD FLOWN OUT OF THE NEST OF
UNITY, AND THAT HAS RESTED IN THE THICKET
OF THE MANIFESTATION OF PLURALITY.

In that lone place in which no life had been revealed,
The world in non-existence' corner lay concealed,
Of no pair to itself this being thought,
Nor "we" and "thou" into its speech had brought.
Beauty that needed no exhibitor to show,
And manifested to itself by its own glow.
Of unseen bridal chamber beauty she,
Her skirt of sin from all suspicion free.
Never might mirror back reflect her face,
Nor the comb's hand her locks in order place.
The zephyr of her hair ne'er broke a thread,
Nor *Surma* dust around her eye was spread.
The spikenard (83) with her Rose might never blend,
Nor beauty to that rose her verdure lend.

Her face of down and ev'ry mole was free,
Nor could the eye her ev'n in fancy see.
But from herself she heard a charmer's voice,
And for herself she threw a lover's dice. (84)
And yet, wherever loveliness holds sway,
A beauty with a veil will not away,
For to a beauty modesty's a bore;
She's at the window if you close the door.
Behold the tulip in the time of spring,
How sweetly in the hills 'tis blossoming;
Beneath the rock it splits its flow'r in twain,
And in this wise it makes its beauty plain.
Should now this secret penetrate thy mind
(Such thread of mysteries you rarely find),
Thou canst not ever drive away the thought:
In speech or writing 'twill be forward brought.
Wherever beauty is 'twill this demand:
Beauty on this took from of old its stand.
It pitched its tent the holy realm outside,
Displaying to all souls and spheres its pride.
In ev'ry mirror (85) it displayed its face;
It conversation held in every place.
On king and angel there flashed out its flame, (86)
Angels as whirling spheres perplexed became.
All heav'nly things that in the pure rejoice
Incontinently raised their holy voice,
And by the divers (87) in the sea of heav'n
Shouts of " Praise to the Angels' Lord" (88) were giv'n.
Of atoms of the earth were mirrors made;
On each reflected was their faces' shade.
A ray of light fell thence upon the rose,
And in the nightingale's heart tumult rose.
Itself the candle with that fire illumed;
In each abode a hundred moths consumed— (89)
When with its light the sun in splendour blazed,
Out of the flood its head the lotus raised—

When Leila with its face adorned her cheek,
Must Majnoon for her hair in phrensy seek—
With sugared smile when Shirin's lips would part,
It ravished Farhad's life, Parviz's heart.
Beauty displays itself in every place,
Though it be veiled from earthly lover's face. (90)
When Canaan's moon raised from its breast its head,
Out of Zuleikha's soul her senses fled— (90)
It holds each hiding veil that thou mayst see :
What renders captive hearts is its decree.
In love for her alone the heart can live,
Strength to the soul her love alone can give.
The heart with longing to the fair that turns,
Knowing or not, for her with passion burns.
Beware! make no mistake or e'er aver :
"Love lies with us, and goodness rests with her."
Mirror art thou : what decks the glass is she :
Whilst thou art hid, she ever clear will be.
As thou art good and art approved in love,
In thee appears what first in her did move.
If thou look well, the mirror's self is she,
Not treasure only, but the treasury.
For me and thee, our business here is naught ;
We can have nothing here but futile thought.
Be still! The tale will not continue long,
And no interpreter requires her tongue.
'Twere better we in love should still remain :
Without this converse we are all in vain.

### The Palm Tree of setting forth the Excellence of Being in Love, and the Branch of the Commencement of the Reason for the Composition of the Book to Attach to it.

That heart's no heart that is without love's pain :
Without it bodies moistened clay remain.

Tow'rds passion's pain thy face turn from the earth;
The world of passion is a world of mirth.
Of love's sweet pain may never heart be free,
On earth without love may man never be.
With passion's tumult full of strife the world,
The heav'ns from love's desire (91) are madly whirled.
Be passion's captive! Be this aye the thought,
That all the pious this pursuit have sought.
Be passion's captive, that thou mayst be free;
Lay on thy breast its burden, glad to be.
Love's wine with warmth and ardency will bless:
All else brings melancholy selfishness.
Freshness may lovers in love's memory claim;
In its recital aye gain greater fame.
Had Majnun of this cup not drunk the wine,
How in both worlds would thus his glory shine?
Both wise and good full many men have gone,
Who of love's passion naught have ever known,—
Their name remains not, and no trace as well;
In time's hand of them there's no tale to tell.
Sweet and melodious there is many a bird,
Whose tale from people's lips is never heard.
When feeling people tell of love the tale,
They speak of moths and of the nightingale. (92)
Though in the world thou many things essay,
Love only takes thee from thyself away.
Turn not thy face from love, though it be feigned;
Access to God's truth through it may be gained,
On board (93) the alphabet hast thou not read,
To learn the Korán how canst thou be led?
A pupil to his *Pír* (94) I once heard say,
That he should help him in the righteous way.
" Thy foot love's path has never trod," said he.
" Go, be a lover: then come back to me.
" Of form the wine-cup until thou hast quaffed,
" Thou canst not taste of mystery the draught. (95)

"But in the form (96) thou shouldest not delay,
"Across the bridge but quickly take thy way.
"If at the stage thou wouldst lay down thy load,
"Thou shouldst not stand upon the bridge's road.
"Thanks be to God that, living in this cell, (97)
"Light on my love's path my footsteps ever fell.
"Without musk saw the nurse my navel's cord,—
"She quickly cut it of love with the sword.
"When to my lip my mother placed her breast,
"Love's sorrow in my mouth with milk she pressed.
"Though now my hair of milk is as the hue,
"That passion's flavour to my heart clings, too.
"Nothing in age and youth compares with love,
"And me its magic power will ever move.
"Jámi, since thou in love art growing gray,
"Be merry still, and in love pass away.
"Now of love's wantonness a tale relate,
"That in the world thy traces may be great.
"With point-creating pen a figure trace
"That when thou goest still may keep its place."
From love when came this voice my ear to greet,
My sense met her without (98) with honour meet.
The girdle of obedience on my soul I bound,
And of enchantment a new mode I found.
Now if God give me favour, I agree,
And if my palm of truth should fruitful be,
Love's pain will I depict in subtle wise,
That wit shall burn the baggage of the wise—
Smoke will I spread throughout the azure sphere,
And the stars' eyes shall fill the swelling tear;
The word on such foundation will I place,
That it shall fill my heaven with thy grace.

## The Gathering of the Nosegay of Flowers from the Mead of Excellencies of Love, and the Twisting upon it of the Finishing String of the Reason for Compiling the Book.

The word's the preface of the book of love,
It is the new wine, too, of passion's grove.
Whatever, old or new, has borne the earth,
Has in the word, the wise man says, its birth.
No manager has wisdom like the word;
Equal memento has the world ne'er heard—
Of *Káf* and *Nún* (99) the word breathed to the pen,
On being's page it took to writing then.
As the pen's *Káf* from *káf* (100) to being grew,
A generous fountain from its spring it drew.
The people of the world, both high and low,
Are in mad tumult from that fountain's flow.
When in this heat the lips in speech unclose,
From mystery's garden it becomes a rose.
Seizing its skirt, the spirit's breath will lead,
And with all grace convey it from its mead;
Then to the ear's gate it will make a way,
And at its coming sense will go astray.
The mind will greet it then with honour due,
Tight as a bud the heart embrace it, too.
At times it brings the lip a smile of joy,
Presses at times grief's moisture from the eye.
On lip of those who mourn a smile appears,
Or from the smiling lip rain down the tears.
With it when I thus see God's power blend,
That I withdraw from it may God forefend!
Attention to this wine has made me gray;
Be now my task to drive old age away.
No more the secret in my heart I'll keep,
But make the world laugh or will make it weep.

Old is the tale of Khusro and Shirín ;
In sweetness shall a Khusro new be seen.
Leila and Majnun's time is fully spent,
Yet will I now produce a new event.
Like parrot to eat sweets my mood I'll move
In Joseph's beauty and Zuleikha's love.
God calls the tale the fairest one can say,
And I will tell it in the fairest way.
When that fair beauty shall revealed appear,
For lies there will remain no entrance here.
The wind with falsehood's not content, forsooth;
Though thou shouldst tell it as a seeming truth,
The word with truth is aye adorned the most ;
The moon but at its full can beauty boast.
The first of morning's dawn is never bright,
For it boasts falsely of the beam of light.
When the true dawn in heav'n itself displays,
As the sun's beam in heav'n its flag 'twill raise.
And if with his thy art thou shouldst adorn,
From that lamp to the heart no ray is borne.
On ugly form why dost thou sew brocade ?
Not fair thereby the ugly may be made. (101)
From gold stuff ugliness assumes no fairer hue,
But towards ugliness reverts the gold stuff, too.
A rosy hue becomes a rosy face ;
Its fairness waxes through the rose-hue's grace.
A dark rose-colour if on it you paint,
The eye sees nothing but a darksome taint.
His beauty more than all the fair ones' there,
With Joseph not one beauty could compare.
She who no second has 'mong beauties all,
Her can they but a second Joseph call—
Of lovers none was like Zuleikha fair ;
Zuleikha passed them all in passion there.
From childhood up to age her passion grew ;
In rule and beggary did she love renew.

After old age and poverty and pain,
Of fresh youth when the time came back again,
Faith and love's road she trod and none beside,
Born and bred up in it, in it she died.
Although Zuleikha was beloved by all,
Joseph's the greater beauty one might call.
The tale of both of them this book shall teach,
And my pen scatter round the gems of each.
With ev'ry coin of theirs that I may spend
A casket of fresh wisdom will I blend.
If some good man, such is my hope indeed,
In this love-book of mine some word shall read,
Leaf-like, he may not turn from me his face,
Nor with his finger's pen my words efface:
If here and there an error he should see,
This accident he may not lay on me;
As far as may be, to amend may try,
Or else in silence he may pass it by.

## THE STORY OF THE LIGHTING OF THE CANDLE OF JOSEPH'S BEAUTY IN THE NIGHT-PLACE OF THE HIDDEN WORLD, AND THE BURNING OF THE MOTH OF ADAM'S HEART BY ITS FLAME.

To whom of mystery's sea the pearls to weigh is given,
Those who the pages read of the Divine Word of heaven,
The world's tale to recite when they began
'Twas thus of Adam that the story ran.
When his eye opened to behold the day,
Revealed, his progeny before him lay.
Behind there and before, the prophets' race,
Each in his order stood and fitting place:
And separate the saints in order meet,
Stood, one beside another ranged their feet.
The throng of earthly monarchs of renown,
Each ruler wearing there his glorious crown;

Whilst other mortals, rank on rank stood they,
In fitting fashion and in fair array.
When Adam tow'rd that crowd had turned his eye
And saw of each the varied company,
Joseph, that moon, then came into his sight ;
No moon, a lofty sun of honour's height !
A light selected from that company,
Above the crowd a torch erected high,
The beauty of the fair before him lost,
As in the sun's ray is the starry host.
The cloak of charming to his shoulder mete,
A hundred mantle-clothed ones at his feet.
Beyond all thought was his perfection found,
The thought itself of sense beyond the bound—
God's robe of favour on his shoulder borne,
Upon his head a crown of glory worn.
The morn of blessing on his forehead lay,
Night's darkness from his face the martyr's day.
Before him and behind the prophets all,
Made pure of earthly darkness from the pall,
Free of defect all souls of purity,
To right and left their standards lifted high,
On that sun-candled altar place they raise
The sounding melody of prayer and praise.
Adam, astonished at the glorious show,
In manner of amazement whispered low :
"God, from whose rosebud did this flower spring ?
" Whose is this play, the eye enlivening ?
" Why on him shines this fortune's brilliant ray ?
" This dignity and beauty, whence are they ? "
A voice : " Of thine own eye he is the light,
" Thy heart which grief has seen that renders bright,
" Of Jacob's garden thou a plant dost see,
" From Abram's desert a gazelle is he.
" His hall of state is raised above the heaven ;
" To him the throne of Egypt's land is given.

"And the great beauty that his face displays
"The envy of the fair of earth shall raise.
"She holds a mirror up before thine eyes:
"What treasure, then, thou hast give him as prize."
He said: "Of grace, see, open is the door:
"Of beauty's six parts I have given four—
"Now of that beauty which the fair possess,
"What others have with two do Thou him bless.
"His casket (102) opened idols to destroy,
"For beauty's type he may all 'Suls' (102) employ."
Tow'rds his own bosom then he Joseph drew,
From loving heart inspiring virtue new.
Of his own love he made him then aware,
And as a father kissed his forehead there.
Like nightingale upon his rose for blessing prayed,
From his son's love as opening rose himself displayed.

THE BRINGING OF THE PLANT OF BEAUTY OF JOSEPH FROM THE SPRING-GARDEN OF THE HIDDEN WORLD TO THE GARDEN OF MANIFESTATION, AND WATERING IT WITH THE WATER OF JACOB'S EYE AND NOURISHING IT WITH THE AIR OF ZULEIKHA'S HEART.

In changeful life where mere show rev'rence meets,
And each in turn of life the tymbal beats,
On each day (103) something clear for truth is shown,
And on the world a light from some name thrown.
Were the world ever in the self-same plight,
There would remain still hidden many a light.
Were in revolving the sun's light not lost,
Would lack their beauty of the stars the host.
Should winter never leave the flowering plain,
At spring's touch would the rose not laugh again.
When from this temple (104) Adam turned his face,
Seth in the *Mehráb* sat, and took his place.

When he departed, Idris (105) then began
In fraud's (106) house purity to teach to man.
When Enoch's (107) teaching was transferred to heav'n,
Faith's guardianship was then to Noah giv'n.
When Noah perished in destruction's flood, (108)
This door was opened to the friend of God. (109)
When from the world his table had been moved, (110)
For Isaac then his office was approved—
To non-existence' path (111) he turned aside,
And from salvation's mountain Jacob cried—
When from this business Jacob then withdrew,
His flag in Canaan from Syria flew.
When permanent in Canaan he remained,
Increase of wealth and children he obtained,
Whilst of his cattle, sheep and goats the tale
Exceeded ant and locust in the vale.
Thus prophet after prophet, on they came,
In prophecy distinct as shining flame.
Joseph himself eighth in descent appears,
For whom the world remains dissolved in tears.
Joseph beside, Jacob had sons eleven :
But now to Joseph was his whole heart given. (112)
When Joseph from his mother came to birth,
In face the moon an equal had on earth.
In the heart's garden was a plantlet reared,
A crescent in the heav'n of souls appeared.
Of God's friend in the grove a rose there grew,
A tight robe round its tender form it drew. (113)
A star from Isaac's constellation bright
Arose the eye of heav'n to deck with light.
In Jacob's mead its flag a tulip bore,
A wound and plaster both for Jacob's sore.
A deer to Canaan's breeze that perfume lent,
Tartary at Canaan's wastes in envy went.
Whilst in this life his mother yet remained
His sweet mouth from her milk its nurture gained. (114)

Him she embraced up to the age of two :
Into her food then Time its poison threw.
An orphan of its mother thus bereft,
The pearl from bounty's sea was tearful left.
His father, when he saw his pearl distressed,
The place of oyster gave his sister's breast. (115)
His soul's bird from his aunt its food obtained,
In her joy's rose-bed wings and feathers gained.
His form assumed the way of graceful walk ;
His lip soon formed the way of pleasing talk.
To him his aunt's heart clung in such degree
That from that bond she could be never free.
As her own soul each night upon her breast,
By day on him as sun her eye would rest.
His father longed as well to see his face,
And in his love he ever took his place.
He in his sorrowing heart had none beside,
Nor seeing him at times was satisfied.
And he desired that moon his heart to light
With him should present be both day and night.
He told his sister : " Thou for my love's sake
" Around my head dost like a willow shake.
" I can no longer Joseph's absence bear ;
" Do thou me from his separation spare.
" Send him of mystery to my secret place,
" Send him to where in prayer I turn my face."
His sister heard the word that Jacob said,
Nor from it outwardly she turned her head,
Prepared herself a pretext to invent
That back from Jacob he might yet be sent.
Of Isaac with her there a girdle lay,
In God's own service rubbed and worn away.
Whoever on his hand that girdle bound
Free of the spheres' oppression would be found.
When towards his sire she Joseph's face inclined
Did she the belt in secret round him bind.

Secret the girdle she around him drew,
So that its presence there he never knew.
Thus girdle-bound he to his sire was sent,
Whilst she delayed no more to make lament :
" The girdle from our midst is lost," she said,
And on them all around suspicion laid.
Then under each one's garment must she look,
And in his turn each one in order took.
Thus when it came to Joseph's turn at last,
She loosed the belt that round his waist was fast.
On those at that day who the Faith obeyed,
This precept by the holy law was laid :
" Whoever in the act of theft is caught,
" To the goods' owner captive must be brought."
Once more again, then, through this false pretence,
Which she made up, she bore him homewards thence.
Fixed on his face, her eye was rendered bright ;
But death in brief space closed that eye to light.
From seeing him his eye no longer closed,
Then Jacob's mind in happiness reposed.
In Joseph's countenance his *Kiblah's* (116) place,
He from his other children turned his face.
In Joseph only was his soul at rest,
Alone in Joseph's light his eye was blessed.
In Joseph all then centred that he did,
Joseph's the only market where he bid.
Wherever may the moon its light display,
The sun itself can never find its way.
How shall I tell that loving beauty's mead,
Huris' and Paris' that surpassed indeed ?
It was a moon whence heaven friendship gained,
Whence brilliance space and being both obtained.
No desert moon, it was a shining sun,
From which the heav'n itself its brilliance won.
That he was like the sun how shall I say ?
A mere mirage the fountain of its ray,

A holy light from bonds of "what" and "when"
Raised from the veil of form its head again.
A form when that Incomparable gained,
By way of veil was Joseph's name obtained.
In Jacob's heart although his love concealed,
It was in heart and soul to him revealed.
Though, envious of Zuleikha, Huris pale,
She in the West sits hid in virtue's veil.
Yet of his sun-like face unseen the beam,
She of his image captive was in dream.
Love's pain controls e'en those who are afar,
'Twill not be far from those who nearer are.

## Concerning the Lineage of Zuleikha, from the Rising of the Sun, of whose Perfection the West became the East, and moreover passed beyond it by Thousands of Degrees.

Thus speaks that learned weigher of the word,
He in whose treasure wealth of words is stored :
There was a Western king, renowned of fame,
Who beat the drum of rule ; Taimus his name.
Of kingship all the wealth had he obtained ;
Of him no heart's wish unfulfilled remained.
Prosperity the crown had from his head ;
Firm basis for the throne his foot had laid.
Orion in his host his loins had bound,
And round his sword-knot victory was wound.
He had one child, Zuleikha, fair of face,
Against the world with him who held her place :
No girl—a star she of the royal sign,
A gem did she in royal casket shine.
Not into words can her charms' praise be brought, .
I make a simple trial of the thought.
If to her feet I like her hair descend,
To my mind brilliance would her image lend—

I from her pleasant lip assistance seek,
The merits that I know that I may speak.
Her palm-like stature was of grace create,
In sweetness' garden with its head elate,
That from a lordly river water drank,
And bore the palm from cypress on the bank.
The wise became entangled in the snare
Of her not far from musk-beperfumed hair.
In middle placed of head so tender, soft,
Of her fair locks the comb made partings oft.
Cleft the heart's bag of musk that head in two,
And thus the musk-bag's office harder grew.
Her jessamine-scented ringlets, downwards spread,
Threw on the rose's branch at foot a shade.
Of her two ringlets Indian ropes were made,
On her tall box (117) that like rope-dancers played.
The heavens to describe her beauteous grace,
A silver tablet on her forehead place,
And of that silver tablet by the side
Musk-scented, two inverted *Nûns* (118) provide:
Beneath those *Nûns* of *Swáds* (119) a beauteous pair,
Which the Creator's pen had written there.
Down to *Mîm's* (120) ring from what the Nûns enclose
Straight as an *Aleph* drawn the silver nose:
*Aleph* beyond, by the mouth's Naught's (121) increased
The evil of the world ten times at least.
Her *Sîn* (122) is clear her smiling lip beneath,
When her *Mîm's* knots she loosens with her teeth.
Her face a type of Iram's garden fair,
Flowers of many kinds are blooming there.
Its mark a mole on every side there shows,
Like a black child upon a bed of rose.
Not liable to tithes (123) her silver chin,
A well from which life's water springs within.
That chin beneath a wise man wandering round
Had from that well the water flowing found.

Ease for his heart he had not there obtained,
The well a whirlpool and a well contained.
Purer than ivory, her neck was fair ;
The deer upon their necks brought tribute there.
Reproach (124) on jessamine her two shoulders threw ;
Hid in its breast itself the rose from view.
Resembling domes of light her two breasts swell,
Or bubble risen up from Káfur's well.
Two fresh pomegranates growing from one stem,
No daring hand of hope had handled them.
Like silver store her arms her form embrace ;
Pure silver by its side is metal base.
On that pure pearl to ward off future ill
The pure on earth at heart poured blessings still.
To make their soul her rue the fair inclined ;
With their life's vein her amulet to bind.
Plunder of throned kings diadem that wore,
Her two arms fill her sleeve with silver store.
Full rest to those who toil her hand conveys,
And on each wounded heart a plaster lays.
Of her own fingers she has made a pen
To write her words upon the hearts of men.
To hearts in ev'ry nail of her it seems
Above the full moon that a crescent beams.
With fingers five she struck the moon a blow
From her hand's force that it might trouble know. (126)
Her waist a hair, a split hair 'twould appear ;
Of that hair's fineness aye she had a fear :
She could not bind her loins e'en with a thread
Lest it might chance to break it in the dread.
Her belly like a board with ermine spread,
So soft the midwife had her navel shred.
Her hips a hill, but of pure silver found,
Down from her waist as if a fallen mound :
So soft, if with the hand 'twere gently pressed,
Like dough, 'twould not between the fingers rest.

From golden hand-ball (127) silent pass away,
Of silver hand-ball (127) hear what I shall say.
Below the navel to above the knee
Nothing, nor old nor new, be said by me.
To that chaste fortress and forbidden place
I give not fancy e'en the road to trace.
The fashion of her legs should I declare,
Pillars of silver they her charms to bear,
By God! a wondrous nosegay, full of light,
But of all blind ones hidden from the sight.
The mirror that revealed her purity
Fell from respect itself upon its knee.
The mirror thus together with her knelt
That from her face the grace of light it felt.
Whoever knelt down with her on the ground,
The face of fortune there reflected found.
In grace her foot would with her leg, too, vie,
For this in pleasure has no constancy. (128)
For thus it was, when smart and quick she moved,
Her foot from heel to toe so tender proved,
That if upon a lover's eye 'twere placed,
The tears as bubbles on its sole were traced.
Of gold and gems I know not how to speak:
Whate'er I say my words would still be weak.
Who would that *Pari* as a jewel praise?
Her beauty would gems' lustre even raise.
Upon her head a jewelled crown she wore:
Each gem the tribute of a province bore.
From pearl and ruby pendant in her ear
From heart and soul sense, joy disappear.
If from her neck a jewel thou shouldst pull,
Both breast and skirt of jewels would be full.
The jewelled band that fastens back her hair
Is worth a thousand knots of jewels fair.
With her own hand should she her wrist not hold,
With fraud to clasp it who would be so bold?

Henceforth can I of gold no tale repeat;
An anklet made of it lay on her feet.
At times upon a couch herself she laid,
Arrayed in Grecian or Chinese brocade;
Graceful at times within the hall she paced
With robes of Syria or Egypt graced.
And every day, when fresh appeared the sun,
Naught but a new robe did she e'er put on.
Twice from one vest her head she did not raise:
Moon-like, each day she took a newer phase.
From kiss of great men she her foot withdrew;
Such fortune 'twas her skirt alone that knew.
And to her shift alone was given grace
To hold her body in its close embrace.
The cypress-formed ones all her nod obeyed:
To her the *Pari*-faced ones worship paid,
While of her sisters of the *Huris'* race
Thousands served day and night before her face.
Her heart of sorrow never bore the yoke,
And in her soft foot a thorn never broke.
She had not loved nor had she been beloved,
Nor passion ever had her feeling moved.
At night Narcissus-like her eyes would close,
And in the morn bloom as the smiling rose.
With the young silver-bodied ones in sport,
With fair gazelles there in the palace court,
Her heart no games of fortune to annoy,
In naught but sport would she her time employ.
Thus light of heart and frolicsome was she,
And from all weight of grief and sorrow free.
What fate will on her from fell Time alight?
What from her womb bring forth the pregnant night?

### THE SEEING BY ZULEIKHA FOR THE FIRST TIME OF THE SWORD OF THE SUN OF THE BEAUTY OF JOSEPH IN THE SHEATH OF A DREAM, AND HER BEING KILLED WITH LOVE OF HIM BY THAT SWORD.

One night as pleasant as life's morning rays,
And joy-enhancing as of youth the days,
From movement were both bird and fish at rest,
And fate within its skirt its foot had pressed.
In this house (129) seers many that contained,
None but the stars' eyes wakeful had remained.
Had stol'n the watchman's sense the thief of night,
The ringer the bell's tongue had fastened tight.
Their tails the dogs their necks had twisted round;
In that ring for their voice no way was found.
Its feather-sword had drawn the bird of night,
And cut its reed that should proclaim the light.
Where royal dome its battlement upreared
And to the sentry poppy-head appeared,
No strength remained in him his watch to keep,
The poppy-head had lulled him off to sleep.
The drummer's drumming now was at a stand,
Sleep's onslaught to his stick had tied his hand.
Nor had *Yá Hai!* the Caller's message, sped
The beds to roll up of the careless dead.
With sugar-clear lips there Zuleikha lies,
With sugar-sweet sleep seated on her eyes.
With spikenard rubbed her locks her pillowed head;
On her couched form the rose's harvest spread.
Her locks the pillow in disorder threw;
Their silk threads on the roses pictures drew.
Closed fast in sleep her outward eyes may lie,
Yet from her heart looks out another eye.

Sudden a youth comes to her from the door;
A spirit 'tis, I say a youth no more.
That form auspicious from the realm of day
To Eden's mead the *Huris* steal away.
Their charms and beauty all away he took,
And snatched away from each her amorous look.
His stature like the young box raised on high,
The cypress tall his slave in dignity.
As chains his ringlets, falling him around,
Both wisdom's hand and foot of counsel bound.
Shone from his brow a light of brilliant ray,
The moon and sun before him prostrate lay.
His eyebrows' bend the *Mehráb* of the pure,
For drowsy men a perfumed shade secure.
With softness' *Surma* was his eye anoint,
Piercing all men's hearts with its eyelash point.
Smiles shedding sweets upon his lips abode,
And from his mouth speech mixed with sugar flowed.
His bright pearls, from those lips that jewels shed,
Were lightning flashing in the twilight red.
Light from the Pleiads by his smile was spread,
And salt his lip in agitation shed.
A dimpled apple from his chin was hung,
Or like a quince upon an apple strung.
With moles of musk was his cheeks' rosebed dressed,
As crows that in a garden build their nest.
A crescent new from Eden's heav'n that face
In Archer's sign made with its brow a place.
Silver his side and arms, a mighty pair,
Not so his loins, thin drawn out as a hair.
Upon his face Zuleikha cast one look,
And there took place at once what place there took.
Beauty she saw beyond all mortal range,
Unseen by *Pari* and to *Huri* strange.
To his fair form and pleasing traits as well
She with a hundred hearts a captive fell.

In dream she saw him at the age of seven;
Bound as with rope, her heart to him was given.
His stature's image in her heart embraced,
Affection's plant she in her spirit placed.
Fire burning from his face her breast illumed,
Of her heart's patience all the goods consumed.
To those sweet locks that scattered amber round
With every hair her own soul's rope she bound.
At his arched eyebrow she lamenting wept,
And at his drowsy eye in blood she slept.
Her heart her lip then into sugar made,
Her teeth her eye-lash in gem-necklace laid.
Her silver forearm washed from sense her hand,
And wound around her loins a service band.
She saw the sweet musk-mole upon his face,
And on the fire she took, like rue, her place.
She saw life-pain in apple of his chin:
Such apple lightly who can gather in?
In God's name, what a beauteous form appeared,
Sown in an outward form, in mystery reared!
Zuleikha with Zuleikha was oppressed,
The mystery gone, upon the form at rest.
If of the mystery she had been aware
Upon its road had she been moving there,
But captive to the form when she had grown,
At first that mystery she had not known.
We in the bonds of fancy all are laid,
And by appearances are captive made.
Once from the form turned tow'rds the inward part,
When tow'rds the form would ever turn one heart?
There's moisture in the jar, the thirsty knows
Full well, as on its neck his hand he throws:
Once overwhelmed within the limpid sea,
Weeping, the jar no more remembers he.

## The Blowing of the Morning Breeze on Zuleikha, and the Opening of Her Drowsy Eye.

At morning when took flight of night the crow,
And early cock's cry sounded clear below,
The nightingales with song melodious grew
And from the rose its coverlet withdrew.
Its face the jessamine with dew had wet,—
Its amber locks had washed the violet.
Zuleikha still her face to turn would seem
Towards the *Mehráb* of her last night's dream,
No dream, a sweet insensibility,
From the night's blackness a perplexity.
Her maidens at her feet all clustered stand,
And her attendants throng to kiss her hand.
Now her moist tulip's veil she lays aside,
Her eye, half drunk with sleep, too, opens wide:
Her breast of sun and moon the rising-place,
She lifts her head and all round turns her face.
Of the night's face of rose no trace she saw,
And bud-like would within herself withdraw.
'Twas thus that cypress by her grief down borne,
Rose-like her vest had from her body torn,
But shame of others held the hand of pride,
And thus her foot to skirt of patience tied.
Hid in sad heart her secret close she folds,
As in hard rock the mine the ruby holds.
Like buds the blood she swallows in her heart,
Nor outwardly betrays the smallest part.
Her lip still with her maids in talk engaged,
Yet at the talk her heart in secret raged.
With friends her mouth in sweet smiles aye resolved,
Like cane in hundred knots her heart involved.
Though with her friends her tongue had aye its jest,
Love with a hundred tongues burnt in her breast.

Whilst upon others' forms was turned her eye,
Her heart was with her lover constantly.
How in her hand were her heart's reins retained,
When with that charmer always they remained?
Hearts to love's crocodile that are a prey
Gain not their object, seek it as they may.
She has not one wish from her love apart,
And not with any is at rest her heart.
Each word she says she to her lover speaks,
All aim she seeks she from her lover seeks.
Times thousands to her lip her soul arose:
" Oh that the night this day of pain would close!"
Night comes to soothe him who in love abides;
Night comes that lovers' secrets ever hides.
For this to day with them night preference bears,
The one a curtain-hangs, the other tears.
At night towards grief's wall her face she leant,
Her back with weeping like a harp was bent.
Her tears upon the harp as strings she laid,
To her own heart attuned its chords she played—
With weeping raising her pathetic cry,
Treble and bass she uttered sob and sigh—
Her lover's form before her constantly,
She scattered jewels both from lip and eye.
" From what mine art thou, gem of purity,
" Whence jewels fall around, encircling me?
" My heart thou stol'st; thy name thou didst not tell,
" Nor hast thou left a trace where thou dost dwell.
" Thy name I know not of whom to enquire,
" Nor one from whom thy dwelling to require.
" If thou art king, tell me at least thy name,
" And if a moon, the place from whence it came—
" Oh! may none ever like me captive be!
" No lover mine, there is no heart in me.
" I saw thy form, that robbed me of my sleep:
" My heart's pure blood it caused my eye to weep.

" And now, deprived of rest and sleep, I lie,
" With thy hot flame my fever burning high.
" If on my fire thou water pour, what then?
" Like fire, wilt not thou blaze and burn again?
" I was a flower in youth's garden fair,
" And like life's water fresh was blooming there.
" No wind had ever blown upon my head,
" Nor had my foot from piercing thorn-point bled.
" Thou gav'st me to the wind with one caress,
" And on my couch a thousand thorns didst press.
" Tend'rer a hundred times than leaf of rose,
" On bed of thorns how could my form repose?"
Thus till the morning came her night was spent,
Against her lover's image this complaint.
To lull suspicion, when night turned to day,
The blood tears from her eye she washed away.
Her lip was moist with the blood-feast of night,
But what had been was hidden out of sight. (132)
Upon her pillow rose-leaves fresh she spread,
With silver cypress freshened her soul's bed.
As in this manner she passed night and day,
Straight to a hair's breadth she held on her way.

### The Knotting with Perplexity of the Rope of Anxiety of her Maids from their Seeing the Change in the Condition of Zuleikha, and the Unloosing by her Nurse with the Point of the Finger of Enquiry of the Knots of that Rope.

Where'er an arrow shoots of love the bow,
The shield of counsel wards not off the blow.
Inside the house when that dart finds its way
A hundred signs its presence there betray,

And pleasant is this saying of the wise
That love and musk-scent one can not disguise.
If upon musk a hundred folds you lay,
Through many screens the scent will find its way (133).
Zuleikha ever kept her love concealed,
Nor grief's seed in her breast sown e'er revealed,
Yet ever from its place 'twould raise its head,
And from within its signs and traces (134) spread—
Her weeping eyes at times would water shed:
No, not with water, but pure blood they bled—
In every drop that from her eye-lash flowed,
There outwardly a hidden secret glowed.
At times from burning heart she heaved a sigh;
Rising, its smoke was wafted to the sky.
In ev'ry sigh that from her heart she drew,
Of a hot, burning heart the scent they knew.
Sleepless and foodless sometimes day and night,
To yellow tulip turned her red rose bright.
In any garden, (dost thou this not know?)
Without a spot can never tulip grow.
Her waiting maidens, when these signs they knew,
Would their perplexity for aye renew.
Yet what its reason was was never clear,
Nor did what caused her cruel lot appear.
"The like was never seen," first some one cries;
"Perhaps an evil eye upon her lies."
Another to this fancy gave belief:
"Some *Div* or *Pari* had brought her to grief."
"No, no! some sorcerer," would some one say,
"Has tied her skirt-fringe in some magic way."
"These are all signs of love," another says:
"'Tis love that on her all this burden lays.
"As she sees no one in her waking hour,
"In sleep this evil holds her in its power."
Thus of the matter differing thought had each,
All with each other holding varied speech.

Still was the secret of her heart untold,
Nor to one thing could they together hold.
Her nurse a sorceress among the rest ;
Of magic she the capital possessed.
The ways of passion she herself had seen,
Sometimes had loved, and sometimes loved had been—
Lover and mistress had to union brought,
And had to differing lovers concord taught.
One night she came, of service to repeat
Her tale, and kissed the ground before her feet.
"O rose-bud of the royal mead," she cried :
"Glow at thy beauty all the fair with pride.
"Thy lip be full of smiles, thy heart elate,
"Propitious from thy glory be my fate !
"In beauty's garden thou that cypress art
"Whence pheasant turns the parrot of my heart.
"I am the river of that faithful sea,
"Fortune upon whose shore has nourished thee.
"'Twas I that first beheld thy face in life,
"And cut thy cord with my affection's knife—
"I with rose-water bathed thy form and hair,
"And for thy dye (135) musk-water did prepare.
"Of my heart's veil thy swaddling clothes I wove,
"A hundred tender threads of life I rove.
"My milk did I provide for thee as bread,
"That body nourished which thy spirit fed.
"When night arrived I slept but for thy sake,
"To deck thy face my morning task I'd make.
"As fringe in walking on my shoulders worn,
"And in my arms in sleeping wast thou borne.
"When thy rose-branch to graceful cypress grew,
"Not from thy skirt yet I my hand withdrew.
"Still ever in thy service did I wait,
"Early in thy affairs employed and late.
"Thou couldst in no place that fair cypress find,
"But I as shadow followed close behind.

"When thou didst sit waiting I stood by thee;
"In sleep upon thy feet my head would be—
"In thy affairs employed still as before,
"In all sincerity I still adore.
"The secret of thy heart why dost thou hide,
"And as a stranger hold me from thy side?
"Who into this has thrown thee? Speak at last.
"Who stole thy sense? This load on thee who cast?
"Why so afflicted and thyself beside?
"Why with such grief and pain art thou allied?
"Why does thy red rose yellow turn as gold,
"And thy warm breath become in this way cold?
"Thou art the sun; as moon why sink as yet,
"And in the morning hour desire to set?
"Surely I know, some moon stands in thy way;
"Then who that moon is, to me plainly say.
"If in the heav'n above an angel he,
"And his pure essence formed of light should be,
"Urgent with supplication will I pray,
"Till he from heav'n to earth shall find his way;
"A *Pari*, if in hill and wood he dwell,
"To read spells for thee's my affair as well—
"By incantations will I him compel
"Shut in a bottle (136) here with thee to dwell,
"And if he should be born of human kind,
"Quickly with him will I rejoice thy mind.
"With this alliance who would not desire?
"Not slaves alone but those whose place is high'r."
Zuleikha knew her sympathetic heart,
Her incantations' power and magic act;
And saw no way but to the truth to keep,
And took her moon among the stars to weep.
"Invisible my treasure is," said she;
"My treasure's door-key, too, is lost to me,
"How can I show of that bird any trace
"That with the Anká has its dwelling-place? (137)

" This bird, indeed, mankind the Ankâ call,
" But this my own bird has no name at all.
" To him who's disappointed what delight
" That he his wish's name should know aright!
" In absence disappointment though he meet,
" The name the bitter of his tongue makes sweet.
Her secret to the nurse then open laid,
Her trust's foundation she far higher made.
Out of her dreaming she awoke her then;
In place of ignorance she made things plain.
When of her book the nurse had read one word,
No remedy to her perplexed occurred.
Of every fancy this the picture true:
'Tis vain to search for what one never knew.
If from the first thou know'st not thy desire,
Of what avail yet farther to enquire?
When from its bonds her heart she could not save,
She loosed her tongue and admonition gave.
At first she said: " This is of *Dívs* the way;
" *Dívs*' business is to cheat and to betray.
" To men they put on an appearance fair,
" To open them the door of black despair."
Zuleikha said: " How could a *Dív* presume
" The form of a beloved one to assume?
" She who malignant tumult would prepare,
" May God forbid that she an Angel bear."
" It is an evil dream", the other said:
" For such an ill astray why art thou led?"
The other said: " Then if this dream be ill,
" The pure how should it be misleading still?
" For men of learning clear this maxim state:
" Crooked with crooked goes and straight with straight."
The nurse replied: " Thou art a clever child;
" Then drive out from thy thoughts this fancy wild.'
Zuleikha answered: " Rested it with me,
" How should this load obtain the mastery?

'The thing can no more by my hand be done;
"The reins of power from that hand are gone.
"Than on the stony rock more deeply yet
"Engraved upon my heart an image set,
"The waves may rage, or howl the wind and storm,
"Yet not efface that deeply graven form."
The nurse, who saw what force her love had gained,
From words of admonition now refrained,
But told her father secretly her state.
Her father, greatly troubled at the tale,
Since all device appeared of no avail,
Left the whole matter in the hand of Fate.


### THE SEEING BY ZULEIKHA OF JOSEPH FOR A SECOND TIME IN A DREAM, AND THE SHAKING OF THE CHAIN OF HIS LOVE, AND CASTING HIM INTO THE WHIRLPOOL OF DARKNESS.

Happy that heart where passion comes to birth,
That in its passion scorns the things of earth;—
Their coruscating flash of lightning bright
Burns sense and patience harvest with its light.
Salvation's pain (138) no more a thing of awe,
Reproach's hill less weighty than a straw,
A feather weight his soul reproach will know,
That with the blame his love will stronger grow.
For a whole year Zuleikha's moon then waned;
Her full moon to its crescent form attained.
With back bent like the crescent she one night
Sat with her bleeding eye in semi-light,
And spoke: "O heav'n, with me what hast thou done,
"That should already 'gin to pale my sun?
"Now like a bow becomes my bleeding frame;
"I am a target for the darts of blame.

"My reins on restive hands didst thou bestow,
"The restiveness of which alone I know.
"He cast into my heart of love a ray,
"And in dreams treats me in a niggard way.
"In waking hours he does not sit with me,—
"His form in dreams not such that I may see.
"A sign of making fortune in my dream,
"A moon I see of world-enlivening beam.
"Sleep gives no comfort to my weary eyes;
"Of fortune but the form my dream supplies.
"If fortune in my dream would but awake,
"My lover in my dream would substance take."
Thus said she till a watch of night had passed;—
Upon her lip her soul rose up at last.
Sudden, a dream her fancy bore away:
It was no dream; insensible she lay.
Her form upon her couch was not at rest,
Hope came in from the door her soul that blessed;
That form that had appeared to her at first
Brighter than moonlight on her vision burst.
No sooner did her sight the vision meet,
Than leaping she fell down before its feet,—
Kissed then the ground and cried: "O cypress-rose,
"That from my heart rob'st patience and repose,
"By Him who has created thee from light,
"From all contamination pure and bright,
"Who thus has given kingship o'er the fair,
"And than life's water greater grace to bear,
"In stature as a rosebush in life's mead,—
"Of the soul's food thy lip a source indeed,—
"Thy heart-enlivening face my light illumes,
"And like a moth my bird of life consumes.
"Hid in thy scented locks a lasso lies
"Enfolding every hair of mine that ties.
"Thy waist has made thy body as a hair:
"Thy mouth's *Mim* drives my sad heart to despair.

" Pity my wretched soul without a hope,
" And thy sweet mouth to give me answer ope.
" Say with that grace that ravishes my heart,
" Who thou mayst be and of what race thou art.
" Where is thy mine if thou a gem shouldst be?
" A king, where is thy hall of majesty?"
Then answered he: "I am of mortal birth,
" Of water made and of the dust of earth.
" Thou say'st thou hast of love a claim on me,
" If these thy words be in sincerity,
" My right of love and faithfulness preserve,
" Unmarried still, do thou my will observe.
" Thy sugar by no tooth shall bitten be,—
" No diamond thy jewel pierce for thee.
" If on thy breast my sign-inscribed shall be,
" From that brand think not that I can be free.
" My heart as well is captive in thy snare,
" And of love's branding, too, the scar I bear."
Then when Zuleikha saw his loving mood,
And from his lip the mystery understood,
Her maddened seized the *Pari* (139) once again,—
The fire fell on the moth with greater pain.
From her dream's thought infatuate, she leapt,
With heart and mind in burning madness kept.
Her grief for him at heart still greater grew,
Up to the spheres her grief's smoke (140) quicker flew.
A hundred-fold her madness had increased
Beyond all bounds; her wailing never ceased.
Down from the hand of wisdom fell her rein,
She freed herself of counsel from the chain.
Like rose-bud, her soul's robe in tatters shred—
Like tulip, in the dust her lip's blood shed;
Sometimes from love for him her face she'd tear,
Or root out, thinking of his locks, her hair.
On every side attendants on the ground
Sat like a halo drawn the moon around,

And if a gap were left in any part,
Straight as an arrow would she through it dart.
And had the circle held her skirt not fast,
Into the fields the cypress would have passed:
Round her, as round a bird, should it not close,
Gone to the market like an unveiled rose.
Informed of these events, her sire each sort
Of med'cine sought for from the wise at Court:
Of all devices every road run through,
Better than chains no remedy they knew.
A twisting serpent made of gold they brought,
Which was with precious pearls and rubies wrought.
The snake, around her silver leg entwined,
Made rings, near treasure as you serpents find.
Treasure of grace Zulcikha was indeed,
And every treasure of a snake has need.
Beneath her skirt there as the serpent slept,
Thus she exclaimed, as pearly tears she wept:
" Fast in the bonds of love my heart's foot lies,
" Yet dearer than the world those bonds I prize.
" Why should quick fate, dear life that wears away,
" Loading my feet, me in such fetters lay?
" To me no power in my foot is left,
" To go and come I am of sense bereft.
" Why with such heavy bonds my foot confine?
" Why wound with cruel sword this heart of mine?
" Fast in the mire my cypress foot they bind,
" And movement for my foot is hard to find.
" And what the benefit the gardener gains,
" When round that foot he draws the water chains?
" That charmer's foot should surely chains control,
" Who in a moment all my senses stole,
" And lingered not so long there in my eye
" As with his tulip hue to satisfy.
" As flashing lightning did he then depart,
" And raised the smoke from out my burning heart.

" If lofty fortune me its aid would lend,
" Round his own foot this chain of gold I'd bend.
" Then as I wished would I upon him gaze,
" And he would render bright my darkened days.
" What of that tender beauty shall I say,
" Upon whose foot if ever dust there lay
" Grief on my soul would like a mountain be,
" And would roll up my couch of joy for me?
" When did I wish a load were on his mind,
" His silver leg from bonds should trouble find?
" A hundred heart-stabs sweeter far to me
" Than that his skirt one thorn should pierce would be."
Now of those pleasing tales that lovers tell,
One suddenly upon her target fell.
Dust from her wounds upon her bosom fell,
Like wounded game into the dust she fell.
For a short time insensible she lay,
But soon to sense her spirit found its way.
With spells imagined in her maddened heart,
Again her charms began to bear their part.
Sometimes she laughs, and sometimes takes to tears,
Sometimes alive and sometimes dead appears.
Each moment varying from grave to gay,
In varying mood a whole year passed away.

## The Seeing of Joseph (on him be Peace!) by Zuleikha in a Dream for the Third Time, and her Asking his Name and Place, and the Return of Zuleikha to Wisdom and Sense.

Full of deceit and charms, thou, Love, appear,
At times to peace, at times to war who'rt near—
At times the wise distracted rendering,
At times thou dost the mad to wisdom bring.

Of beauties when thou bindest up the hair,
The wise fall into fetters of despair.
And if those ringlets thou shouldst e'er untie,
The lamp of wisdom gains in brilliancy.
One night Zuleikha as she senseless tossed,
A twin to sorrow and to patience lost,
Drinking the dregs out of the cup of grief,
From love's fierce agony found no relief.
Now from her perfumed hair the veil she drew,
Dust on her head with burning heart she threw.
Her tender cypress back she bowed in prayer;
Earth made of Iram's grove the envy there—
Tears red as *Arghaván* (142) poured forth her eyes,
With lily tongue she uttered happy cries.
Grief and affliction filled her sorrowing breast
As to her lover she this tale addressed:
" O thou who robbest me of sense and rest,
" And hast with misery my days distressed;
" No comfort giving, though thou broughtest grief;
" Stealing my heart, thou bringest no relief;
" Thy name I know not, that I thee might name:
" Thy place I find not, that I thee might claim.
" In my own state I smiled so cheerily,
" But now like cane I am in bonds to thee.
" As bud from grief for thee blood was my food:
" Now like a rose I fall out from my hood—
" I say not in thy eyes that I am dear;
" No: least am I of all thy handmaids here.
" If thou wouldst cherish her how would it be,
" And wouldest her from bonds of sorrow free?
" May none be e'er defiled with blood like me,
" Or among people thus dishonoured be!
" My mother grieved that I was of her race,
" And I, his child, my father bring disgrace.
" My waiting women all are from me gone,
" A prey to grief have left me all alone.

"Thou to my wretched spirit hast a torch applied ;
"Like me in friendlessness burns none beside."
Till she was held in slumber's soft caress
Thus her soul's object did she then address.
Her eye inebriate with sleep's cup became,
And in a dream to her sleep's robber came,
In form more fair than I could e'er portray,
Nor do I know henceforth what more to say.
Her hand upon his skirt she weeping kept,
With eyelash at his feet heart's blood she wept.
" Thou with the anguish of whose passion fly
" Ease from my heart and slumber from my eye,
" By that pure Being, Who thee pure has made,
" His choice from both worlds' fair ones on thee laid,
" Shorten the period of my grief for me :
" Tell me thy name and where thy town may be."
" If that suffices for thee," he replied :
" In Egypt I am Vazír and abide.
" Among those trusted by the king I stand :
" He gives me rank and honour in the land."
Zuleikha from her love this sign obtained :
As dead a hundred years fresh life she gained.
She drank as 'twere a new draft from life's bowl :
Her body strength, and patience gained her soul.
Fortune awake, when from that dream again
She waking rose, the mad one rose up sane.
To her hot heart of that moon came the word,
And her to sense and intellect restored.
She called her handmaids in from every side :
" Ye who have felt my sorrow," then she cried :
" News of good fortune to my sire convey ;
" Drive sorrow's burning from his heart away.
" Knowledge and wisdom have returned at last ;
" My stream comes flowing that away had passed.
" The gold chain from my silver by be laid ;
" No more of madness shall I be afraid.

"No more in miser's bonds my silver leave;
"With thy own hand my leg from chains relieve."
When to her father the good news was brought,
He went to meet her, much as one distraught.
Like lover first himself away he threw,
Then towards that cypress on his way he drew;
Loos'ning that double snake that round her wound,
Her silver breast from bonds of gold unbound.
Her handmaids 'neath her feet their foreheads laid,
A throne of gold beneath her feet they made.
Tender upon a couch they laid her down;
Made her head lofty with a golden crown.
The fairy-faced ones all together drew;
As moths around that candle all they flew.
When of her comrades in the midst she sat,
Her lip like parrot's sugar broke and ate.
The cover of her tale box she unloosed,
As tales of every city she produced.
Of Rome and Syria she wove the thread,
With sugar mixed what she of Egypt said.
Tales of Egyptians now come to an end,
She named him who in Egypt was her friend. (144)
When of this name came from her tongue the sound,
She fell, as would a shadow, on the ground.
A flood of blood fell from her clouded eye,
And up to heaven rose her wailing cry.
By day and night she had this work on hand,
Spoke ever of her friend and of his land.
Such converse in her ear aye sweet remained;
On every other topic silence reigned.

## The Arrival of Ambassadors to demand the Hand of Zuleikha, and their Return Disappointed.

Though through her love Zuleikha's state confused,
Her beauty's fame was through the world diffused.
Where'er that beauty's tale men might relate,
Was he who heard at once inebriate.
Eager desire was she of monarchs crowned;
At royal feasts her fairness was renowned—
In hope in marriage he might gain her hand
Each moment came from some king a demand.
When, then, of madness she escaped the chain,
And sat recovered on love's throne again,
Envoys from kings of every land around, (145)
From Syria's kingdoms and Rome's countries bound,
More than ten persons there the journey made,
And at her shrine of majesty delayed—
With royal letter one and goods a store;
The seal of Solomon another bore.
From some world-conqueror a gift each brought,
A sign in wedlock that her hand he sought.
Wherever turned that envy of the sun,
A throne, and on her head a crown was won.
Whatever land with grace she might adorn,
As her road dust would royal crowns be borne.
If moonlike she in Syria (146) deigned to rest,
From morn till even (146) she would aye be blessed.
And if towards Rome she should take her way,
From Rome to Zanzibar all would obey.
Each courier a message thus conveyed,
A name auspicious from his lip was said.
News of their purport reached Zuleikha there:
Her heart from fear was driven to despair. (147)

" With these from Egypt is there no one now?
" Beneath Egyptians' love my back I bow.
" Towards Egyptians is my heart constrained :
" If Egypt envoy send not, what is gained?
" The breeze that from the land of Egypt blows,
" And in my eyes the dust of Egypt throws,
" A hundred times more dear that wind to me,
" Than the musk-laden breeze of Tartary."
Her father summoned her.  Before his face,
Absorbed in thought she sat down in her place.
" Light of my eye!" he said ; " heart's joy to me,
" That frees from grief thou deed of liberty!
" In beauty's chief seat of those crowns who own,
" Of kings who wear a crown upon the throne,
" At heart the scar of thy desire they know,
" The seed of longing in their bosoms sow.
" From every realm in hope of thy consent
" Does an ambassador himself present.
" I tell of every messenger the tale
" To see among them who will now prevail—
" And of that land tow'rds which thy heart may lean,
" That of it quickly I may make thee queen."
The father spoke and she more silent grew,
And turned her listening ear to sound she knew.
Happy is one when one can turn the ear
The words of well-known friends alone to hear.
One after other did he of kings tell,
Of Egypt only there no mention fell.
Zuleikha saw from the Egyptian's land
No messenger had come to claim her hand.
Before her father hopeless in despair,
She rose, like willow trembling in the air.
With her eyes' spear she pierced the pearls she shed,
Out of her eye she rained her tears and said :
" Oh that a mother I had ne'er possessed.
" Or that she ne'er fed me from her breast!

"What star my fate rules is to me unknown,
"Or by that fate I whither have been thrown.
"If a cloud, rising from the ocean's bed,
"On every thirsty lip should water shed,
"Tow'rds me with thirsting lip if it should turn,
"In place of water 'twould rain fire to burn.
"Tow'rds me I know not, heav'n, what is thy mood,
"In blood that cloth-like (148) my skirt is imbrued.
"If to my friend thou wilt not let me fly,
"So far from him, oh! do not let me lie.
"If thou desire my death, behold, I die;
"By thy injustice lifeless here I lie.
"Or into sorrow if thou wouldst me throw,
"Thou castest on me many a hill of woe.
"Beneath a hill what is a blade of grass?
"Through waves of grief how can a straw e'er pass?
"A hundred wounds upon my heart through thee,
"Still is it in thy hand to pity me.
"What is't to thee if I am glad or greet?
"What is't to thee if I am sour or sweet?
"Destroy the wind my crop, say 'let it be'!
"Two hundred harvests are one grain to thee.
"Who am I? What from me can ever rise?
"Exist or not, what is it in thy eyes?
"Destroying many a rose that freshly bloomed,
"Thou hast to fire with death's brand on them doomed.
"Where would thy feelings ever be distressed
"That I should ever differ from the rest?"
With grievous groaning both by night and day,
And with heart filled with blood, like bud, she lay.
Tears from her moistened eye would ever flow,
Dust on her head her angry hand would throw.
Her father saw her restless discontent,
And heard for Egypt's Vazír her lament,
The messengers in royal robes arrayed
Dismissed, excuses with his lips he made.

He said : " For this my precious child as bride,
" To Egypt's Vazír long my tongue is tied.
" Ye who are learned all will understand
" His right is first who did the foremost stand.
" Better than this can time's tongue never say :
" The hand that's foremost carries aye the day."
Thus lost the hope of gaining their desire,
With wind in hand (149) the messengers retire.

## The Sending by Zuleikha's Father of a Messenger to the Vazir of Egypt, and the Bringing Forward of Zuleikha to him and his Acceptance of her.

A scar upon her heart Zuleikha bore :
Despair increased it ever more and more.
Each day will ever clothe its face in white,
Save day of hopelessness, as dark as night.
For Egypt grieved her father saw her mind,
And but one remedy for this could find,
That down to Egypt some wise man should go,
From the Vazír its remedy to know ;
That he to him a message might convey,
And for Zuleikha's union pave the way.
He chose a man for wisdom from the Court (150),
Gave to his wisdom praise of every sort.
A hundred gifts he gave to him of every kind,
To the Vazír his road with counsel how to find.
" O thou whom time" (he gave for message this)
" Revolving must thy threshold's dust aye kiss,
" May the spheres' favour to thee never cease !
" Thy greatness aye from day to day increase !
" There's in my sign of chastity a sun,
" Whence in her heart the moon a ray has won.

" Higher than is the moon's her base is laid,
" Yet has the sun's eye never seen her shade.
" Purer than pearl that e'er in oyster lay,
" Than star in honour shedding brighter ray.
" Only when veiled will she the moon behold,
" For fear the stars to look on her be bold—
" Only the mirror sees her features fair,
" The comb alone lets loose her flowing hair.
" That hair alone is with the fortune blessed
" At times its head upon her feet to rest.
" When the house-courts she walks in loveliness
" Naught but her skirt may those sweet feet caress.
" Nor does her chin the bride-adorner dress,
" Nor does her lip the cane with finger press :
" Her beauty from the rose her skirt withdrew,
" Whose robe disgracefully was torn in two.
" Nor at her cheek may the narcissus pry :
" It loves the cup and has a wicked eye.
" She walks not in the light of moon or sun,
" Lest in pursuit of her her shadow run.
" She passes not by fountain or by stream,
" Lest her reflection's eye should on her beam.
" Her station ever though within the veil,
" Outside a hundred strifes for her prevail.
" All kings desirous to obtain her hand
" But ruin at her will demanding stand.
" The high from Rome and up to Syria's bound
" Drinking their hearts' blood through her love are found.
" Yet towards no one does she turn her mind,
" In Egypt only can she comfort find.
" At Rome with mind content she would not smile :
" To her are Syria's dust and water vile.
" Towards Egypt only does she long to go ;
" Her tears, a second Nile, for Egypt flow.
" Why she for Egypt longs I cannot say,
" Nor who it is that draws her heart that way.

"Her native land as if they there declared,
"Or for her food there royal briefs prepared (151).
"If thy exalted mind to this consent,
"She shall to that attractive land be sent,
"By beauty's right should she the throne not share,
"To sweep the house, then, be her service there."
When Egypt's Vazír heard the grateful word;
With his pride's head-dress were the heavens stirred.
Deeply he bowed and cried: "Then who am I,
"That in my heart such thoughts are sown and lie?
"Yet since the king has raised me from the ground,
"My head may rightly pass the heavens' bound.
"I am that earth which the fair cloud of spring
"Is with its goodness ever watering.
"A hundred tongues should now my body raise
"Like grass, could I enough such goodness praise?
"Yet through the favour that the king now lends,
"My duty is, if fortune me befriends,
"To make my head his foot, my eyes his shoes,
"With head and eye my road to him to choose.
"And yet with Egypt's king, that wisdom's mine,
"So tight the bonds of service me entwine,
"If for one hour only should I absent be,
"With sword of power he would punish me.
"Do ye this service not from me demand; (152)
"Absolved from pride's suspicion let me stand.
"By way of gratitude, should he allow,
"Two hundred golden litters send I now;—
"A thousand waiting-maids, a thousand slaves,
"Pine-statured, moving as the *Tubá* waves.
"The slaves of disposition sweet and kind,
"In Paradise no purer could one find;
"From smiling mouths they naught but sweetness breathe,
"While pearls and rubies round their hair enwreathe.
"With girded loins and jaunty caps aside,
"They in their golden saddles smartly ride.

" The waiting-maids of light and bright array,
" *Huris* of earthly water free and clay.
" Their perfumed locks their rosy cheeks adorn,
" With arching eyebrows o'er a moon upborne.
" Of many gems their ornaments they bind,
" In golden litters gracefully reclined.
" With these, too, such as are possessed of wit,
" And skilled in horsemanship, as may befit,
" I send, that her with honour they convey,
" To my retirement gently lead the way."
When the wise messenger had heard his mind,
Prostrate he kissed his feet, on earth reclined,
And said : " Though Egypt glory great may see,
" Beneficence arises fresh in thee.
" Our sovereign requires not pomp or state ;
" Of what thou say'st he has enough to sate.
" The slaves and all the handmaids of his Court
" Would, shouldst thou reckon them, be counted short.
" Those robed with honour (153) at his banquets found
" More than the leaves upon the trees abound.
" The glittering gems presented by his hand
" Are more in number than the desert sand.
" Acceptable is his desire to thee,
" Happy the man with whom thou dost agree.
" Since now thy table it would seem to suit,
" Towards thee will he quickly send that fruit."

THE BLOWING OF THE BREEZE OF ACCEPTANCE FROM THE DIRECTION OF EGYPT, AND THE PASSING OF ZULEIKHA'S LITTER, LIKE THE LITTER OF THE ROSE, TO EGYPT.

When the wise man returned from Egypt's land
From off Zuleikha's soul to loose the band,
Of the Vazír good news he brought indeed ;
With him he filled her, from herself he freed.

Her fortune's rose-bud then began to bloom,
Its flight her destiny's *Humá* to resume.
In dreams on her affairs the bonds that fell,
Imagination came to loose as well.
Indeed, wherever sorrow is or mirth,
They come from dreams or fancy on the earth.
From dreams and fancy happy he who's passed,
Out of such whirlpool lightly saved at last.
Her father saw Zuleikha glad again,
And to prepare her trousseau turned his rein.
And for the bridal then did he prepare,
From Roum and Russia, thousands of the fair,
Pistachio-mouthed, and of pomegranate breast,
Cheek and breast garden on rose-garden pressed.
On each ear-lobe a knot of jewels tied,
Encircling musk from ear to ear applied.
As rose-leaf in the morning fresh their face,
Free of dye's shame, and of red paint's disgrace.
Locks as of amber on a tulip hung,
And on each ear a pearl of price was strung.
Thousands of male slaves to excite men's strife,
With charms blood-shedding, robbing men of life.
Jaunty the red caps on their heads aside,
And of their scented hair the knots untied,
Whilst of the locks around their caps each hair
As twisted hyacinths 'neath tulips fair.
With coloured coats on body fitting right,
As tender bud or cane of sugar tight.
Their hair-like waists with jewels hung around,
A hundred hearts to each hair hanging bound.
A thousand well-formed horses, full of grace,
Obedient to the saddle, fierce in pace,
Than *chougán*-driven ball more swift to pass,
More mild than dew that lies upon the grass.
Upon them if the whip but cast a shade,
Out of time's plain to leap all haste they made.

Like the wild ass that scours the desert plain,
Or water-bird afloat upon the main :
That with the hoof the stony rock would cleave,
Or with the tail in canes a knot would weave ;
On hill that passed as light as o'er the plain,
Yet never lost the guidance of the rein.
A thousand camels might that never lack,
Mountain of mountains, hills upon their back ;
Not without pillars, standing as a hill,
With wind-swift coursers' speed advancing still.
Like hermits with but little food content,
With lordly patience under burdens bent.
A hundred deserts passed in God's repose,
Whilst eating thorns like spikenard or like rose.
For travel's love without food, without sleep,
In desert bounds to music step that keep.
Upon a hundred camels precious things,
Whilst every load a country's income brings.
Two hundred coverlets of rich brocade,
In Roum and Syria and Egypt made.
Caskets of jewels that reflect the light,
Badakhshan rubies, pearls and sapphires bright.
Two hundred trays of musk from far Tatár (154),
With amber pure, and aloes of Kamár (155).
With camel-drivers for each stage and place,
Like China's desert was of earth the face.
And for Zuleikha as a bride apart
They made a litter pleasing to the heart.
With aloe carved and sandalwood was made,
The house, and on its planks was gold inlaid.
Like Jamshid's tent its roof with gems was bound,
Like the sun's globe aye shedding gold around.
Without, within, as full as it could hold,
Were drops of pearl and many a nail of gold.
Its hangings all of woven gold brocade,
Of hues enchanting, beauteous form were made.

In that bride's chamber they Zuleikha place
And towards Egypt gently turn her face.
On back of camels swift of foot made fast,
In the spring breeze like rose the litter passed.
Jess'mine in face and scent, of jessamine form,
Thousands of cypress, box, and pine trees swarm;
They started off, as if the early spring
From place to place the plain were traversing,
And to whatever stage that idol came,
There Iram's garden hid its face from shame.
The boys excited, leaping here and there,
And ogling from their litters maidens fair.
Of her own locks each girl a noose had thrown,
And made a boy a captive of her own.
Each boy had of his eye-lash made a dart,
And made an opening in his prisoner's heart.
To charm on one side and caress desire,
On the other longing and a lover's fire.
Thousands of lovers and beloved were by,
Goods everywhere and hundreds there to buy.
After this manner staging day by day,
They towards Egypt took their lengthy way.
Zuleikha happy, pleased with fate indeed,
The road towards Egypt would be passed with speed;
The night of sorrow would be turned to day,
The pain of separation pass away;
Not knowing this, that still the night was black,
From that till morn of many years the track.
Through darksome night and through the daylight clear,
On, on they drove till Egypt's self was near.
A courier quickly forwards thence they sent,
And he before them on his camel went,
That he tow'rds Egypt on his road might go
And Egypt's Vazír might the tidings know,
" Thy fortune, lo! is here before thine eyes;
" If thou wouldst go to welcome it, arise!"

### The Hearing by the Vazír of Egypt of Zuleikha's Approach, and his Arising with the Intent to go to Meet her, and Adorning himself with Ornaments with his Egyptian Attendants.

To Egypt's Vazír when the tale was brought,
Tow'rds his desire the world had turned, he thought.
Then he proclaimed that forth from Egypt's land
To march the army whole prepared should stand;
That what by way of ornament each thing
Each of them had he should produce and bring
The army then came forth from foot to head
In gold and ornaments and gems (157) arrayed.
Thousands of slaves and maids assembled soon,
With face of rose and cheek that vied the moon.
Boy slaves with collar golden and with crown,
Like golden palm-tree from the saddle grown.
With their seven (156) ornaments the girls arrayed,
In litters that were curtained with brocade.
Singers, sweet-lipped, conceits repeating choice,
Congratulating all with pleasing voice.
Musicians, tuned of pleasure's harp the string,
Commenced the song of merriment to sing.
When to attune it the lute's ear is wrung,
Its sweet chords echo to the cheerful song.
Good news of meeting brings the flute's sweet sound,
And for the soul the hope of union's found.
Freed by rebeck the soul from string of woe,
Its dulcet tones evokes the sounding bow.
The drum awakens too the friendly sound,
That in the travellers' hand the skin is found. (158)
As in this manner on their way they went,
Due meed was to the road of pleasure lent.

When like the moon two stages they went on,
They came of all those fair ones to the sun.
They found a country not removed from light,
A thousand cupolas had made it bright,
As if the cloud of heaven, without a bound,
Had rained full many stars like hail around.
Here, in the midst of royal tents displayed,
Of maidens fair an army was arrayed.
When Egypt's Vazír's sight that tent fell on,
He smiled as morning at the rising sun,
And lighting down from off his royal steed
Towards that tent he went with joyous speed.
The servants of the *Haram* might and main
To kiss his foot's dust ran, to honour gain.
Welcome he spoke to each assembled there,
And smiled upon them as a flower fair.
Of that fair moon he due enquiry made,
By air and toil how on the road delayed.
Then gave the offerings that he had brought,
Things to the eye with special pleasure fraught,
Of smiling girls all sweetness to behold,
Of loin-begirded youths with caps of gold,
Of horses on whose saddles gold was laid,
From tail to ears in jewels all arrayed,
Of garments, some of silk and some of hair,
And of rare jewels, all beyond compare :
Of sweets of Egypt what was rare and new
And of sweet draughts to drink of every hue ;
With such the desert was adorned and laid,
Pleasant words spoken and excuses made.
Now for their march was fixed the coming day,
As to his own camp then he made his way.

## The Seeing of the Vazír of Egypt by Zuleikha through a Hole in the Tent, and her Raising a Cry that this is not He whom I Saw in My Dream, and for whom I have been Troubled for Years.

That ancient juggler, this revolving sphere,
To trouble men its tricks devises here.
Of hope it binds the wretched with the chain
To hopelessness to lead him back again;
Fruit to the palate shows in distant view,
That unfulfilled hope he may sadly rue.
When on the tent the Vazír threw his shade,
Zuleikha was within there with her maid.
Desire to see drew from her hand the rein;
She said: "O ancient sharer of my pain,
"Contrive it so that I may have one look,
"For now no longer patience can I brook.
"And never greater the desire to see
"Than when one's love 'neath the same roof may be.
"Of thirsty souls should water touch the lip,
"They burn the mouth to moisten with a sip."
When her nurse saw disturbed Zuleikha grew,
Her mistress round the tent she slily drew,
And in the tent with cunning and design
She made a hole as eye of needle fine.
When to that hole Zuleikha fixed her eye,
From a grief-laden heart she heaved a sigh.
"Alas", she cried; "strange things do me befall;
"Still uncompleted now falls down my wall.
"Whom in my dream I saw, this is not he,
"In search of whom I bore this misery.
"Not he, my sense and wit away who bore,
"And to unconsciousness my reins gave o'er.

F

"Who told his secret, 'tis not he again,
"Who made my consciousness resume its reign.
"Alas! my slack fate brings me hardship still,
"The rising of my star has brought me ill.
"I planted palms for dates; thorns only grew.
"I scattered seeds of love that brought me rue.
"Much grief I suffered for a treasure's sake,
"And to my hand has fallen but a snake.
"Towards the garden drew me roses' scent;
"The thorn's spear caught me and my skirt was rent.
"I wander thirsting in the desert sand,
"For water hastening on every hand.
"Upon my lip my dry tongue falls through thirst;
"Pustules upon my lip in blood-waves burst.
"Sudden afar had water on me shone;
"In desperate rise and fall I hurried on:
"In place of water in a pit I find
"Shining in sun-light salt earth left behind.
"I am that traveller lost upon the hill
"For want of food below a mount of ill.
"Stones from my feet have torn the flesh away,
"Nor strength have I to move nor wish to stay.
"All of a sudden through my bloody tears
"This image whom I long have lost appears.
"As tow'rds him to advance I make me bold,
"A raging lion fate makes me behold.
"I am the merchant whose bark rocks have torn,
"Who on a plank sits naked and forlorn.
"My place through waves can I no moment keep,
"Now to the sky they bear me, now the deep,
"When suddenly a boat there comes in sight,
"And glads me that my task may yet be light;
"But it approaches me without delay,
"And is a crocodile sent me to slay.
"On the whole earth there's no more wretched wight,
"Of wretched ones none in more hopeless plight.

"No heart is left me, charmer none I know,
"Stones on my heart, dust on my head I throw.
"Pardon for God's sake, heaven, on me bestow,
"In love show me a gate through which to go.
"Beneath my friend's skirt if I be not laid,
"Let me be captive to none other made.
"Do not thou tear the vest of my repute,
"And let no other hand my skirt pollute.
"My purpose have I vowed within my soul
"And ever strive to keep my treasure whole.
"Consume me not with pain who helpless stand,—
"Give not my treasure to a dragon's hand."
After this manner she for long complained,
And blood from every pointed eye-lash rained.
From soul and rent heart uttering cries profound,
In grief she rubbed her face upon the ground.
Of mercy then arose in flight the bird,
And from the hidden world a voice she heard.
"Raise from the dust, O wretched one, thy face:
"Ease shall of difficulty take the place.
"Egypt's Vazír is not thy heart's desire:
"That wish without him mayst thou not acquire.
"Through him thou seest the beauty of thy friend,
"Thou gain'st thy heart's aim through him in the end.
"Let not his friendship terror bring to thee;
"In safety will he keep thy silver key.
"For his key's teeth are all of waxen mould;
"Of waxen key the business may be told.
"To guard thy jewel, then, what is thy need?
"In diamond's work soft iron fails indeed—
"If of a light thorn they a needle make,
"How will a hard rock its long stitches take?
"Where of a hand the sleeve is void, 'tis clear,
"There of a dagger there need be no fear."
Zuleikha, when she heard these words of grace,
Rubbed on the ground in thankfulness her face.

Tongue free from moans and lip from cries, her blood
She girded up her loins to swallow, like a bird.
Through eating blood she only breathed with pain;
She burnt with grief and yet did not complain.
Fixed on the road her eye, awaited she:
"When shall this matter's knots all loosened be?"


### The Arrival of Zuleikha with the Vazír of Egypt and the Coming out of the Egyptians and making Offerings of Golden Boxes on the Litter of Zuleikha.

When on its golden drum the starlit arch
The signal beat for the night's morning march,
The stars their own assembly rendered void (159).
And joining with the night their burdens tied.
Of that gold-scattering drum was from the light
The peacock's tail with parrot's hue bedight.
With royal pomp the Vazír forward went,
Placed in her litter that moon from her tent.
To right and left, before, behind her, too,
The army he arranged in order due,
With gold umbrellas that o'er beauties' head
Was as of golden trees a shadow made;
A jewelled saddle beneath every tree,
A throne for every fair one there would be.
And in the midst of tree, and shade, and throne,
The fair one sitting there went moving on.
The singers now attuned their voice to song,
The camel-drivers shouting (160) pushed along.
With sound of melody and *Huda* shout
Heav'n's vault and desert plain were filled throughout.
From steeds and camels moving on amain
Of moons and crescents full were vale and plain.

At times from every side in headlong pace
The crescent, wounding, cut the full moon's face:
At others, from the full moon rising clear,
The crescent would then wane and disappear; (161)
Wounded by horses' hoof where earth had bled,
The camel's foot a plaster there would spread.
Drives to their saddle-seat the rampant deer, (162)
The horses' neigh, as bell resounding clear;
The girls at ease in litters borne along
Follow the camel-drivers' cry and song;
Zuleikha's handmaids were in mirth and glee
That she of separation's fiend was free.
The Vazír, and his people, too, were glad
His house for mistress such an idol had.
Zuleikha, bitter in her litter pent,
The heav'n with cries and lamentation rent.
" O fortune! why hast thou me so oppressed?
" Why hold me so impatient, without rest?
" Nor do I know what I have done to thee
" That thou hast thrown me into misery.
" In visions first didst thou despoil my heart,
" Waking, a thousand woes didst thou impart.
" At times of madness binding with the chain,
" At times in bounty loosing me again.
" When thou didst break me, I myself was free:
" I erred in seeking remedies from thee.
" How should I know that when a cure I sought,
" To exile thou wouldest me have brought?
" Enough for me the pain myself I knew,
" The pain of exile thou hast giv'n me, too.
" Be melting souls a remedy for thee,
" What, God defend us! will that melting be?
" Fraud's snare, upon my road, oh! do not place;
" Nor throw stones on my bowl of patience' face.
" Promise that henceforth thou in happiness
" With ease of life wilt thy own soul possess.

"Well with that promise should I be content:
"Who knows if such a lot for me is meant?"
As thus Zuleikha spoke to Heaven's ear,
The time the baggage to unload came near,
And from the guides there rose the hasty cry:
"Lo! Egypt's city and Nile's bank are nigh."
Thousands of souls Nile's margin round about,
On foot and horseback standing raised a shout.
Egypt's Vazír by way of gratitude
With bounteous hand before that litter strewed
Gold caskets full of *dirams* and of gold,
Caskets of jewels and of pearls untold. (163)
Jewels the offerers were scattering
As on the flowering mead the clouds of spring,
From gold and gems those many hands that shower,
The litter hid as in a jewelled bower.
From many jewels that men threw around
Upon the road no horse-hoof touched the ground.
Horse-shoes and rubies clashing as they passed,
As stone and iron fire around them cast.
Their presents scattering there mile on mile
The people line in rows the banks of Nile.
And in the Nile pearls deck each fish's ear,
As in the oyster royal gems appear.
Whilst from the *dirams* (164) scattered in the stream
The crocodiles themselves all *dirams* seem.
Thus moving forwards all in kingly state
With pomp they soon drew near the royal gate.
A Paradise on earth the palace reared,
Before it sun and moon mere bricks appeared.
Within that palace had a throne been placed,
Than other thrones with far more beauty graced.
The master goldsmith to that throne applied
Gold by the ass-load, all the gems beside.
To that gold-cradled seat they led her on,
Placed like a jewel on a golden throne.

From her heart's scar she yet was never free : (165)
Sitting in flames of gold she seemed to be.
A jewelled crown upon her head they placed,
And throne and crown both with her beauty graced.
Beneath that heavy diadem was still
Her heart as weighed down as 'twere 'neath a hill.
Those plenteous jewels poured upon her head
A very rain of sorrow seemed instead,
And from those gems, the envy of the sun,
Naught from her eye but pearls of tears would run.
With separation he whose heart is torn
But for a moment (166) tow'rds a throne is borne.
Who on that plain wears on his head a crown
Where heads in hundreds go to ruin down?
When fills the eye with tears of sheer despair,
What room is there for pearls and jewels there?


### The Passing of her Life by Zuleikha in Separation from Joseph (on whom be Peace!), and her Lamentation and Sighing by Night and by Day.

When with one charmer the heart gains its ease,
How can with any other union please?
When does the loving moth fly tow'rds the sun,
When its own light its face in hope has won?
Place scented herbs the nightingale before,
It loves the rose's perfume and no more.
When on the water-lily falls the sun's bright fire.
To see the moon why should it e'er desire?
When longs the thirsty soul for water pure,
It profits not clear sugar to procure.
In that abode of happiness and bliss
Of luxury could naught Zuleikha miss.

The Vazír ever as her slave at hand,
Both wealth and gold were aye at her command.
Rose-bodied servants, all perfumed with rose,
Looked for no ease in serving or repose.
Handmaids, enchanting and beloved of all,
Stood ever ready to obey her call.
Slaves all loin-girded, clad in rich brocade,
As sugar candied sweet from foot to head,
With black men also, all of amber hue ;
Like angels of pure skirt, no lust they knew.
The *Haram* (167) they frequent in harmless play,
True to the *Haram's* service day by day.
With Egypt's ladies sitting in one place,
For goodness known and delicate in grace,
Of equal dignity and equal birth,
Associating with her in her mirth,
Zuleikha, seated in her audience hall, (168)
Where friends and strangers entered, equal all,
Enjoyment's carpet had spread out, the while
Her heart was bleeding, on her lip a smile.
While holding converse outwardly with all,
Her heart was in another place a thrall. (169)
To talk with people she her lip would lend,
Whilst heart and soul were ever with her friend.
In grief and joy but to that burden tied,
A lasting bond she sought with none beside.
She seemed to sit with those of mortal kind,
But inwardly from all had freed her mind.
This was her mood till night from dawn of day,
Among her friends was ever this her way.
When night upon her face the veil had thrown,
Moon-like, behind the veil she sat alone ;
Till morn within her chamber would she oft
Place her friend's form upon a cushion soft,
On honour's knee before it once again
Would there relate it all her grief and pain,

And as she tuned her harp to trouble's air,
The song commence to sing of sheer despair.
She said: "O thou the object of this life of mine,
"Who of thyself in Egypt gavest me the sign,
"Of Egypt's Vazír didst thou give the name:
"For ever may endure thy greatness' fame!
"My head with honour's crown thy love will grace,
"Thy handmaid's service fortune there may trace.
"Lonely and strange in Egypt I arrived,
"Of union with thee by hard fate deprived.
"Oh! with this flame how long shall I consume,
"And with this fire my lamp of woe illume?
"Come! Of my heart's garden the adornment be!
"May my heart's wound be salved in meeting thee!
"Hopeless became the matter of my love:
"Gave me new hope a message from above.
"When from that hope my life new being took,
"Dust of despair from off my skirt I shook.
"From light thy beauty on my heart has cast,
"I know that I shall win thee at the last.
"From thy desire although my eye should bleed,
"Tow'rds four of six sides (170) does my eye give heed.
"Happy the day when thou approachest near,
"When to my eye as moon thou shalt appear.
"When I shall see thee, I shall cease to be
"And my life's carpet be rolled up by me.
"Of my own thoughts then shall I lose the thread,
"In madness shall myself astray be led.
"Me in my place again thou wilt not see.
"Coming as life, in my soul's place thou'lt be.
"In this and in the next world thou my hope,
"When I win thee, of self to speak what scope?
"I lay aside all thoughts of us and me,
"Why should I seek myself in finding thee?"
Thus speaking, morn to night she turned again
Nor until morning would her lips restrain.

And when the morning breeze began to rise,
Began to speak again in other wise.
She said : " O Zephyr of the morning, blow ;
" In jess'mine's bosom make musk-scent to flow.—
" Of cypress and of lily deck the place ;
" With spikenard's moist locks rub the roses's face.
" Stirring the branches, leaves ring bells of mirth ;
" The tree will dance, though fast its foot in earth.
" Thou bearest lovers' messages to please,
" And with the motion lovers bringest ease.
" By thee are charmers' soothing letters borne ;
" Comfort thou bearest to all those who mourn.
" None in the world more sorrowful than I,
" And none more pained by parting's misery.
" My heart is sick : affection bring to play :
" My sorrow 's great : oh ! drive my grief away !
" There is no place upon the earth below
" Where thou some time or other canst not go :
" Thy way through iron doors thou couldest take,
" Were the doors closed, through windows entrance make.
" Have mercy on me helpless, gone astray,
" And make a search for me in every way.
" Of ruling monarchs pass thou through the town,
" Pass by the throne of those who wear a crown ;
" In every city seek this moon of mine,
" Search of my king on every throne the sign.
" On every sweet spring garden cast a look,
" Step on the margin of each purling brook.
" On any river that thou passest by,
" That charming cypress may there meet thy eye.
" On Tartar desert thy kind foot be pressed ;
" In China's picture-houses stay and rest.
" Look for a model that his tale may tell,
" And from his perfume capture the gazelle.
" To leave that country should the thought prevail,
" Where'er thou pass in every hill and vale ;

"There graceful moving should a partridge stand,
"Rememb'ring him, strike on its skirt thy hand.
"If on the road thou meet a caravan,
"With at his head a heart-enchanting man,
"See in my eye of my own life that king,
"That caravan into this country bring.
"It may be so, that charmer when I see,
"That from hope's bush a rose may gathered be."
From morning's dawn until the shining sun
Into the plain of day in haste moved on,
With eye blood-shedding and heart full of pain
She to the morning breeze addressed her strain.
When the sun lit the world with its bright ray,
She lit up her assembly as the day.
Attendants stood before her in their rows,
And in her beauty her friends found repose.
With those pure-bosomed ones of cleanly heart
As yesterday she took her common part.
Such her condition every night and day,
The moons and years aye passing thus away.
When tedium in the house was hard to bear,
She in all haste would to the fields repair.
At times heart-scarred with sighing and lament,
She in the plain like tulip pitched her tent :
To tulip there that rose's secret spoke,
And from her scarred heart would sad speech evoke.
At times like flood she gave her torrent head,
And tow'rds the Nile with weeping eyes she sped :
Before it casting her own woe awhile,
She washed her mourning garment in the Nile,
And in this fashion as she passed the day,
Her eye fixed firm on expectation's way ;
Her lover by what road would he draw near,
Rise as the sun or as the moon appear?
Come, Jámi ; let us exercise our thought,
That Canaan's moon from Canaan may be brought.

With hope implanted in Zuleikha's breast,
Upon the royal road her eye at rest.
Her longing has beyond all limits passed.
Give me her cure, her love to meet at last.
After long expectation, oh! how sweet
That with her hope the hoping one should meet!

## The Commencement of the Story of the Envy borne towards Joseph by his Brothers, and of their Arranging to take Vengeance on him in Concert.

The scribe of this pen from some master old
Such words as these has in this volume told.
As Joseph now to greater beauty grew,
Was Jacob's heart enchanted with the view;
Saw him the very apple of his eye, (171)
His other sons neglected passing by—
His love to him would more and more renew,
So that each day their envy greater grew.
There was a tree that in his palace seen
Increased his pleasure with its freshness green.
Whose base was in its place so firmly laid,
It threw upon the ground its bounty's shade,
Like those cell-dwellers who are robed in green
And moved with frantic ecstasy are seen.
Each leaf to utter praises was a tongue,
By which due praises to God's name were sung.
Beyond the azure dome its branches fair,
As sparrows sitting, angels rested there.
With every son that God did him provide,
From that glad tree that with the *Sidrah* (172) vied,
A fresh branch sprouting would there come to view
Which with the infant's stature equal grew.

And when the child arrived at age mature,
A green rod from the tree would he procure.
Yet not for Joseph, on whom fortune beamed,
For whom no stick from that tree worthy seemed.
He of life's garden was a plant, unfit
That any wooden branch should vie with it.
He to his father one night said aside :
" O thou to whose arm conquest is allied,
" Pray thou that He in Whom our surety lies (173)
" A rod for me may grow in Paradise,
" Which from the time of youth till I am old
" Where'er I fall may ever me uphold,
" And both in sport and in the battle field,
" Over my brothers me the palm may yield."
Then humble prayer to God his father made,
As Joseph wished, his supplication laid.
Down from the *Sidrah* tree a jasper rod
A heav'nly messenger conveyed from God.
This by time's axe had never wounded been,
Nor from fate's saw had it e'er trouble seen.
Strong and of weighty price, yet light the while,
Nor oil nor colour might the rod defile.
He brought word down that by the grace of God
Pillar of royal house should be the rod.
When new strength Joseph from this gift obtained,
Struck down with grief the envious remained. (173)
From being's source the stripes by that rod dealt
More heavy than a hundred blows were felt.
Each one within himself conceived a thought,
Into his heart the plant of envy brought.
This to their nature first might vigour lend,
But of disgrace would bear fruit in the end.

## The Beholding by Joseph in a Dream of the Worship of the Sun and Moon and the Eleven Planets, the Hearing of the Same by his Brothers, and the Increase of their Envy against Him.

Blessed he from outward form who freedom gains,
Whose eyes are not closed by magicians' chains.
His heart awake, his eye sweet slumbers close,
None e'er so wakeful in such calm repose.
His eyelids, closed to what will not endure,
Open to what eternal is and sure,
Lay Joseph before Jacob's eyes one night,
Loved in his eye more than his very sight.
His head on pillow laid in slumber mild,
His lip of beauty there in sweetness smiled.
His tender lips with that sweet smile apart,
Brought sweet excitement into Jacob's heart.
Joseph's moist eyelids from their sleep unclose,
And as his fortune he from dreams arose.
His father said: "Sugar is shamed of thee:
"Of that sweet smile what may the reason be?"
"I saw in dream," he said, "the moon and sun,
"With the eleven planets, all as one,
"Their heads in salutation lowly place,
"And bow in reverence before my face."
"Such speech as this," his father warned him, "shun:
"Tell not, beware! thy dream to any one.
"If this, which God forbid, thy brothers know,
"They'll wake thee with a hundred times more woe;
"A thousand furies in their heart ne'er cease:
"When in their passion will they give thee peace?
"The dream's interpretation is too clear:
"With it in patience they will never bear."

The father's warning thus; but Fate ordains,
And with a breath it breaks device's chains.
The tale which Joseph told in some one's ear,
Told by that man his brothers came to hear.
Hast heard that what by more than two is known,
Common to every tongue will soon have flown?
A wise man says: "Of lips there are but two;
"It is not right that secrets pass them through."
Secrets that from between two lips are freed
May cause a hundred warriors to bleed.
Well said that utterer of maxims deep:
" He who would keep his head should secrets keep."
The wild bird from his cage who freedom gains,
With tales thou canst no longer bind in chains.
Now when his brothers had heard Joseph's tale,
They tore their very robes, with anger pale.
" What are our father's thoughts, O God", they cried,
" On gain and loss that he can not decide?
" Does he not know what from a child can come,
" That children only childish things become?
" From weaving falsehoods he will never cease
" That his own dignity he may increase.
" The poor old man deceit finds at his hands,
" In his companionship unsettled stands.
" Our sweet connection with him would he break,
" Our father's love would from his children take.
" Our father now has raised his head so high,
" He cares not for so much of dignity.
" He would that we, in darkness robed profound,
" To worship him should fall upon the ground—
" Father and mother, too, as well as we.
" This pitch of self-exalting may not be;
" We are our father's traffickers, not he:
" He wishes not our father well, but we
" By day in deserts guarding flocks aright,
" We are the guardians of his house at night.

"Both against foes his arm of strength are we,
"And among friends from us his dignity.
"What has he ever seen in him but tricks
"That he above us all on him should fix?
"To cure this, come, let us provide a way,
"That on some road he may to ruin stray.
"Between us since there is no sympathy
"But him to exile there's no remedy.
"Gird we our loins to find some helpful way,
"Before the power from us pass away;
"Or ere the thorn grows up in infamy,
"Tear up its root ere it becomes a tree."
To find a fitting remedy in league
They sat themselves together to intrigue.

### The Conspiring of the Brothers with each other, in order to remove Joseph (on whom be Peace!) from his Father.

When difficulties happen to the wise,
In his affairs whence trouble may arise,
To his own sense he adds another's wit,
That aid he may procure in solving it.
Should with one candle the house not be bright,
He places in its midst another light.
For the right-seeing ones these words, forsooth,
For those who sit upon the seat of truth:
Not for the crooked-thinking, crooked face;
Crookedness between two such grows apace.
When Joseph's brothers conference began
In Joseph's matter to concoct a plan,
"He has through sorrow shed our blood", one said:
"We need a stratagem his blood to shed.
"When a fierce foe one has in hand, and sure,
"By killing him one may be quite secure."

One said : "Of wickedness this is the way,
"One innocent that we should think to slay.
"If we of cruelty should drive the steed,
"Are we not faithless (175) in his death indeed?
"To drive him from this house our only aim,
"Not that he die, or we should kill or maim.
"'Twere well he from our sire should far be led,
"Alone, deserted, in some valley dread—
"Some desert where but snares and beasts are had,
"With naught but wolves and foxes, good or bad,—
"But tears of hopelessness no water there,—
"Except the sun's round orb no loaf to share,—
"Except night's darkness where would be no shade,—
"No couch but what on thorns' sharp points was laid.
"For some time if on them to rest he lie,
"He of himself without doubt soon would die.
"Nor with his blood our swords would coloured be ;
"From wound of tales and tricks we should be free."
Another said : "'Tis death of other kind ;
"Any worse death than this one could not find.
"I've heard 'tis best to perish with the knife,
"Not to yield up to thirst and hunger life.
"'Twere better, then, that we should seek and mark
"Some well, or far or near, but cramped and dark.
"There from his seat of honour will we throw
"Him with a hundred piercing slights below.
"Perhaps some caravan may see the place,
"And there may halt to rest themselves a space.
"Some one may lower in the well a cup,
"And in the place of water draw him up.
"Some one may take him as a son or slave,
"And make all haste to bear him off and save.
"Connected with this place he will not stay,
"Whilst that we injured him they cannot say."
When thus was told the tale of that dark well,
They all themselves into it headlong fell.

Their own well of deceit they did not know,
And all without a rope went down below.
Moving as hypocrites their father's heart,
In lying they agreed to bear their part.
To their own business then they went their way,—
Postponing this until another day.

## The Asking by the Brothers for Joseph from their Father, and the taking of Joseph (on whom be Peace!) before their Father.

In self-oblivion's corner aye confined,
Happy are they whom self's bonds never bind;—
From nature's bonds free and deceits of lust,
Who in pain's road and love's street are but dust.
To vex men's heart no dust from them will rise,
Nor on them from mankind a burden lies.
Under the world's obstructions aye content,
To burdens all that come their backs are bent.
Sleeping at night who anger never keep,
Awaking in the morn are as they sleep.
Joseph's detractors in the morning gay,
Rejoicing in their thoughts of yesterday,
Love on their tongues, their hearts still hatred keep,
As wolves are hidden in the form of sheep.
Seeing their father, the *Ihrám* (176) they bound,
Respectful kneeling down upon the ground.
Opening the door of fraud to over-reach,
They of hypocrisy began the speech.
They talked of everything, both old and new,
Till to the point they wished the story drew.
" From weariness at home we suffer grief,
" And in the desert air would seek relief.
" If thou wilt give us leave, we all intend
" To-morrow in the desert out to spend.

" Joseph, our brother, that light of our eyes,
" Is young and seldom in the desert lies.
" Our dignity to heighten with intent,
" How would it be if he, too, with us went?
" In the house-corner sits he night and day ;
"' Send him to-morrow out to sport and play.'
" Sometimes with him the desert path we'll tread :
" To hill and wood at times shall he be led.
" At times we'll draw the sweet milk of the sheep,
" And drink while laughter shall us merry keep.
" Of the green sward we'll make a place to play,
" Or to the tulip beds will lead the way.
" From off the tulip's head its cup upborne,
" With it will we our Joseph's head adorn.
" With skirts as those of partridge lifted high,
" Graceful upon the sward shall he pass by.
" At one place for the grazing deer we'll care,
" Or of the wolves he might in pieces tear.
" Perhaps we thus his spirits may revive,
" And weariness of home away may drive.
" With wonders though you every effort use,
" Can nothing but his play a child amuse."
When Jacob heard what they had all to say,
The collar of consent he rent away.
" That you should take him how can I agree?
" 'Twould mean but sorrow in my heart for me.
" I fear for him lest you should have no care,
" And of his state should be neglectful there,
" And on that ancient plain, so full of woe,
" To him some old wolf his sharp teeth should show.
" Those teeth may close upon him in the strife,
" And rend his tender body and my life."
When those deceitful ones these words had heard,
Another tale to tell to them occurred.
" Of purpose all so weak we do not live,
" That we ten corpses to one wolf should give.

"Were he no wolf, but lion men to eat,
"Soon like a fox he'd lie beneath our feet."
And when these words to Jacob's ear attained,
From making more excuses he refrained.
Joseph he let them to the desert bear
To his own realm inviting woe and care.

### The Carrying away of Joseph by his Brothers from before his Father, and Throwing him into a Well.

Woe to this trickey sphere, which every day
Casts in a well some beauteous moon away.
Gazelles that feed in pastures of the soul
Of some wolf's claw it places in control.
When Joseph to those ravening wolves was giv'n,
"Wolves carry off the lambs," exclaimed the heav'n.
Whilst they remain before their father's eyes
Each with the other in affection vies.
One holds him on his head or back at rest;
Another to his bosom tightly pressed—
When on the desert's edge they placed their feet
Then with the hand of cruelty they beat.
No more upon the back of kindness borne,
They threw him on the hard rock or the thorn.
His foot in thorns and mud that naked went
With thorns and grass as if with nails was rent.
His shoes thrown off, upon the rocky road
His silver foot the stones tore as he trod.
His foot's sole, tightly which the mud retained,
Amongst the thorns and rocks with blood was stained.
Behind those ten hard hands stayed he to rest,
With slaps and blows his fair cheek was distressed.
(May soon the sword cut off the hand of those,
Who with a tender moon could come to blows!)

If he went on, like flood would pour the blow,
A Nile behind him as the face of foe.
('Twere better that that man should pinioned be
Who such a fair neck could e'er broken see!)
If he proceeded with them side by side
They pulled his ear for him on every side.
(He with his finger who would rub that ear,
Of all but fingers may his fist lie bare!)
Wailing, the skirt of any if he pressed,
Open he cruelly would tear his vest.
Weeping if he the foot of one embraced,
Laughing upon that head a foot was placed.
To whomsoever he with groaning spoke,
Naught but abusive songs he would provoke.
Hopeless from them, when he would weep and moan,
Blood from his eye on tulip flowers was sown.
Sometimes in blood, sometimes in dust he lay;
Shattered his heart with sorrow, he would say:
" Where hast thou gone, my father? Where, oh! where?
" That thou for my misfortune dost not care?
" Come! Of thy handmaids now the sons behold,
" Fallen from wisdom, from thy Faith of old—
" Come, see the wretched plight in which I stand,
" Ground to the dust of envy by the hand.
" Thou hast thy precious one thyself brought low,
" And by the hand thou maimest of his foe.
" To claws of those that know no mercy thrown;
" Of wolves the power thy gazelle must own.
" See with thy hearts' hope what desire have they,
" And how thy favours they would now repay.
" In thy life's garden the sweet rose that grew,
" Aye watered of thy bounty with the dew,
" Through thirst, dried up with fever, it remains,
" And neither hue nor moisture it retains.
" The soft plant reared as Paradise's own,
" That in the garden of life's house was sown,

"Through cruel wind has fallen in the dust,
"And thorns and grass their heads above it thrust.
"The moon that lit the darkness of thy night,
"And was of gloomy fate far from the sight,
"Has heaven overcast in such a way
"That from the crescent moon it seeks a ray."
Thus for three leagues was he then dragged afar,
Peaceful, but with those stony hearts at war.
Harsh looks from them in him with mildness meet,
And cold abusive words from him with heat.
Of a well suddenly they reached the head,
And at its head there were their footsteps stayed.
A well, dark, narrow as a tyrant's tomb,
That e'en on wisdom's eye would cast a gloom.
Then were its lips as dragon's mouth agape,
That men from outside for its food would rape;
Inside of men-oppressors as the mind,
And full of serpents to torment mankind.
Its circle was the centre-point to grieve;
Its depth beyond man's power to conceive.
Full of impurity its depth profound,
Fetid its air, brackish its spring was found.
And if a breather there an instant stayed
A bar across his breathing's road was laid.
When they that rose-faced moon to drive away
Approach the well, all horrid as it lay,
Against their cruelty he cried once more,
And wept and wailed in such a measure sore,
That if the rock had understood the moan,
Softer than wax would have become the stone.
Yet as the pleading voice became more shrill,
Their stony hearts grew ever harder still.
How may I tell how cruel they became?
My heart will not permit to give it name.
Upon those arms which, if the silk of heav'n
Had touched, it would great pain have giv'n,

Of goats' and sheeps' hair made they bound a string,
In every hair of which there was a sting.
His slender waist, with finest hair that vied,
They with a woollen rope made fast and tied.
His robe from off his body then they tear,—
Like rose without its bud that form was bare,
But with reproach their own robes cut away
From their own stature for the Judgment Day.
Then him within the well that day they hung,
And half-way to the water downwards slung.
As the world-lighting sun in beauty clear,
They cast into the wave that shining sphere.
Above the water in the well a stone
He made a place for him to sit upon.
Behold what blessing to that rock there came,
That it a mine of precious gems became!
Whilst from his lip, as fresh as sugar new,
That brackish water to sweet honey grew.
Lit by his cheek, the well at once grew bright,
As the earth lit up by the moon at night.
The odour from his *attar* (175) shedding hair
Removed the smell from the well's putrid air.
Each noxious thing, when that light rose revealed,
Down in another hole itself concealed.
He had a garment that contained a charm,
That saved his grandsire from the fire's alarm.
From *Rizván* (179) down to Abraham it came;
Into a bed of roses it turned flame.
Soon from the *Sidrah* Gabriel came to view
And from his side the amulet he drew.
Forth from that place he brought out then the vest
And that pure body with it robed and dressed.
Then said: "O thou with parting's sorrow rent,
" By me the Eternal has a message sent,
" Some day those on thee who this evil wrought,
" That band who have such evil in their thought,

"Heart-wounded more than thou shalt ever be,
"With bowed heads will I bring them here to thee.
"Thou shalt these cruelties to them recite,
"Nor thy condition shalt thou bring to light
"These as thou knowest shalt thou all declare:
"They shall not know of thee a single hair."
From Gabriel this promise Joseph gained,
And by his brothers' deeds was no more pained.
It seemed to him a throne, that slab of stone,
And Joseph sat as monarch on his throne.
And whilst he sorrowed stood the Faithful Soul (180)
To wait upon him and his heart console.

## The Arrival of the Caravan at the Well, and the Bringing up of Joseph (on whom be Peace!) like the Moon.

In God's name, what a fortunate caravan,
From which for water came a knowing man.
He drew up from the well his bucket soon,
And from Aquarius' sign arose a moon.
For three days in the pit did that moon dwell,
As dwells the full moon in the "*Nakhshab*" well. (181)
As the fourth day upon this azure sky,
Rose the lost Joseph from the well on high.
With goods prepared from many cities round,
For Egypt with propitious fortune bound,
A caravan had wandered from its road,
Pitched tents and there to rest undid its load.
Happy the wand'rer who might lose his way
And come where such a guide as Joseph lay.
Around the well they made their camping-place,
And seeking water thither turned their face.
There came one first who was by fortune blessed,
And tow'rds life's water there who forward pressed.

In the dark well that one of *Khisr* (182) face
Let down his bucket on the water's trace.
To Joseph Gabriel faithful said: "Arise!
"Pour mercy's water which the thirsty prize.
"Like the bright sun sit in the pail at rest,
"And hasten to the East from tow'rds the West.
"Make the well's edge thy own horizon bright,
"Illumine that horizon's veil with light.
"Throw from thy face upon the world a ray;—
"Illumine once again the earth with day."
From the well's stone then Joseph leapt in haste,
Himself as water in the pail he placed.
The strong man then the bucket upwards drew,
And what a pail of water weighed he knew.
"To-day the pail is heavier," he cried:
"Than water there is something more beside."
As rose that world's moon from the well on high,
Rose of good tidings from his soul the cry,—
Glad news that from that dark well came to birth
A moon that should illumine many an earth;
Glad news that from a brackish well obscure
Water there should arise so fresh and pure.
A rose had in that desert been revealed,
Yet from the rest he kept it there concealed.
To the encampment he conveyed him then,
And handed him in secret to his men,
Just as with luck one may a treasure gain,
And yet unless concealed 'twill bring him pain.
Those envious ones as well were standing by,
What might become of him to promptly spy,
There constantly they lingered round to wait,
To learn what possibly might be his fate.
When of the caravan the news they found,
To know in haste the well they gathered round.
In secret they called Joseph by his name,
But nothing from the well but echo came;

And thence towards the caravan they went,
Into their power to bring Joseph bent.
And after searching with much pain and care
Amidst the caravan they found him there.
"This is our slave," in seizing him they said,
"Out of faith's collar who has wrenched his head.
"For work and service he is not inclined,
"But tow'rds flight for long has set his mind.
"He has no wish to do his service well;
"Thus him, though of the house, we fain would sell.
"The service of a bad slave in his mood
"Is more of evil service than of good.
"Better that thou shouldst sell him ev'n for naught:
"Into restraint from ill he'll not be brought.
"Much pains we will not take on his account:
"'Twere best to sell him for some small amount."
Thus the young man who from the well had brought,
Joseph from them at some small value bought.
The young man was to Málik fully known;
He for a trifle made the slave his own.
With fastened loads the caravans then went,
On reaching Egypt on their aim intent.
Wrong he who sells a soul as merchandise
Who sells for trifles such a goodly prize.
All Egypt's income for one look from him!
And a life's goods for but one word from him!
Yet of his costliness can Jacob tell;
At what to purchase knows Zuleikha well.
Sells fortune's treasure he who's void of sense,
And frowning gives it but for some few pence. (183)

## The Bringing of Joseph by Málik into the Neighbourhood of Egypt, and the Sending of the Vazír by the King to meet him.

When Málik without labour in his trade
His foot by chance upon such treasure laid,
Upon the ground before that charmer's face
Through joy it on that journey found no place,
But his soul feeding on a distant scent,
Turning two stages into one he went.
From far when he came near to Egypt's bound,
The tale 'mong Egypt's people passed around:
" Málik's long road to-day will find its end :
" A Hebrew slave he's bringing as his friend.
" No slave is this, but 'tis a brilliant sun,
" For the world's capital that's fortune won,
" A shining moon of goodness on the height,
" In realm of love a king of omens bright.
" The heav'n with all its eyes could never see
" Like picture in earth's picture gallery."
The rumour reached the King of Egypt's ear,
And he from jealousy was vexed to hear. (184)
" A garden of fair beauty 's Egypt's earth :
" No other land can give such roses birth.
" Roses above in Paradise that grow
" From shame before their face are shed below."
He said to Egypt's Vazír : " Do thou go,
" To meet the caravan and honour show.
" With thy own eyes do thou behold this moon ;
" Bring him thyself here to the palace soon."
Towards the caravan the Vazír went,—
His look upon that case of heart he bent.
And so that single look did him enthrall,
In worship he would fain before him fall.

But Joseph raised from off the ground his brow;
Before his face he would not let him bow,
And said: "Before Him only bend thy head,
"Who on thy neck from first hath blessing shed."
Then the Vazír of Málik asked this thing,
That he would bring him to the conquering king.
He said: "In coming I should have no fear,
"And hope that I should find thy favours near;
"I pray that thou wilt my excuses take,
"And leave me in my camp for quiet's sake.
"For two or three days let us be at rest;
"From want of sleep and food are we oppressed.
"Our face from dust, from dirt our bodies free,
"Cleanly will we attend his Majesty."
When Egypt's Vazír heard this subtle thing,
He went back to the presence of the king.
Of Joseph's beauty he a trifle said,
And the king's soul to jealousy was led.
He gave a sign that thousands of the fair,
The monarchs of the realm of beauty there,
With heads with gold caps all of which were graced,
And clad in robes with gold embroidery traced,
With waists that gem-bespangled belts adorn,
And mouths with lips on which sweet smiles are born,
From beauty's grove like roses to collect,
From Egypt rosy-faced ones all select,
When Joseph to the market came, that they
Before the purchasers should him display.
Then with such forms and qualities should those
To Joseph's boasted claims themselves oppose:
Were he the world-revolving sun of old,
His market through those fire-faces would grow cold.

## The Coming of Joseph to the Water of the Nile and Washing off the Dust of the Journey and Sitting on a Lofty Seat.

On the fourth day, as promised, when the sun,
Joseph, above heav'n's Nile its place had won,
To Joseph Málik said : "O heart of grace,
"Make, like the sun, on the Nile's bank a place.
"Go ; from thyself the road's dust wash away,
"And to Nile honour with thy dust convey."
At Málik's own command that shining sun
Alone towards the Nile then hastened on.
Raising his hand within his vest, was seen
On jessamine the water-lily's screen.
When from his head he took the golden cap of light,
Rose from sun's golden egg the crow of night.
As from his head he draws the clinging vest,
His skirt's the East, the Western moon his breast.
From his skirt's side the back and breast appear,
As from the circling sky the morning clear.
Binding in haste his linen drawers of blue,
As silver cypress tow'rds Nile's edge he drew.
From the blue sky, a cry there echoed round ;
"From that moon's feet is Egypt prosp'rous found.
"How would it be if I, in place of Nile,
"Could kiss his foot and rest me there awhile!"
Forward the sun resolved himself to throw,
That his own spring upon the Nile should flow.
He sees the sun's spring for himself not meet,
And with Nile-water washes hands and feet.
From bank his feet towards the stream incline,
Just as the moon might enter Pisces' sign.
As the world-lighting sun in its ascent,
As water-lily in the wave he went.

Into the water as he naked dived,
From him the flowing stream fresh life derived.
As he unloosed his curling locks again,
His foot the flowing stream held with a chain.
For every kind of game he might prepare
From crescent to full moon an amber snare.
Water sometimes he pourd upon his head,—
The Pleiads' gems upon the moon were shed.
At times he rubbed with hand his cheek so fair,
Or combed with hands as comb his spikenard hair.
Dust from face cleaned and dirt from body, too,
Like cypress on the banks of Nile he grew;—
From Málik's carpet-spreader called for vest,
His rose of jessamine with a fillet dressed.
Drew on his bosom then the fair brocade,
With many a pleasing figure that was made;—
The moon eclipsed by his gold diadem,
Put on his waist-belt decked with many a gem.
Two ringlets hung down so enchanting fair,
That filled with amber scent was Egypt's air.
That fair one on a litter then they place,
And to the royal castle set his face.
Outside the fort a platform there appeared,
Where for the king a daïs they had reared—
Before him many beauties standing there—
To gaze on Joseph's beauty all prepare.
Now on the daïs high the litter lies:
The whole world on that litter fix their eyes.
Perchance that day the heaven was concealed,
And to the world the sun was not revealed.
"O charmer", then to Joseph Málik said;
"Out of thy litter to the throne be led.
"Thou art the sun: raise from thy cheek the veil,
"And let thy own light o'er the world pervail."
When from the litter (186) Joseph took his way,
And on mankind threw like the sun his ray,

"It is the sun", the seers thought awhile,
"Or 'tis a vapour rising from the Nile."
The world-illuming sun was full in view:
This brilliance was not thence, they fully knew.
Hidden by clouds the sun was not yet bright.
In Joseph's face they knew this shining light;—
Beating their hands, amazed, on every side,
All people there who saw him loudly cried:
"Who is this star of fortune, God," they said,
"Sun, moon, before whom hang with shame the head?"
And Egypt's beauties, their heads hanging down,
Their own destruction on his tablet own.
Wherever the bright sun appears beside,
Is *Suha's* remedy alone to hide.


### THE COMING OF ZULEIKHA TO THE KING'S COURT, AND ASKING THE REASON OF THE ASSEMBLY, AND SEEING THE BEAUTY OF JOSEPH.

Of this Zuleikha had been unaware
That but two stages might bring Joseph there,
Yet to her inmost soul the tidings came;—
The scar of love had set her heart aflame.
She knew not her desire from whence it rose,
And sought by many stratagems repose.
Out to the desert went she, in belief
That from her heart it might expel her grief.
There for some days she stayed and lived distressed,
Her teeth together in her trouble pressed.
Luxury and pleasure in her train,
Yet every moment but increased her pain.
When there her harvest the flood bore away,
Again towards her home her longing lay.
Then once again she on her litter rode,
And took the way towards her own abode.

To her own house although she turned her face,
She passed along the castle's open space.
She saw the crowd and said: "What are these cries?
"Methinks to-day the dead in Egypt rise!"
One answered her: "He of auspicious name,
"The joy of Canaan's land, a slave there came.
"No slave is this, but lo! this shining sun
"In beauty's capital has fortune won." (187)
Zuleikha of her litter raised the screen:
She saw the slave and knew whom she had seen.
All undesired, a cry from her escaped,
A cry unconsciously her heart had shaped.
All haste the bearers of the litter made,
The litter to her private rooms conveyed.
Of her own house she the seclusion gained,
And sense from her unconscious state regained.
Her nurse said: "Lighter of my soul, say, why
"Thou from a burning heart didst raise a cry?
"And when thy sweet lip opened with the call,
"Why with its pain didst thou unconscious fall?"
She said: "O mother kind, what can I say?
"Whate'er I speak, there's woe in every way.
"The slave in that assembly thou didst see,
"Whose praises Egypt's people sang to thee,
"In all the world my shrine of worship he,
"My soul for him, my love, an offering be!
"'Twas he whose face to me in dreams was shown,
"The patience of my soul was overthrown.
"Body and heart through him I fevered lie,
"And in a sea of blood is drowned my eye.
"In longing for him to this land I come,
"And make in his desire this town my home.
"Of my own family 'twas he bereft,
"And in this exile me has wretched left.
"In all my trouble thou hast seen for years,
"This world's peace broken for me through my tears,

"All this was in the hope his face to see,
"And longing for his gracious symmetry.
"More than a mountain's weight my load to-day;
"How will my matter end I cannot say.
"The royal hall of whom does my moon grace?
"The light of whose night-chamber is his face?
"Whose eye in brightness will through him unclose,
"Whose house becomes through him a bed of rose?
"Who from his sweet lips his desire may gain,
"Or find peace 'neath his cypress free from pain?
"Who of his scented hair may tie the bow,
"Or with his silver palm-tree union know?
'Who on his value all her gains would stake,
"Her eyes' collyrium of his dust who make?
"Through him shall my state benefit or not?
"This fortune shall my hand attain or not?"
When her nurse saw this fire and whence it came,
Sadly she wept, as candle in the flame.
She said: "O candle, this thy heat conceal,
"Nor thy day's grief, nor thy night's pain reveal.
"For long hast thou with patience borne the ill:
"Now hold the matter in thy patience still.
"Thou mayst with patience yet thy hope attain,
"And from dark clouds thy sun may shine again."

### The Coming of Joseph to the Place of Sale, and his Purchase by Zuleikha at Double Price.

The time how happy and the day how sweet,
When of their union lovers fruit may eat!
When friendship's bright lamp is again a light,
And pain of separation's put to flight.
The market brisk had Joseph's beauty made;
Itself to buy him Egypt open laid.

With anything that any hand acquired,
In that bazaar to buy with all desired.
There an old crone, I heard, excited sped,
Bringing with her some yarn she'd spun, and said:
" Enough, though little there be in my hand, (188)
" Among the purchasers to let me stand."
The criers right and left now loudly cry :
" A slave without defect, come, who will buy ?
" Like beauteous rising of the dawn his face ;
" His lip a jewel from the mine of grace.
" His face with virtue's signs is full of light :
" His breast on bounty's nature based aright.
" Upon his tongue there's naught but what is straight ;
" In twisted, crooked words he'll nothing state."
One, from the midst of them the first to try,
For one bag of red gold proposed to buy.
If of that bag thou wouldest count the tale,
Of gold a thousand pieces would not fail.
While others, their steed's victory to boast,
A hundred bags laid on the winning post. (189)
Another rich man then as much would pay
In fragrant musk as Joseph's self should weigh ;—
Another wiser one, outbidding them,
With equal weight of ruby and of gem.
After this manner they bid and more
Of every kind of precious things a store.
Zuleikha, from whom this had not been hid,
Doubling their offers, all at once outbid.
Then they closed their lips, all those buyers there,
And sat them down on the knees of despair.
" Of counsel good," to the Vazír she said :
" Let the full price to Málik now be weighed."
He said to her : " All that there hidden lies,
" Musk, jewels, gold, my treasures that comprise,
" Even to half his price would not extend,
" How can I, then, the whole of it expend ?"

A box of gems Zuleikha there possessed,
A constellation full of stars, no chest. (190)
The price of every jewel in that store,
Equalled all Egypt's revenue or more.
She answered him : " These jewels for his price,
" Give jewels of my life, his sacrifice."
The Vazír an excuse then made once more :
" The age's king tow'rds him a liking bore :
" That in his house one of such purity
" Head of the list of all his slaves should be."
She said then : " Go thou to the conquering king,
" Before him all thy service rendered bring.
" Tell him : Of sorrows I have only one,
" That these my eyes may never see a son.
" Exalt me with this single grace, I pray,
" That this one slave may my commands obey ;
" That in my constellation he may shine,
" Be the king's slave and as a son be mine."
Thus at Zuleikha's word the Vazír came ;
Before that lofty king he said the same.
The monarch heard the words and hearing weighed,
Nor did he turn from the request his head.
To purchase him at once he gave the leave,
And as a son to love him and receive.
Rejoicing homewards he then Joseph bore.
Zuleikha from her pain was freed once more,
And piercing pearls of joy with eyelash thread,
Weeping, her own two eyes she rubbed, and said :
" Am I awake, O God, or in a dream,
" That from my love my soul's desire should beam ?
" When had I ever hope in that black night
" That in this way my day would e'er be white ?
" Upon my night has followed azure day :
" My daily grief and pain have passed away.
" Now that my darling they with me unite,
" The heav'ns that I should now caress were right.

" In this sad world of pain who is like me ?
" After decay who's freshened up like me ?
" I was a fish for water sore distressed,
" Writhing on sand, with water's grief oppressed
" Yet from the cloud of grace a flood at hand
" Safe to the river bore me from the sand.
" Lost in night's darkness I was straying round ;
" In wandering my soul upon my lip I found.
" From the horizon rose a moon and shone,
" And to my street of fortune led me on.
" Upon death's couch I slumbering had lain,
" Death's lancet pricking of my life the vein ;
" When sudden *Khizar* came in from the door,
" And did upon me his life's water pour.
" Thanks be to God that fortune proves my friend
" And Fate its troubling of my soul will end.
" A thousand lives for him an offering,
" Who to my market now such cash could bring !
" To break into my jewel-box what pain,
" Of fine gems when a mine my hand shall gain ?
" Before a soul's cash what are gems to me ?
" A friend's security, whate'er it be.
" I gave some lifeless things a soul to keep,
" And in God's name I bought them wondrous cheap.
" What profit does he gain for cash who sells
" *Isá* himself and picks up paltry shells ?
" Although these paltry shells all I expend,
" I make a gain if *Isá's* still my friend."
These secrets in her sieve of thought she strained,
Whilst from her eyes tears bright as jewels rained.
Silent, at times on Joseph turned her eye,
She yet was free of parting's misery.
Sometimes rememb'ring partings left behind,
With thoughts of union she rejoiced her mind.

## Yusuf and Zuleikha.

THE STORY OF A GIRL BY NAME BAZIGHA, OF THE RACE OF THE ÁDIS, WHO IN SECRET BECAME ENAMOURED OF THE BEAUTY OF JOSEPH (ON WHOM BE PEACE!), AND IN BEHOLDING IN THAT MIRROR THE BEAUTY OF TRUTH PASSED FROM WHAT IS FEIGNED TO WHAT IS TRUE.

From sight alone will love not always rise :
'Twill come from speech sometimes, as well as eyes.
Through the ear's door will beauty entrance find ;
It takes ease from the heart and sense from mind.
No need is there for procuress's art,
That she should tell her tale on beauty's part.
Though through the eye no influence may be,
Love sometimes finds its way in secretly.
There was a girl in Egypt's land, in grace
Who held the lordship of the *Ádis'* race.
Pearls (191) from her ruby mouth put on a smile ;
With sugar filled her laugh the land of Nile.
And from the sweetness that her smile possessed,
The cane's heart ev'n was with her chain oppressed.
When her sweet lips sweet smiles around her threw,
The cane between its teeth its finger drew.
At her mouth sugar's heart in narrow pass,
And sweets from envy on a stone as glass—
Should pleasure's sweets her saucy lip inflame,
Sweets in the bottle's heart a knot became.
Although the sweets gave to the bottle heart,
Against her lips it could not bear its part.
Wine-bibbers with that mouth could not contend :
In the defeat of brave men it would end. (192)
That *Huri*-envied one the world brought strife ;
Egypt her sweetness made with tumult rife.

The country's heads her favour all would seek,
The beauties of the town before her weak.
But as her crown in grandeur grazed the heaven,
Equality with her to none was given.
In honour, wealth, and in the pride of place,
Would she tow'rds no one ever turn her face.
When Joseph's tale and all his praise she heard,
Towards that moon-face all her love was stirred.
One on another as the rumours flew,
Her heart in his ideal firmer grew.
From hearing turned her mind to seeing round;
In hearing is the seed of seeing found.
She knew the price that should for him be paid,
Her heart its reck'ning for that payment made.
A thousand camels of high lineage foaled,
Laden with musk, brocade, and gems, and gold,
All kinds of precious things that she possessed,
To offer as his price which she deemed best.
To march on Egypt's road these all prepared,
Of everything her treasury she bared.
The rumour spread she came to Egypt nigh;
Itself in Egypt rose a fresher cry.
She came to Egypt following Joseph's way,
And made enquiries of where Joseph lay.
When news she had obtained of Joseph's place,
Gladly she thither turned her reins and face.
Beauty beyond the range of thought she saw,
A soul of earthly stains (193) without one flaw.
She never saw his like upon the earth,
Nor had she heard of one of equal birth.
She swooned, unconscious, at the sight away;
Out of her senses from delight she lay.
Back to her sense unconsciousness she brought.
Out of her careless dream she waking sought.
Loosing her tongue in questioning to speak,
Gems from that treasure store she 'gan to seek

She said : "O thou whom only fitting actions grace,
" Who with such beauty has adorned thy face ?
" Who threw the sun's bright ray upon thy brow,
" And of moon-clusters gleans the harvest now ?
" Thy form has from what artist's brush been known ?
" Thy cypress fair what gardener has grown ?
" Who with his compass thy arched eyebrow lined ?
" Who did in graceful curls thy ringlets bind ?
" Its water whence did thy moist rose derive ?
" With it who made thee in the garden thrive ?
" Who taught thy cypress fair its graceful gait ?
" Whence learnt thy lips sweet stories to relate ?
" Thy moon-face on their tablet who indite ?
" The letter of thy locks what pen shall write ?
" Who thy narcissus opened to day's beam,
" Of non-existence woke thee from the dream ?
" Who thy pearl's casket locked with ruby key,
" That heart and soul of thine might strengthened be ?
" And who that dimple in thy chin has made,
" In which life's water to the full is laid ?
" Who with that amber mole thy cheek has graced ?
" That raven who in that rose-garden placed ?"
When Joseph in his ear had heard this word,
Out of his fountain sweet soul's food was poured :
" I am the Great Creator's work", he cried ;
" With one drop from His ocean satisfied.
" The heaven's but one dot from perfection's reed,
" The earth but one bud from His beauty's mead.
" The sun a spark out of His wisdom's light,
" The sphere a bubble from His sea of might.
" Pure is His beauty from all charge of sin,
" Of the invisible the screen within.
" Of the world's atoms He has mirrors made,
" Of His own face on each an image laid.
" Whate'er of good thou seest with thy eye,
" Look well ; His own reflection there will lie.

" The image seen, haste to the source away ;
" Feeble before the source the imaged ray.
" Forbid God from the source thou far remain ;
" The image gone, thou wilt no light retain.
" In but short time the image will have passed ;
" One cannot trust the rose's hue to last.
" Have to the original for life recourse,
" And seek faith only at the very source.
" To long for anything may pierce life's vein ;
" Sometimes it is—at times 'twill not remain."
In mysteries when Joseph thus replied,
Joseph's love's carpet, wise, she rolled aside.
" Thy praises hearing", she to Joseph said,
" To long for thee in pain my heart was led.
" For thee of hoping I pursued the way,
" And on my foot my head in searching lay.
" I saw thy face and headlong there I fell,
" My thought to perish at thy feet as well.
" Of mysteries the pearls then didst thou string,
" And gavest me the sign of light's fair spring.
" With truth of my words hast thou split the hair,
" Nor wouldst thou me permit thy love to share.
" Thou from my face the veil of hope hast riv'n,
" From atoms to my sun the road hast given.
" Now that thy secret's door stands wide to me,
" It were deceit to bandy love with thee.
" Now that truth's way is clear before my eye,
" From longing that 's profane 'twere best to fly.
" May God reward thee that my eye is clear,
" That to the Soul of souls thou bring'st me near.
" From all strange love hast thou withdrawn my heart,
" For holy union set my house apart.
" If every hair of mine a tongue became,
" Thy tale should every one of them declaim.
" Thy pearls of gratitude I cannot string,
" Nor e'er a hair's point of thy praises sing."

Then bidding him farewell she went away;
Freed of desire, she would no longer stay.
Then after she in haste had left him there,
Upon Nile's bank she built a house of prayer.
From rule and from the world and riches freed,
She patronised all such as were in need:
Through these her wealth and kingdom went to waste;
At night there was not left enough to taste.
No crown had she that jewels bright adorn;
Contented with a *makna* (194) old and torn,
A golden fillet she no more would bind,
But woollen stockings round her head would wind.
She freed herself from silk and from brocade;
Of felt a garment for herself she made.
As bracelet on her wrist with jewels gay,
As rosary she counted beads of clay,
And in the corner of that praying-place
Turned from the world towards that shrine her face.
A sheet of ashes from the furnace brought,
In place of ermine she for bedding sought;
Under her head for pillow laid a stone,
And at her pain the earth would even moan.
Thus in that house of prayer she passed her days,
And firm she made her feet in prayer and praise.
In service when her life was thus complete,
She like a hero joyed her death to meet.
Oh! think not that she gave her life in vain,
To die, her loved one's face seen, was no pain.
Learn, heart, from her a hero's part to take,
And as she mourned thy sorrow true to make.
Swallow the grief, hast thou no cause to groan;
And make thee mourning if thou hast no moan.
Vain show in worshipping thy life has passed;
Thou thoughtest aye of things that do not last.
Each moment outward beauty knows decay,
All things revolving change from day to day.

On other stones place ever not thy feet,
Nor constant change from branch to branch thy seat.
Above the universe aye take thy rest;
Beyond the dome of spirit make thy rest.
There are a thousand forms, but spirit one:
Those who on outward forms count ever shun.
There is in numbers ever misery;
Thy stronghold ever make in unity.
Canst thou not bear the onset of thy foe,
'Twere best thyself safe in a fort to know.

### THE PREPARATION BY ZULEIKHA OF THINGS FOR THE EASE OF JOSEPH AND HER PERFORMING SERVICES FOR HIM.

When fortune to Zuleikha's net was given,
In her own name was money coined by heaven.
Thenceforward to all earthly longings blind,
Did she her loins in Joseph's service bind.
Gold 'broidered robes of beaver and brocade,
According to his stature fair she made.
Waist-belts of gold, with gold-wrought diadems,
Each one of them adorned with glittering gems.
Three hundred, sixty, as a year of days,
Prepared, her finished task aside she lays.
And every morning, as new broke the day,
A robe of honour on his shoulders lay.
The Eastern lord put on his crown each morn,
With a new crown she would his head adorn.
When the fair cypress raised its head each day,
She in new fashion would his waist array.
His face, that ever heart-deceiving sun,
From the same collar never two days shone.
Nor twice that cypress from the garden fair
Would the same coronet of beauty wear.

Ne'er, like the cane, that sugar lip would find
By the same belt its slender waist confined.
When with gold crown his forehead she would dress,
A thousand kisses on his head she'd press.
And say : " My crown may dust be from thy feet,
" To rise to lordship's heights a ladder meet !"
And when upon his form she drew the vest,
In secret she the garment thus addressed :
" Thine and my body, may they one thread be,
" And from that form may I eat fruit like thee !"
When she placed the coat on that cypress' height,
She addressed it thus, as she pulled it tight :
"I hope from that cypress of rosy face,
"Him may I hold, like thee, in tight embrace."
When round his waist she made the girdle fast,
Upon her tongue this longing floated past :
" If my hand were that belt, how would it be ?
" If union I enjoyed how would it be ?"
When she his curling locks with combs would part,
She found a healing for her maddened heart.
Of amber pure she would a net prepare,
Her own soul captive in that amber snare.
To eat at morn and in the eve again,
In her own chamber she would him retain ;
Tables of various hues would she prepare,
Adorned with varied kinds of viands rare.
Candy and almonds for him sweets to get,
To his own lip and taste she went in debt.
By way of fruit of every kind and hue
The model of his silver chin she drew.
Into roast meat the breasts of fowls were made,
And like her own heart there sometimes were laid.
Then like his juicy mouth would she prepare
Conserves especial and of flavour rare.
Drinks would she make of sugar fine and new,
And water turned to candy at the view.

And to whatever thing he was inclined,
That would she, as for life, that instant find.
At night when thought of sleep he entertained,
Faint at his day's labour she herself remained;
A heart-enchanting coverlet she spread,
And made of silk and of brocade his bed.
Of rose she made a bed for his repose,
Jess'mine or tulip pillow for his rose.
She told him tales and stories ere he slept,
Dust from his mind by telling tales she swept.
Then when the veil of slumber closed his eye,
In fever with the candle would she vie.
Her two enraptured deer (195) until the dawn
That moon grazed of his beauty on the lawn.
At times the secret of his eye she knew,
Or of his mouth at times the breath she drew.
A tulip from the bed now would she take,
A purchase from his rose-bed now would make.
With his sweet fount at times her lip would play,
At him around his chin like dewlap stray.
Sometimes conversing gently with his hair,
At times his rosebud's secrets she would share.
"Now from my eyes I tears of blood could weep,
"That such a *Div* should with a *Pari* sleep!"
Thus speaking the back of her hand she'd bite,
And pass the night, dark as her locks, till light.
Days passed into nights: her trouble the same,
No quiet or rest to her ever there came.
She soothed his grief and to him comfort gave,
And, though his mistress, was indeed his slave.
Yes: a lover will sell his soul indeed,
The loved one will serve with his soul at need.
Out of her path thorns with his eyelash put,
Although his eye should suffer from her foot.
With his soul's eye he waits on her intent,
In hope her heart towards him may relent.

## The Setting forth by Joseph of the Story of the Pain of his Journey, and the Trouble of the Well, and the becoming aware by Zuleikha that the Sorrow she had had that Day had arisen from it.

And now the orator in language meet
With the tale proceeds of his stories sweet,—
That ere she met with Joseph, on a day
Strange pain and burning on Zuleikha lay.
Patience of heart and rest for body none,
Care for the end, too, from her soul had gone.
At home no business would she undertake
Herself, nor to a stranger pleasant make.
Water on eyelash, with heart full of woe,
Both in and out she never ceased to go.
Her nurse, on whom the star of fortune shone,
Said to her: "Moon, thou shadow of the sun,
" May heaven's cruelty not injure thee;
" From Fate's unjust disturbance be thou free !
" I know not what to-day thy state may be :
" For drowned thy soul seems in misfortune's sea.
" Thou art that leaf which every wind that blows
" Turns round, and settled no one knows.
" It falls upon its back or on its face,
" In this or that direction takes its place.
" In one abode it does not rest at ease,
" But to turn round has no desire to please.
" Say, of this restlessness who is the cause,
" All this fresh trouble who upon thee draws ?"
She said: "Bewildered all am I to-day—
" In my own business, too, have gone astray.
" I have a sorrow, but I do not know
" Whence springs up in my soul this source of woe.

"Yet, secretly, it robs me of my rest;
"My days are with its cruelty oppressed.
"I am the earth that self-contented lies
"Until the stormy whirlwinds wake and rise.
"In its own being though it movement knows,
"It knows the tempest not, nor whence it blows."
When Joseph to Zuleikha nearer drew,
Their intimacy each day closer grew.
One night to her his secret to disclose,
He told her all his grief and all his woes.
In converse intimate his tongue would tell
The story of the journey and the well.
When of the well the tale Zuleikha learned,
Like twisting rope round on herself she turned,
And knew within her heart 'twas on that day
Her soul to burning grief had been a prey.
The day and month when she to reckoning brought,
She was assured it happened as she thought.
Now every heart that is watchful can say,
From heart to heart there is ever a way.
From the rent hearts of lovers, it is sure,
Whose faith to their loved one is clear and pure,
From every rent a road opens wide,
To carry their sight to their loved one's side,—
And of their loved one's state this road a ray
To their weak souls and bodies will convey.
Thus if the loved one's foot should pierce a thorn,
The lover's soul will be with anguish torn.
On the belovèd's locks each breeze that blows
Wafts to the lover's heart a hundred woes.
If on her cheek a speck of dust descend,
Her lover's back beneath the load will bend,
One day a lancet, I have heard (196), indeed,
In her hand *Leila* took herself to bleed :
To bleed when Leila pricked herself in *Hai*,
Bled in the vale *Majnun's* hand by-and-bye.

Come, Jámi, from thy very being shrink,
Nor of thy own existence ever think.
'Tis His (197), if thou hast honour and repute;
And scent and colour, these are His, to boot.
Away let thy own love and hatred pass;
And of thy own reflection cleanse thy glass.
Let beauty from the unseen be thy light;
And shine like Moses, from thy bosom bright!
Clear in thy heart's eye if that light abide,
From thee thy darling's secret 'twill not hide.


## The Desiring by Joseph of the Office of a Shepherd for the Reason that there had been no Prophet who had not performed a Shepherd's Office.

Happy the hopeless one allowed by Fate
On his belovèd, wandering round, to wait!
To his own wish he is no longer thrall,
But to her wishes he surrenders all.
'Tis on his lip if she his life desire;
Her dust he'll kiss and will himself expire.
Should she desire his heart, by grief oppressed
He through his eyes pours out blood from his breast,
And in her service honoured to be led,
When she says "Rise", he makes her foot his head.
Driven, like pen, he will not turn his look,
And called he twists his face not like a book.
Of all enlightened people in the view
Sheepfolding is to prophets suited, too.
Joseph, as many rulers of his kind,
To fill a shepherd's office had a mind;
And when Zuleikha heard of Joseph's will,
She turned her reins that longing to fulfil.

First from art-masters did she this demand,
That they should make a sling for Joseph's hand.
Like sun with gold adorned its rope they rove,
And like to amber-scented ringlets wove.
Rose in Zuleikha's mind the wish again,
To be as hair entangled in the strain.
"To him without some cause myself I cannot bind:
"And thus to kiss his hand occasion I may find."
"Oh! how would I desire," again she said,
"To bind him by one hair from off my head!"
Jewels upon it then she fastened round,
Like the pearls and gems on her eyelash found:
A ruby if she found of beauteous hue,
This like a worthless stone on it she threw.
Then did she give the shepherds her command,
In hills and deserts grazing flocks at hand,
That they should from those flocks some lambs provide,
And those without an equal set aside,
Like Tartar deer on hyacinths that grazed,
In whom alarm a wolf had never raised.
In armour clad of wool like black men's hair,
In colour than fine silk more fresh and fair.
In fatness were their tails of equal weight,
The lambs through weightiness of graceful gait,
In every valley where they grazing stood,
It was as waves of butter in a flood.
The wind upon the waves' face (198) in its pride
To making watery chains itself applied.
Among these flocks did Joseph hastening go,
In Aries' sign as is the sun aglow.
Like the musk antelopes that lonely stray,
He to those flocks of sheep went on his way.
Zuleikha all her sense and heart and care
Sent, like a tailed dog, with the shepherd there.
And other guardians, too, did she provide
To watch lest him some evil should betide.

Thus as it pleased him he proceeded still,
And uncontrolled by any other's will.
At will a shepherd in the desert he,
Or of her soul's realm might the monarch be.
That fairy-born one in his purity
From kingship both and shepherdhood was free.

## THE DEMANDING BY ZULEIKHA OF UNION WITH JOSEPH, AND JOSEPH'S INDEPENDENCE.

When a fair form is stamped in any breast,
He in his business never can have rest.
The cash of union if he cannot find,
He on love's credit gambles in his mind.
When from his heart the thing goes to his eyes,
Blood trickles from his heart that bleeding lies.
When profit gains his tearful eye from this,
He falls to thinking of embrace and kiss.
Should he to kiss and to embrace attain,
In fear of parting he has constant pain.
In love there is of happiness no hope;
For purity of life there is no scope.
In drinking blood it aye begins alone:
And at the last comes death when this is done.
In case when can the heart of him rejoice,
Of eating blood or death who has the choice?
Ere Joseph came before Zuleikha's eye,
In dream or fancy she could blissful lie.
Only to see his form could she aspire;
To seek and find him was her sole desire.
But when she saw him and that profit knew,
Her longing then for something higher grew.
After long search 'twas this she longed for in the end,
That that hope with a fond embrace might blend,

With kisses from his lips she might be blessed,
And in his cypress bosom find her rest.
The eye when of a grove a sight it gains
For roses' love it bears, like tulip, stains.
At first to see the rose it is content,
From sight on plucking it the hand is bent.
Zuleikha every plan for union tried,
Though Joseph from her ever stood aside.
Zuleikha tears of blood pours from her eyes,
Whilst Joseph ever from before her flies.
Zuleikha's heart was scarred with misery,
But from her fancy Joseph yet was free.
On his fair face Zuleikha's cheek would lie,
Turned tow'rds his foot was ever Joseph's eye.
Zuleikha's heart with every glance would burn,
Whilst Joseph from her look his eye would turn.
For fear of strife on her he would not look,
Nor would his eye her glance of passion brook.
The lover keeps that form not in his sight,
When eye to-eye he cannot see its light.
He can not ever weep and heave the sigh,
His love to see who hopes not by-and-bye,—
When of her lover's state she will not know,
That from her lover's heart his blood should flow.
When to Zuleikha this grief found its way,
She in brief time in grievous ruin lay.
And in the autumn when it trouble knew,
Her red rose took the yellow tulip's hue.
Upon her heart there stood a heavy load of woe;
With sorrow bent her cypress like a bow.
From her red lips the lustre passed away,
And of her cheek the light extinguished lay.
She never combed her amber-scented hair,
But that her hand it from its roots would tear.
Towards her mirror she scarce turned her face,
But ever on her knees her cheek would place.

From the fresh blood that from her heart would bleed,
Her cheek of pigment never had a need.
The world was to her eye all dark and drear,
Then how should "*surmá*" on that eye appear?
"*Surmá*" to dye her eyes would she not lay,
Tears from her eyes would wash the stain away.
And when Zuleikha's heart with grief was sore,
Reproaches on herself her tongue would pour.
" O thou on thy affairs who shame hast brought,
" By longing for a slave that gold has bought,
" A king upon a throne him far above,
" Why thy own slave dost thou thus stoop to love?
" Seek for a lover like thyself in state,
" For monarchs only should with monarchs mate.
" Than all strange things there is one stranger still,
" That to thy union he bends not his will.
" Thy state if Egypt's women were to know,
" On thee reproofs a hundred would they throw.
" Their tongue in cursing would be loosed full soon
" A thing to point at as the crescent moon."
Yet that unequalled one, though thus she'd say,
Dwelt not within her heart in such a way
That she could drive him from heart at will;
And with this tale increased her sorrow still.
A lover's soul once knit with lover fond,
That soul can never then unloose the bond.
Of soul with body you may loose the tie,
But ever firm remains their unity.
How well said he, love's anguish whom had rent :
" Its hue the rose may lose, and musk its scent,
" But that a lover from his love should shrink,
" That were a think impossible to think."

## The Questioning of Zuleikha by her Nurse as to the Reason of her Melting away at the Sight of the Candle of Joseph's Beauty.

Zuleikha when her nurse saw on this wise,
She asked, while tears were pouring from her eyes:
"O thou from seeing whom my eye has light,
"From whose cheek's image my heart's rose-bed's bright,
"Thy heart is full of pain, thy soul of woe:
"What thy condition is I may not know.
"Ever before thee thus thy soul's desire,
"Why without rest art ever thus on fire?
"What time from thee he still was far away,
"Thou wert excused when thy heart burning lay,
"But since to union with thee near he came,
"Burns thy soul's candle why with such a flame?
"What lover ever with such favour's graced
"That as slave near him his own love is placed?
"Propitious omen to thee Fortune gave,
"That to thee came thy Sultan as a slave.
"A moon to royal crown that might aspire
"Is in thy hand: what more dost thou require?
"Before his face be happy, glad of heart,
"And let all sorrows of the world depart.
"His cypress tulip-hued thy longing make,
"And in his graceful gait thy comfort take.
"Look on his lip; nourish with him thy soul,
"And hope's pure water drink thou from his bowl."
When from her nurse Zuleikha heard this thing,
She made her heart's blood of her tears the spring.
From her eye's cloud her heart's blood then was shed,
And her sad story thus it was she said.
Said: "Thou who e'er art as my mother kind,
"Thee skilled in secret things do I not find.

" Dost thou not know what of my heart's the care,
" From this world's life what I may have to bear?
" He stands to serve before my face, 'tis true,
" But no true service will he ever do.
" Though distant from me he may ne'er remain,
" To look upon me yet he will not deign.
" One should with weeping of the thirsty think,
" On whose lip's water that they can not drink.
" Like beauty's torch although my face should shine,
" His eyes towards his feet will aye incline.
" 'Tis not for this that he my blame should bear,
" His instep than my face is far more fair.
" When him I look on with world-seeing eye,
" Upon his forehead fair a frown will lie.
" Yet for that frown I can not blame him long,
" For what there comes from him can not be wrong.
" His eyebrow in my heart such knots has bound,
" That knotless my affairs are never found.
" Such heavy knots in my affairs it ties,
" I can not gaze upon him with my eyes.
" From speaking to me when his mouth refrains,
" But to drink blood what then for me remains?
" My mouth if from that red lip water flood,
" The water in my eye is turned to blood.
" His form, the plant where all my hope would be,
" But seldom casts a kindly look on me.
" I hope to pluck an apple from that tree;
" The apple brings a hundred woes on me.
" If from his chin's well I should seek relief,
" My place of ease he turns to well of grief.
" That sleeve I ever envy in my breast,
" That it with fraud upon his arm should rest.
" As for his skirt, I hide my torn soul in my breast
" That at his feet before him it in dust should rest."
And when the nurse had heard these words, she wept
That in such case she yet alive was kept.

By fate such absence as may be enforced
Union excels whence sweetness is divorced.
The pains of parting are but heavy blows,
And such a union brings two hundred woes.

## THE SENDING OF HER NURSE BY ZULEIKHA TO JOSEPH IN SEARCH OF HER OBJECT, AND HIS REJECTION OF IT.

Zuleikha in her grief reliance laid
Upon her nurse's pity and her aid.
She said: " A hundred times thy help I own,
" Who to my wishes hast devotion shown.
" Now once again do thou thy aid bestow ;
" Once more of sorrow ward thou off the blow. (199)
" On my head's part take thou to him thy way,
" And thus to him, as my tongue acting, say.
" Say: O thou plant that hast been reared in grace,
" On roses casting sweetness from thy face,
" From beauty's garden, bed of luxury,
" No lofty cypress ever grew like thee.
" Water they mixed from soul and heart with clay,
" Planting therein from *Sidrah's* branch a spray,
" Did it of loftiness the leaf unfold,
" To call it graceful cypress they were bold.
" Thee when the bride of Time bore on the earth,
" Was never born a son of purer birth.
" Bright at thy birth the eye of Adam seen,
" At thy fair face, of earth the rosebed green.
" Thy perfect form beyond all mortal bound,
" From it no gain has ever *Pari* found.
" Were not abashed at thee the *Pari's* pride,
" She would before thee not in corners hide.
" Though angels dwell above in golden sphere,
" Yet are their heads in dust before thee here.

"Since thy foundation heaven has raised so high,
"On thy poor captive let thy shadow lie.
"For though Zuleikha so enchanting be,
"She is a captive in thy noose to thee.
"From childhood is thy scar upon her breast;—
"From thy desire that old grief has no rest.
"Three times at home in dreams did she thee meet,
"And now her life consumes at fever heat.
"At times in chains as water fastened tight,
"At times as breezes wandering at night.
"From longing for thee, as a hair she's thin;—
"But she—she has no wish her heart within.
"The cash of her life has she lost for thee:
"'Tis sweet to be kind: have pity on me.
"Thy lip is of life's water pure the fount:
"To shed a drop on her what would it count?
"Grant from thy lip she her desire may gain:
"May be that this may ease her of her pain.
"Of stature to bear fruit thou art a tree:
"If she should eat that fruit, how would it be?
"Where she may lay her head advance thy foot,
"That from thy palm-tree she may gather fruit.
"How would thy royal dignity become the less
"If with a single glance thou her wilt bless?
"Before thy handmaids, too, in serving thee,
"Who art so dear, would she a handmaid be."
When from the nurse he heard this, by-and-bye
Joseph his gem-lips opened in reply—
He said : " O thou who secrets knowest well, (200)
"Weave not around me to deceive thy spell.
"Bought with Zuleikha's gold, I am her slave,
"To me who many and many a favour gave.
"Of clay and water she this building made,
"And on her faith my heart and soul are laid.
"Her favour to requite though life I spend,
"My gratitude to her would yet not end.

"I lay my head on line of her command,
"And in her service ever will I stand.
"Yet bid her not of me thus e'er to think,
"That I shall from my God's commandment shrink—
"From lust's bad counsels that are born of sin,
"To evil's straits that I should enter in.
"As his son I, so the Vazír has said,
"And of his household reckons me the head.
"On grain and water fed, his bird am I:
"How in his house can I act wickedly?
"By the pure God in every nature sown
"Are some peculiar habits of its own. (201)
"He of pure nature ever does what's good,—
"Adulterer he is who is base of brood.
"Not dogs of man or man of dogs is born,
"Not from wheat barley, nor from barley corn.
"My breast bears the secret of Israel,
"And I have the wisdom of Gabriel.
"To wear a prophet's mantle am I fit;
"'Tis Isaac's grace I have to thank for it.
"A mystery-enshrouding rose I am,
"In the rose-garden reared of Abraham.
"And God forbid that I a deed approve
"Me from that family that might remove.
"Go; bid Zuleikha now the wish refuse,
"And her own spirit both and me excuse,
"For in the pure God aye I hope to be
"Chaste, and from all lustful feeling free."


### The Going of Zuleikha to Joseph and Humbling Herself, and Making Excuse to Joseph for the Fulfilment of her Object.

These words the nurse then to Zuleikha said
And she was as the wild hair on her head.

## Yusuf and Zuleikha.

Poured on her cheek her eye-lash her heart's blood,
And her black almonds shed the jujube's flood.
With graceful gait, then, that tall cypress sped,
And threw its shadow on her darling's head,
And said: " Dust at thy feet may my head be,
" And of thy air my heart be never free !
" Void of thy love have I no single hair,
" And of my own hair am I unaware.
" Within myself as soul thy image lies,
" And round my neck thy noose the collar ties.
" Have I a soul? it breathes thy sorrow's air ;
" A body? thou dost bring it to despair (202).
" What of the state of my heart shall I say?
" Of thy blood-shedding eye it is a spray.
" Deep in the sea of thy love do I drown :
" Immersed in it am I from foot to crown.
" From every vein of mine the bleeder scores,
" Longing for thee, and not my blood, there pours."
When Joseph heard these words, tears filled his eyes.
" Wherefore this weeping ?" then Zuleikha cries.
" Thou art my eye. How can I sit and smile,
" That eye when I see weeping all the while?
" When from thy eye-lash drops of water flow,
" My very soul like fire must be a-glow.
" This of thy beauty's wonders one I know ;
" Fire on my soul dost thou with water throw."
When Joseph heard from her these grievous cries,
Pearls from his lip he shed, as from his eyes.
Weeping, he said : " My heart is aye distressed,
" That no one's love for me is ever blessed.
" On my love's road when first my aunt there came,
" She as a thief's spread in the world my name.
" When my sire's love my brothers greater knew,
" Within their souls the plant of hatred grew.
" Far from my father's side did they me send,
" An exile's days in Egypt's land to end.

"My heart must in this bosom constant bleed,
"Till it see further where thy love may lead.
"For jealous indeed is the lord of love,
"No partner in love's realm can he approve.
"And neither first nor last will he permit
"Another in the same high place to sit,
"Like the tall cypress in its beauty sweet
"That low the shadow casts down at its feet.
"When beauty fair ones' moonlike cheeks illumes,
"The flash of jealousy their sheaves consumes.
"When the sun reaches of the heavens the crown,
"At once towards the West he hurries down.
"When the full moon its form of brilliance gains,
"Seized on by sorrow it in anguish wanes."
"My eye and lamp," Zuleikha then replied:
"Enough of brilliance does thy moon provide.
"I do not say that I am dear to thee:
"A handmaid of thy handmaids would I be.
"Oh! of thy handmaid that thou wouldst be fond,
"Of slavery wouldst free her from the bond!
"I am thy handmaid lower than the rest,
"With but a longing heart and burning breast.
"Thee dearer than my life do I not know?
"Why shouldst thou look upon me as a foe?
"None wretched in his life desires to be,
"Nor wishes for his soul calamity.
"My heart is cleft of thy love by the blade:
"Thus of my hatred why art thou afraid?
"Be sweet and from thy lip my wishes grant:
"Subdued awhile, ease in my soul implant.
"Go but one step upon the road with me:
"Behold what love I ever bear to thee."
"My lady mistress," Joseph answer found:
"A slave before thee I with bonds am bound.
"Beyond thy service nothing in my hand,
"My duty lies in hearing thy command.

## Yusuf and Zuleikha.

" From thy slave rulership forbear to claim :
" With all this favour bring me not to shame.
" Who am I for thy friendship to be fit,
" That at the Vazír's table I should sit?
" A king that slave would rightly grind to dust,
" Who in the salt with him his hand should thrust.
" 'Twere best in any way to busy me,
" That all my days I may devote to thee.
" And in thy service should I ever fail,
" In work a hundredfold I'd make its tale.
" By service only do become slaves free,
" Gladdened with patent of their liberty.
" By faithful service are their hearts made glad,
" Freedom he gains not whose work aye is bad."
Zuleikha answered : " O propitious star,
" Than slaves before thee I am lower far.
" For every service I of thee require
" A hundred workmen will at once aspire.
" How well 'twould be were I to pass them by,
" And on the work should only thee employ !
" The foot is useful but to tread the earth,
" And 'tis not with the eye of equal worth.
" If on thy foot's path where thou thorns may'st see,
" Thou place thine eye, they'll surely injure thee."
Then Joseph, when he heard these words, replied :
" Thy heart and soul are with my love allied.
" If thy love pure as morning breezes be,
" On hope's horizon only breath for me
" Since my desire is only thee to serve,
" Strive not against me, nor from friendship swerve
" For he whose heart is captive to his friend,
" Will further his desire e'en to the end.
" With his own will he sports his friends to meet,
" And his own will he treads beneath his feet."
Joseph these words for this before her laid,
That he her company might thus evade

For in her company was fear of ill,
And at a distance he might serve her still.
When fire against it may itself array,
Well for that cotton that can fly away.


## The Sending of Joseph by Zuleikha to a Garden, and the Preparation of its Apparatus.

He of this tale who decks the flowering meads
Thus with the tale of ancient men proceeds.
When with his lips of sugar Joseph spread
This sugar fresh around Zuleikha's head,
Zulickha had a garden fair, a mead
With envy that caused *Iram's* (203) heart to bleed.
A wall of mud and water (204) this surrounds:
The bright red rose (204) on every side abounds.
Branch within branch the trees there interlace,
In modest boldness, though in close embrace.
Its planes, their foot upon the cypress' skirt,
Like necklace round its neck their arms are girt.
The rose upon its bud as litter laid,
Pomegranates making overhead a shade,
On a wide plain the orange-bushes stand,
Their branch the mace, the orange ball in hand,
And in that plain so free from every ill,
The ball of grace they bear away at will.
In beauteous height the palm-tree bears the date,
And to the garden gives its high estate.
Of sweets a harvest every bunch is there
Provision for the sad at heart to share.
Figs and pomegranates there like nurses stand,
For the mead's children juice as milk in hand,
Each bird the fig's juice that might wish to sip,
Opened just as a sucking child its lip.

The sun's bright light, although at midday seen,
Lit with gold rays the latticed green,
And blending with each other sun and shade
With musk and gold was the plain overlaid,
Whilst in the dark the moving sparks of light
Were as rose cymbals with gold bells bedight.
The nightingale from those bells drew its note,
And opened in that azure vault its throat.
A thousand fish there in the willows' shade
With the wind sporting in the rivers played.
Of good and bad the garden clean to keep
The shadows of the trees like besoms sweep.
On the ground green lines as on teacher's board,
The stream had its margin with silver scored,
And the sagacious, on that tablet scored,
Might read the secrets of Creation's Lord.
The red rose as the gently-nurtured fair:
The yellow rose of lovers as the air.
The breezes twist in wreaths the violet,
And knots of spikenard loosed in freedom set.
The jessamine, tulip and sweet herbs embrace,
And as with silk is decked of earth the face.
In that abode of *Huris* there they placed
Two fountains, clear as glass with marble graced.
These like each other as a pair of eyes,
One with the other in its clearness vies.
No wound of a pickaxe on these is seen,
And never a scratch from a chisel been.
Should his thought thereto the wise man apply,
Neither joint nor crack would there meet his eye.
And all who behold in their minds took thought
That without a joint were the fountains wrought.
Zuleikha, her heart's sorrow to allay,
When to that garden she would make her way,
One of the fountains full of milk was stored,
And in the other tasty honey poured—

There of that heaven-cradled moon each maid
With milk her hunger or with honey stayed.
Between the fountains there was raised a seat,
For one fate-favoured, like to Joseph, meet.
Thus to his company she bade farewell,
And in the garden bade him work and dwell.
The garden's bird told this tale to the flow'r:
"The gardener fair, and more fair is the bow'r,
"As Eden's hall should mead and rosebed be,
"Gardeners should *Rizván* and the *Huris* be."
A hundred jess'mine-breasted handmaids stood,
All virgins pure and all of purest mood.
As graceful cypresses they waited all,
Ever in service ready at his call.
"May my head," she told him, "thy footstool be!
"To delight in these is lawful for thee.
"If I to thee am forbidden, alas!
"(Oh! bitter for me should this come to pass!)
"Of these go to her whom thou mayst desire,
"To her to whose union thou mayest aspire;
"Fulfil thou thy desire with her, for this
"The day of youth is the time of bliss."
Then many commands on her maids she laid:
"Beware, oh! beware now, each sweet-lipped maid,
"In Joseph's service strive with heart and soul:
"If poison come, drink from his hand the bowl—
"Where'er he calls you, go ye there with speed:
"Indulge him with your lives, should there be need.
"Whate'er he order, be ye happy still,
"In every way obedient to his will.
"In gaining him whoe'er may lucky be,
"Let her at once the news impart to me."
As one impatient, one might say she drew
On her hope's tablet a deceitful view.
Whichever of the band he might approve,
At sleeping time she would towards him move,

Herself there in her place would substitute,
And of his pleasant plant would eat the fruit:
Beneath that beauteous palm-tree would she lie,
And eat its dates, though she ate secretly.
As Joseph there she placed upon his seat,
Her heart and soul she offered at his feet.
The maids before him she placed standing there,
And made them bow before that cypress fair.
Her heart and soul before her friend there lay:
Her body tow'rds her own camp took its way.
Happy the lover who content at heart
From the beloved will at her word depart;
Who when his absence good is in her eyes,
In parting will all patience exercise.
To union when one's love will not agree,
Absence than presence will far sweeter be.

## The Displaying of their Beauty to Joseph by the Handmaids.

When like a new bride sporting in delight
Its dark rose-shedding hair spread out the night,
It placed the Pleiads' cluster in its ear,
And took in hand the moon, its mirror clear.
Repeating tales, in cloak of grace arrayed,
With air coquettish stood there every maid.
Breathing of love's enchantment tales, each one
Clustered in ordered rows round Joseph's throne.
First from her own sweet lips one sugar shed,
"Thy palate with my sugar fill," she said.
"From my sweet little mouth the knots unslip:
"Eat, like a parrot, the sweets from my lip."
One said, with a roguish glance from her eye:
"O thou whose praise expression would defy,

"In my world-seeing eye thy home I make;
"In my eye's pupil, come, thy station take."
One showed her cypress form in silken grace,
And said: "To-night this cypress form embrace.
"Where wilt thou sleep in joy's cradle at rest,
"If this fair cypress lie not in thy breast?"
With musky ringlets one a noose would tie:
"A mere ring without head or foot am I.
"Open the door and me to union bring:
"Outside that door nor place me like a ring."
Then one lifted up her delicate hand,
And above her arm let her loose sleeve stand.
"From thy beauty to ward the evil-eye,
"This hand on thy neck as amulet lie!"
One of a hair made a belt round her waist,
An ornament of hair around her placed:
"As girdle place thy hand my waist around;
"My soul through thee upon my lip is found."
After this way of those moon-faced ones each
Joseph for union with him would beseech.
Since he of beauty was a garden fair,
For such grass-handfuls he could never care.
Full of deceit and malice were they all,
In figure idols, who on idols call.
And Joseph had this thought alone in view,
To lead them to a service that was true.
All that he told them in the way of faith
Was to shake doubt, of heavenly truths the breath.
First, then, he said: "O maids of beauteous birth,
"Dear in the sight of every man on earth,
"Thus honoured, follow no path that is base;
"Look of religion only on the face.
"Beyond this world we have our God alone,
"The way to way-lost sinners Who has shown.
"He mixed our clay with His own mercy's dew,
"His wisdom planted there the grain that grew,

"That a fair plant might spring up from that grain,
"And in this mead perfection might attain.
"It draws itself aloft from lowly root,
"And of God's worship yields alone the fruit.
"To God alone be hands of worship raised,
"For He alone is worthy to be praised.
"Come and henceforward bow before His face;
"In every place without Him are we base:
"In adoration low our head be laid:
"The head was only for His worship made.
"And why to anyone should bow the wise,
"When head and foot are equal in God's eyes?
"With their own hands they carve a god of stone,
"And for its love in sorrowing heart they moan.
"What through a stone can happen, only know
"That from such worship but disgrace can flow."
From the first of night until morning broke,
This counsel to the careless, Joseph spoke.
Her lip then opens each in Joseph's praise,
Her head at his feet in obedience lays.
Each he confirms with testimony sure,
All mouths are sweetened with that honey pure.
Blessed be that honey on the finger tip
That bitterness expels for those that sip.
With finger wound of testimony sure,
Alone will blind become the *Div* impure.
And from the evil eye escapes the wise,
With martyr's finger who roots out his eyes.
Zuleikha had awoke at dawn of day,
And towards Joseph made her gladsome way.
Round about Joseph there she saw a crowd,
To his instruction who as pupils bowed:
Their idols broken and their zones (205) were rent;
In telling beads towards true faith they leant.
Upon their tongues of Unity the sound,
And in His service with waists newly bound.

K

She said to Joseph: "Thou from head to foot
"Disturbest hearts, that giv'st fair peace to boot,
"To-day another beauty on thy face,
"Thou from some other place hast greater grace.
"How does the night fresh beauty thee provide?
"Of goodness what new door has opened wide?
"What didst thou eat at night to give thee grace?
"Above earth's fair ones what has raised thy place?
"Perchance their company whom thou dost seek,
"These of the silver lips and jessamine cheek,
"An increase to thy comeliness have earned,
"And have thy beauty to perfection turned.
"For as from one fruit other fruit takes hue,
"So fair from fair ones gain a beauty new."
Though with that bud-like lip thus much she spoke,
No fairer bloom could yet her words evoke.
His mouth to all speech he had closed up tight,
But shame gave to his cheek a rosy light.
In modesty his head he would not raise,
But fixed upon his instep aye his gaze.
Zuleikha saw that he his head withdrew,
Nor on her ever glance of pity threw.
Thus in her soul was lit the fire of care,
Her breast was scarred with the scar of despair.
Thus hopeless, she bade to her life adieu,
And back to her chamber of sorrow flew.

### The Humiliation of Zuleikha before her Nurse, and her Plotting for Union with Joseph.

By Joseph's longing slain, when to her sense
Beyond all bounds passed his indifference,
Secret one night she called her nurse apart,
And seating, with caresses soothed her heart.
She said: "Thou power to my frame dost give;
"Thou lightest my soul's lamp that I may live.

"Nourished by thee each breath my spirit gives;
"On mercy's milk through thee my body lives.
"Such love I from my mother never knew;
"Through thy love to this dignity I grew.
"In parting's woe how long must I be left,
"Of that life of my world so long bereft?
"Oh! would that thou to me wouldst once be kind,
"And my desire's abode that I might find!
"In this way if my love a stranger be,
"In the same house to dwell what gain to me?
"The loved to flee from should her love appear,
"In presence is he far though he be near.
"If heart from spirit still be far away,
"What comes of water's union with its clay?"
The nurse replied: "O thou of *Paris'* kind,
"*Huri* nor *Pari* with whom comes to mind.
"God did create thee in this beauteous wise
"To rob of heart and of his Faith the wise.
"If China's limner longing for thy face,
"Should in a temple e'er thy likeness place,
"The idols with desire at once would live,
"Seeing thy face, to thee their souls would give.
"If on the hill thou shouldst thy cheek reveal,
"The hard rock in itself would love conceal.
"Tread thou the grove with graceful languishing,
"Dead trees thou wouldest into movement bring,
"And in the desert should the deer thee see
"With eyelash they would sweep the road for thee.
"With thy sweet lip shouldst thou intone a spell,
"Birds came from air, from rivers fish as well.
"Why with such beauty dost thou feel such woe,
"And why at last such weakness dost thou show?
"Eyebrows thy bow, thy arrow thy eye's ray,
"Of that enchanting beauty make thy prey.
"Shew but thy cheek and turn his face to thee,
"This secret's thine, and he shall kneel with thee.

"Bring into motion that date-bearing palm,
"Bring him with pleasing gait to road of calm.
"Convert into a noose one lock of thine,
"And round his feet the snare of union twine.
"With thy own silver ball ope thou his eye,
"And like a man raise up his head on high.
"Shed honey round him from thy smiling lip,
"That he in honey may thy sweetness sip.
"Go: to thy face heart-nearing smiles impart,
"And with desire for those smiles sear his heart."
"Mother, what shall I say", Zuleikha cried;
"Or what to me from Joseph may betide?
"Since his eye never looks upon my face,
"Before him how can I appear in grace?
"Circling like moon, me he will never see,
"Nor on the ground my sun in brilliancy.
"Should *Surma* give my eye a brighter ray,
"Scarce to his close-shut orb 'twould find a way.
"If ever he would cast one glance at me,
"He might sometimes my sad condition see.
"If care for me he ever had at heart,
"Of his own care when had he felt the smart?
"Not in his beauty only my misfortune lies;
"It is that I am worthless in his eyes,
"For had that charmer ever cared for me,
"How could he heedless and indifferent be?"
The nurse in answer thus again replied:
"Thou from whose beauty the sun draws fresh pride,
"A thought has just arisen in my breast,
"From which I trust thy heart may find some rest,
"But only then wilt thou this thing behold,
"When camels bear silver and asses gold.
"I will construct a house as *Iram* fair,
"And will appoint a skilful painter there,
"Who shall with skill portray in every place
"Thee and thy Joseph in a close embrace.

"When Joseph for a while is seated there,
"And in his arms shall see thee everywhere,
"His heart shall stir that beauteous form of thine,
"And towr'ds thy union he will thus incline.
"Him will on all sides then affection move,
"And matters turn out as thou wouldst approve."
This secret story when the nurse had told,
Zuleikha all her silver brought and gold ;
All this in her possession then she placed,
As with the capital her nurse she graced.


## THE BUILDING BY THE NURSE OF THE HOUSE IN WHICH WERE THE PICTURES OF JOSEPH AND ZULEIKHA.

Thus state the builders who this tale designed :
To build, when eager turned the nurse her mind,
She brought a man possessed of every skill,
On every finger many an art at will,
In geometric arts well proved and tried,
In astronomic ways a faithful guide.
Did he at hand no compass ready find,
A circle with two fingers he designed.
Hard problems from his figures set at rest, (206)
At his doubts cast was Euclid, (207) too, oppressed—
To draw a line when he evinced desire,
To make it straight no ruler he'd require.
Agile he mounted on the arching sphere,
And upon Saturn built a belvidere.
If he should move his hand toward the pick,
A stone became more soft than unburnt brick.
To architecture when he turned his mind,
A thousand fair foundations he would find,
And the world's buildings without head or base
Upon a single finger-nail he'd trace.

To making pictures when his thoughts he turned,
Was being's tablet by his pen adorned—
And that which from his brush on pictures flowed,
From its mere drops a soul with being glowed.
If a bird's figure he had carved in stone,
Light rising it had left its place and flown.
As the nurse ordered, he of golden hand
Of a gold palace the foundations planned.
Good fortune's drawing were its couches pure,
And in its roomy houses hope secure. (208)
Of marble inlaid were its passage floors,
Of ebony and ivory its doors—
Together in it there were mansions seven,
Like the unequalled cupolas of heaven.
Each one was made of stone of varied hue,
Like polished eye, of pleasing colour, too.
The seventh house was as the seventh sphere—
And lost was every shape and colour here—
Its forty pillars were with gold inlaid,
On which were forms of beasts and birds displayed—
At foot of each pillar of gold was made
A deer with bag where fragrant musk was laid.
Of golden peacocks there was full the plain,
With decorated tails in stately train.
And in the midst there was a lofty tree,
Whose like the wondering eye might never see.
Wrought of pure silver its delicate stem,
Gold boughs, with leaves of turquoise surrounding them.
On each branch a bird, created with skill,
With emerald wings and a ruby bill.
And in God's name that green and pleasant tree
From autumn's wind would never blighting see,
And to mankind were all the birds there tame,
And morn and eve at peace together came.
In every place the painter brought to view
The forms of Joseph and Zuleikha too.

As lovers sat together he and she,
As two who in their heart and soul agree.
Both in one place with lips together pressed
One of the other leaning on the breast. (209)
If any passing by had them there seen,
His envious mouth had full of water been.
The roof, moreover, was just like a sphere
On which a shining moon and sun appear.
A wondrous sun and moon, in form as two
Where both from one rent collar came to view.
Upon the wall's face there appeared to sight
As in the time of spring a rose-bed bright.
On every rosebush of that rose-bed placed
Two branches fair with roses interlaced,
And on its carpet everywhere displayed
In cradle roses two in slumber laid.
In short no spot within that house remained,
But it of charmers that sweet pair contained,
And to whatever side the eye was thrown
At once their beauteous forms were clearly shown.
When thus prepared the house appeared in view
Zuleikha's love for Joseph stronger grew.
When she that temple saw, at every turn
Her heart for Joseph would more freshly burn.
When of his darling the face comes in view,
The lover reads the words of love anew;
When from those words his fires fresh force obtain,
He is led captive by that boundless pain.

### THE CALLING OF JOSEPH TO THAT HOUSE BY ZULEIKHA, AND HER DEMANDING UNION WITH HIM.

Op'ning her hand, Zuleikha then arrayed
The house the master there had ready made.
With silken carpets she adorned its floor,
With golden throne increased its beauty more.

Around it lamps with jewels decked were strung,
To give sweet odour scented herbs were hung.
All needful things she had there laid at hand ;
To spread the couch of pleasure, too, she planned.
Of each and all in that abode of bliss
Joseph to summon, there failed only this.
Without the face of her who is adored
By the fond lover's Paradise abhorred.
It came to this that she would Joseph call,
With honour she would seat him high in hall,
In secret would his beauteous self caress,
Towards union's plain she would his courser press.
Would from his life-increasing lip gain her desire,
Would from his haughty ringlets ease acquire.
But towards her beauty art should do its part,
That should demand the love of Joseph's heart.
Her charms had never need of shining gem,
Yet her own beauty (210) she increased with them.
In garden's beauty is well-known the rose,
But with dew-necklace even fairer grows.
With red paint she her roses freshly dressed,
And added to her charm a greater zest.
With dye upon her arching eyebrows laid,
A rainbow of her feast's new moon (211) she made.
Her amber hair in ringlets she combined,
Her Chinese musk locks in each other twined.
Down on her back her locks of musk were laid,
And to the *Arghavān* gave amber aid.
With *surma* her soft eye was tinged anew,
Thence black art's sorcery its pupil drew :
With moles of amber fresh upon her face,
She to her darling there would state her case :
" Thy face into my heart such burning threw,
" That to my heart and soul 'twas just as rue."
Upon her moon with *surma*-wire (212) blue lines she
    drew ;—
That Egypt as from Nile more beauteous grew.

That blue line on that moon's face would not show
But as an iron to make blind her foe.
Had the tire-woman seen that frenzied eye,
The *surma*-wire had she dropped hastily.
Her silver hand she dyed with colour due,
With magic that she might his heart subdue.
An artist drew upon her palm a little thing
With which her beauty to her hand to bring.
Dye of fresh jujube on her filbert (214) spread
Her lover told of blood-red tears she shed.
By art ten crescents (215) to the moon appear.
Out of the veil of twilight shining clear,
That from her fortune's terrace she might soon
Show of her union's feast the crescent moon.
Beside her cheek an earring she had laid ;
The moon had with a star conjunction made,
Of this world and of faith that fortune clear
From that conjunction might to her draw near !
She like a rose in beauty fresh and gay,
Had clothed herself in garments new that day.
Upon her body then a robe she drew,
Its lily skirt was filled with roses, too.
She clothed the rose's branch with jessamine,
Lilies on breast, roses the sleeve within.
No eye could see, though it examined close,
But water on the tulip and the rose. (216)
A stream of wonder, of pure silver made,
Two fish (217) at rest there with two forearms laid.
A bracelet fair upon each forearm bound,
With golden collar girt those fish around.
Both cheek and forearm testimony bore,
From moon to crescent she would fair endure—
When on her body slight the robe was laid,
She decked it with gold wrought Chinese brocade.
With a thousand graces that Chinese fair
In Chinese garb seemed an idol there.

She arranged of dry gold and glistening gem
On her harvest of musk (218) a diadem.
With skirt and bosom all with jewels graced,
Like peacock round the palace court she paced.
Mirror in hand she went on pacing there,
And saw the image of her beauty fair,
And when that fair reflection came to view,
She found it current money, good and true.
Joyed at that cash into her treasure brought,
To purchase it a purchaser she sought.
Some one in search of Joseph when she sent,
Her servant up and down in searching went.
In at the door that moon came suddenly,
In state the sun, in pomp a Mercury.
Traces of clay and water in him none,
Upon his brow a light of lights there shone.
One ray from him a world would lighten still:
One word from him with tales the world would fill.
And when Zuleikha's eye upon him fell,
The fire had seized the cane-brake, one might tell—
She caught his hand, "O being pure," her cry,
" Light of discerning people of the eye;
" Oh! with what faith, in God's name, dost thou serve!
" Favours and gratitude dost thou deserve.
" Of thy good services so proud am I,
" Thy favour's collar lifts my head on high.
" My gratitude, oh! let me now display:
" And let me praise thee for a while to-day.
" The ways of gratitude now let me show,
" That all the world may speak of it and know."
With boundless wiles and stratagems she knew,
Of seven houses to the first she drew.
The moment the first golden door was passed
She made it with a lock of iron fast.
And when the door was closed, her lip revealed
The secret which her heart no more concealed.

She first exclaimed: "O longing of my soul,
" Thou of my heart's wish art the very whole.
" Thy image in my dreams before me lay,
" And in my childhood slumber snatched away.
" In the same house with grief it made me dwell,
" And with great longing maddened me as well—
" Thyself when my eye was opened to see,
" I came to this land, an exile for thee.
" For wandering here no remedy I know,
" And pass wretched days in the midst of woe.
" Though I rejoice at seeing thee again,
" Without thy presence hopeless I remain.
" Pass from unkindness: turn to me thy face,
" Speak one word only to me in thy grace."
Low hanging his head, he said in reply :
" A hundred kings are thy slaves, just as I.
" Make me from this my chain of sorrow free,
" And thus my heart releasing gladden me.
" To be here with thee I no pleasure own,
" To be behind this screen with thee alone.
" Thou art a fire and I am cotton dry:
" Thou *Sarsar's* wind (219); a breath of musk am I.
" How can this cotton with the fire contend?
" How must scent's struggle with the *Sarsar* end?"
These words were to Zuleikha wind, no more :
She to the second house him speaking bore.
Again she locked it firmly as the first,
And with his woe the heart of Joseph burst.
Thence once again Zuleikha raised a cry,
Of many years the veil she lifted high,
" Sweeter than life," she said: "how long shall anger last?
" Me how long at thy feet shall thy rebellion cast?
" I emptied all my treasure for thy price.
" My sense, my Faith to thee I sacrifice.
" So that my medicine thou mightest be,
" Pledged to my collar thou shouldst follow me.

" Not only dost thou not obey my will,
" In every way dost thou oppose me still."
He said: " To do sin is not to obey :
" To live in sin's of wickedness the way,
" For every thing of God that's not approved,
" The chain in service-court may not be moved.
" Nor such a matter may I ever know,
" My hand no power have to strike a blow!"
Few words beyond this in that house were said,
But to another house the way was led.
Zuliekha closed again and locked the door,
And her heart's tale another fashion bore.
In this same way, with wiles and all deceit,
From house to house she onwards led his feet.
In every place she told another tale ;
Some other point minute would there prevail.
In houses six her aim was not attained.
Nor exit from the *Shishdar* (220) for her draughtsman gained.
Thence to the seventh house his feet she brought,
And there the solving of the matter sought.
As yet was she not hopeless in the way,—
Beyond the darkness was the light of day,
From doors a hundred should hope show no light,
Hopeless to eat thy heart still is not right.
Knock at another door ; perchance there may
To gain thy object be another way.

### The bringing of Joseph by Zuleikha into the Seventh House and demanding her Object from him.

He from this house of mystery who writes,
The author, from behind the screen indites.
When tow'rds the seventh house their course they bent ;
Zuleikha uttered thus her loud lament.

"Let thy foot, Joseph, on my eye alight:
"Kindly thy foot place in this *Harem* (221) bright."
In that glad place she seated him again—
Fastened the iron lock with golden chain—
He found a place where strangers could not pry,
And free its neighbourhood from envy's eye.
No road to come and go for strangers there,
And friends to gain an entrance in despair,
A place for lover and his mistress sole,
No watchman's trouble, no fear from patrol.
The loved one's face in all its beauty gay,
Trolling the lover's heart its jocund lay.
The plain was open wide to all desire,—
On the soul fallen, too, of hope the fire.
Zuleikha's eye and heart to frenzy flown,
In the hand of her lover she placed her own.
With words heart-soothing and discourses sweet
She led him gracefully towards a seat.
Upon that throne she threw herself to rest,
And that fair cypress, weeping, thus addressed:
"O rose-cheeked one, toward me raise thy eye,
"And give me now one glance of sympathy.
"Now were the sun himself my face to see,
"Moon-like, would he glean ears from me.
"How long wilt thou see me tortured with woes,
"That on my face thou pity's eye dost close?"
Thus from her heart complaint she constant made,
To Joseph the wish of her soul betrayed.
Still Joseph's eye but on himself was bent;
With head on breast for fear of trouble leant.
Down on the carpet as his eye he brought,
He saw his form with hers together wrought.
Thrown on a couch of silk and gold brocade
The two in close embrace together laid.
Upon those forms he gave a passing look,
And towards another spot his eye then took

If on the door or wall that eye he kept,
Those rosy-cheeked ones still together slept.
If to the God of heav'n he turned his face,
The same upon the ceiling could he trace.
Towards Zuleikha then he more inclined;
He bent upon her face a look more kind.
Zuleikha's hope in that look vivid grew,
As that bright sun his ray upon her threw.
She fell to weeping with a bitter cry
And heart-felt tears of blood rained from her eye.
"O selfish one, grant my desire"; she cried.
" In union medicine for me provide.
" Thou art life's water and I thirst for thee.
" I die: thou art eternal life to me.
" O unfound treasure, I from thee am far,
" As the dead thirsty without water are—
" Thy scar has me for years in fever kept;
" From love for thee I neither ate nor slept.
" No more do thou me in this fever keep;
" No longer foodless leave me without sleep.
" Thee in the name of that God I adjure,
" Who Lord of all Lords is for evermore.
" By that world-conquering goodness he bestows,
" And by that beauty on thy cheek that glows,—
" By that light brilliant that shines from thy brow,
" And at thy feet for which the moon must bow,—
" By the bow to thy brows its curve that lends;—
" By that waving cypress's graceful bends;—
" By that arching eye-brow, to me a shrine;—
" By the wave of those curling locks of thine;—
" By the magic of eyes mankind that snare;—
" That brocade-clothed head and that robe so fair;—
" By that slender waist one might call a hair;—
" By that mouth a secret one might declare;—
" By those musk-like spots on thy rosy cheeks,
" And by that sweet smile when thy rose-bud (222)
    speaks;

"By the tear that flows in my longing for thee;—
"By burning sighs when thou'rt parted from me;—
"Thy absence, that mountain I lie below,
"A captive to many a grief and woe;
"Over me by thy love's great victory;—
"By thy being content if I live or die;—
"Now pity me helpless and in despair,—
"Unloose the knots of this grievous affair.
"My heart for long ages has borne thy scar;
"I look for thy scent from thy garden far.
"For a while the salve of my heart's wound be,
"And scent with thy beauty my mead for me.
"Through parting's famine have I lost my strength:
"From union's table feed my soul at length!
"Mine is the milk, dates, palm-tree fresh, from thee:
"Fail not to spread thy table now for me.
"Food for my soul in milk and dates vouchsafe:
"From perishing by famine make me safe."
Then answered Joseph: "Thou of *Paris'* kind,
"To vie with whom no *Pari* comes to mind,
"Bring not this matter to a cruel pass,
"Dash not a stone against my sinful glass.
"With sinful water wet thou not my robe,
"Nor with the fire of lust my body probe.
"Whose forms men are by Him who has no like; (223)
"To whom inside and out are all alike;
"Foam from Whose bounty-sea the spheres arose,
"And from Whose lightning the sun brightly glows;
"By those pure souls from whom I claim descent,
"From whom this purity to me is lent,
"From whom this spirit pure I gain of mine,
"In whom my star does aye so brilliant shine,
"Thy hand from me, oh! lift thou off to-day,
"And thus release me from this narrow way.
"Then quick my meed of service shalt thou see,
"A thousand deeds of gratitude from me;—

"From my life-giving lip thy wish obtain,
"And ease from my enchanting stature gain.
"Thy longed for food, oh! be not quick to taste;—
"Many delays are sweeter than is haste.—
"Better to snare a noble prey at last,
"Than a good end to lose by being fast."
Zuleikha said: "Himself the thirsty soul
"To drink till to-morrow will not control.
"My life is on my lip from love to-day;
"I have no patience for the night's delay.
"And whence again the power may I find,
"To more delay that I should be inclined?
"To this I know not what can hindrance give,
"For me one moment that thou canst not live."
He said: "Two things will hinder my desire:
"Reproach from God,—of the Vazír the ire.
"This crooked nature should the Vazír know,
"A hundred pains will he inflict and woe.
"In the way that thou knowest he'll bare his blade,
"And bare of life's robe will my form be laid.
"And oh! the disgrace on the Judgment Day
"When fines the adulterers have to pay!
"When they write down the wickeds' recompense
"Will my name among all their list commence!"
"Think not of that foe"; Zuleikha replied:
"He will place me some day at a feast by his side,
"That will plague his soul he a cup shall drain,
"And drunk (224) till Judgment Day not rise again.
"Thou sayest, 'My God is compassionate,
"'And with pity looks on a sinner's state.'
"Of pearls and jewels a plentiful store
"Still lies there buried beneath this floor.
"These for thy sins an offering I stake,
"To God that thy excuses they may make."
He said: "To this can I never incline
"That others should suffer for fault of mine;

" And the Vazír especially, who thee
" Has kindly appointed to wait on me.
" My God, whose favour one can ne'er repay,
" Shall He for bribes His mercy give away?
" He who for giving life takes no reward,
" For bribes His pardon how should He afford?"
Zuleikha answered him: " O happy king,
" Both crown and throne to thee may fortune bring!
" My heart a butt is for the dart of pain:
" Excuse thou heapest on excuse again.
"' Excuse' is crooked-faced, full of deceit:
" In a fair game 'excuse' thou 'lt never meet.
" Now God forbid on false ways that I go;
" Deceit from thee no longer may I know.
" I am strangely feeble; oh! give me rest:
" Willing, unwilling, grant me my request.
" In words on words full many days have passed;
" And yet my hope is not attained at last.
" Thy tongue from bond of idle tales release:
" Move from thy place, that so my woes may cease.
" In my dry cane-brake there has fallen fire,
" Yet in my burning hast thou thy desire.
" What is my gain from all this fire and smoke,
" Since tears in thy eyes it will not provoke?
" Like smoke from fire I upwards curl and soar;
" Come: on this flame of mine thy water pour."
Zuleikha ceased this secret forth to pour:
Joseph began to make excuse once more.
" O Hebrew speaker," she resumed her say:
" Thou hast in talking robbed my time away.
" In this affair oppose no more my will,
" Or else with thy own hand myself I kill.
" Now let my hand around thy neck be laid,
" Or it shall feel of dagger keen the blade.
" If on my neck thy hand thou wilt not lay,
" Upon thy neck wilt thou my blood's price pay.

L

" I'll sheath my lily dagger in my breast,
" Like rose with crimson hue will dye my vest.
" My form shall from my soul know pastime's pain,
" And thus from thy excuses freedom gain.
" Me the Vazír shall find before thee dead,
" And thus to kill thee, too, will he be led."
Before his dart her soul a butt she made,
Herself as oyster for his pearls she laid.
Aim at the target Joseph would not take,
Nor in his search for pearls the oyster break ;
He wished the pearl with diamond to bore,
But his heart held his chastity the more.
Importunate Zuleikha was, but he
Would interpose delay repeatedly.
When in the corner of the house, behold
Sudden a curtain of embroidered gold !
He questioned her : " Why is that curtain there?
" Who sits concealed behind that curtain fair ?"
She said : "While I live in the world below,
" By way of service before him I bow.
" A golden idol, gems he has for eyes,
" Full of pure musk a tray within him lies.
" I fall down every hour before his face,
" My head before him in obedience place.
" And when thou dead behind earth's veil shalt be,
" This longing soul shall fix itself on thee."
Thus saying, from beneath the couch she drew
Like willow leaf a sword of lightning hue ;
And with the fire of grief inflamed and sore,
To thirsting throat that drop of water bore.
When Joseph saw, he leapt up from his place
Her hand like golden bracelet to embrace.
" Zuleikha, from this rashness cease," he said,
" And on this path let not thy steps be led.
" Dost thou desire thy object's face to see,
" Or gain thy wish from union with me?"

Zuleikha, moon enchanting of the sky,
When she saw kindness beam from Joseph's eye,
Thought that, perhaps, her wishes he might grant,
In union might with peace her soul enchant.
Cast from her hand in haste the blade away,
Of concord she essayed another way,—
From his sweet mouth a draught of sugar drew,
His arm around her neck as collar threw. (225)
" I made him up a place within the screen,
" That ever by him I might not be seen.
" That he might not see evil that I do:
" What I am doing now, he may not view."
When Joseph heard the word, he raised the cry:
" Of such *dinars* of cash no *dáng* have I. (226)
" Before the eyes of dead things thou hast shame,
" And from these lifeless ones thou fearest blame.
" The great, wise Seer, why should I not fear?
" Why the Eternal God should I not fear?"
He spoke, and from the midst his way to take,
Arose from that sweet sleeping place awake.
From the *Lám-Aleph, Aleph* stripped away. (227)
Seized camphor lamp on silver stand that lay.
When, with swift footsteps he began to run,
Doors in his flight he opened every one.
Each door when he approached to open it,
Locks here, bolts there, in every place were split.
Point with his finger, he need do no more,
In his hand lay the key of every door.
She saw, and in pursuit Zuleikha sped,
In the last chamber caught him as he fled.
Seizing his skirt to bring him back she flew,
And from behind she tore his vest in two.
Passed from her hand that one with grief forlorn,
His vest was like an opening rosebud torn.
Zuleikha wretched tore her own robe's fold—
Upon the ground as her own shadow rolled.

From her sad heart rose loud Zuleikha's cry,
Her wailing in her sorrow rose on high.
"Ah! woe is me, my unpropitious fate,
"That my love bore his goods from out my gate!
"Alas! my prey escaped my snare in haste!
"Woe for that honey that I could but taste!
"A spider had determined on a day,
"That for itself it would entrap some prey.
"It saw a royal falcon sitting down,
"From hand of one escaped who wore a crown;
"Its web around it it began to spin,
"From flight its wings and feathers to hold in.
"And for a while on the affair intent,
"Its web completely on the matter spent.
"And when away that royal falcon sped,
"Were left the spider but some bits of thread.
"I am that spider, weeping and forlorn,
"Fallen from hope, who far away am borne.
"My soul's vein worn through, just as was that thread,
"My prey, hope's bird, too, from my snare has fled.
"My cord is broken off from every thing,
"And in my hand are broken bits of string."

### The Finding by the Vazir of Joseph outside that House, and the Discovery of her Secret by Zuleikha.

The pen of this tale's writer thus has said:
Out of the house as Joseph flying sped,
Outside the house there met him the Vazír:
A troop of his domestics, too, were near—
When the Vazír saw him with this tumult fired,
Regarding this confusion he enquired,
He in his answer due politeness paid;
No charge was made, no secret was betrayed.

He kindly took his hand within his own,
And to that *Pari*-faced one led him on.
She saw them thus, and to herself she said:
"Joseph the matter has to him betrayed."
In that suspicion loud she raised her wail,
And from her secret's face raised up the veil.
"O scale of justice, what should him betide,
" Who with thy wife (228) would all faith lay aside ;
" In his own evil way without a thought,
" Within the veil such wickedness has wrought ?"
Leave gave the Vazír. "*Pari*-face," he said :
" Say who this crooked nature has displayed ?"
She answered him : " This Hebrew slave, the one,
" Whom from the first thou 'st chosen for thy son.
" Freed from the dust of labour of the day,
" To rest within my chamber here I lay.
" He like a thief around my pillow went,
" To pluck my wild-rose harvest with intent,
" And that I knew it not—such was his thought—
" To that rose-garden glad his footsteps brought.
" Of gardener no leave did he demand,
" Spikenard and rose to plunder with his hand.
" Just as his hand that madman would produce
" The knots of union's treasure to unloose,
" I from my heavy sleep awake became,
" From cup of lifelessness to life I came.
" At my awaking he became afraid,
" And his way quickly from my presence made.
" Towards the door he turned his face in shame,
" And lucky nigh to open it he came.
" Hast'ning behind, I followed in pursuit,
" And reached him ere without he placed his foot.
" Nimble and quick, I seized upon his hem :
" His vest rent as a rose from off its stem.
" With open mouth his tattered garment gapes,
" And what I say with proper meaning shapes.

" Now were it best like those of evil mind.
" That he awhile be in the jail confined.
" Or that in person on his body pure,
" Some pain to grieve him he should now endure.
" If thou approve for him this heavy pain,
" The warning may cause others to refrain."
As she this story to the Vazír told,
He could himself in patience no more hold.
With blame as with a sword his tongue applied,
From path of rectitude he stepped aside.
He said to Joseph: " My jewels were weighed:
" Two hundred treasures for thee empty made
" I chose thee for my son ; in dignity
" Then did I raise thee to a station high.
" I caused Zuleikha, too, to be thy friend,
" Her servants thee to wait on and attend.
" Rings in their ears, they all thy slaves became
" Faithful and pure in faith to thee they came.
" Over my goods, too, I set thee apart,
" Nor did I vex in any way thy heart.
" Was it a wise man's act that thou hast done ?
" Be for thy evil deed God's pardon won !
" It is not right in this our world of woe
" That aught but gratitude the good should know
" Ungrateful thou, though favour thou hast seen
" Hast in ingratitude rebellious been.
" Of gratitude thou passest by the street,
" And breakest the salt-dish, as thou salt dost eat
When Joseph the Vazír's excitement saw,
He shrank as hairs before a flame withdraw.
He said: " O, Vazír, whom doth justice grace,
" Do not impute to me a crime so base.
" Zuleikha's false, whatever she may say :
" Her falsehood is a lamp without a ray.
" God woman from man's left side did create,
" And from the left is never seen what's straight. (229)

"He who knows left and right will know this thing:
"'Tis hard for what is right from left to spring.
"Since we first met, her purpose she retains,
"Until from me her object she obtains.
"Behind me or before to come she'll never fail,
"And ever calls me for some idle tale.
"My eye in seeing her has aye passed by,
"Nor on her envious table have I cast that eye.
"What should I be, then, with thy nature kind,
"In thy *harím* my wicked foot to find?
"But slave, who, when his master is not there,
"To sit upon his cushion shall prepare.
"To exile's pain my heart became a prey,
"Of ease from every corner torn away.
"A messenger to me Zuleikha sent,
"On opening many a door of care intent.
"By many sweet illusions led astray,
"She to this private place bore me away.
"Her hope's fulfilment did she then demand:
"No hope of safety left she in my hand.
"Towards the door in hasty flight I passed,
"And reached it with a hundred woes at last.
"Lo! close upon me from behind she pressed,
"And on my back she tore in two my vest.
"Between us two, I say, from first to last,
"No trafficking but this has ever passed.
"If, then, my innocence thou dost not see,
"In God's name do what thou mayst wish to me."
Zuleikha heard the words as Joseph spoke,
And to prove innocence must God invoke.
And to this other oaths she added more:
By Egypt's king's head and the crown he wore,
By the Vazír's high state and dignity,
Whom the king honoured with his privity.
If in a suit some obstacle arise,
What is an oath in a false witness' (239) eyes?

Of many oaths the swearing will reveal
The evil thoughts the swearer too may feel.
After her oath as from her eyes tears ran,
She cried: " 'Twas Joseph that the thing began."
Their lamps of falsehood when false women light
They need no oil but tears to keep them bright ;
And if upon their lamps such oil they pour,
A whole world may be burnt up in an hour.
Those oaths, those tears shed in the Vazír's sight,
The carpet he rolled up of seeing right.
He gave an officer a sign, a blow
To strike on Joseph's soul, as lute with bow :
To tear his soul's vein with the wound of grief,
Erase from his tablet the verse of relief:
To take him to jail, where he should remain
Till the secret matter became more plain.

### THE TAKING OF JOSEPH TO PRISON, AND THE GIVING OF EVIDENCE BY A SUCKING CHILD AS TO HIS PURITY, AND THE VAZIR LEAVING HIM.

His hand that officer on Joseph laid,
To the labour-place of the jail conveyed ;
The heart of Joseph was rent with despair
Secret he raised to heaven his face in prayer:
" O Thou Who wise art in all mysteries,
" With Thee the knowledge of all secrets lies.
" Falsehood and truth thou ever knowest here,
" And who but Thou can make this secret clear ?
" With the truth's light as Thou hast filled my eyes,
" Oh! let me not be charged through uttered lies.
" May in my claim some evidence appear,
" For in Thy sight my truth is bright and clear."
From thumb-stall of design that might the world subdue,
Directly to the target his prayer's arrow flew.

A woman there, by bonds of kindred tied,
Both night and day was by Zuleikha's side.
A child of three months old her shoulder graced,
Dear as her very soul by her embraced—
Its tongue, like lily, words had never said,
Nor roll of exposition had it read.
It cried: "O Vazír, patiently abide,
" Nor hastily on punishment decide.
" Joseph does not deserve to be chastised
" For loving mercy he is justly prized."
At the child's speech the Vazír was amazed,
And with due rev'rence conversation raised—
" O thou whose lip from milk is not yet free,
" In fairest speech God has instructed thee:
" Tell me now clearly; who has lit this flame,
" And has burnt the veil of my honoured name?"
" No scandalous tale-bearer I," it said,
" Secrets by whom to strangers are betrayed—
" Tell-tale is China's musk, aye black of face,
" Through many curtains whose scent one may trace.
" And see how fresh the roses are in spring,
" Because their curtains still around them cling.
" I backbite not, but yet that thou mayst know,
" To thee this hidden secret will I show.
" Go, look on Joseph's state at once, and see
" His vest, in what way it came torn to be,
" If from the front it has been torn in two,
" Free of his skirt Zuleikha thou mayst view:—
" In Joseph's claim there is no light to view;—
" For his own sake he says what is not true.
" But if the vest has from behind been torn,
" His skirt is free of that wickedness borne:
" Then what Zuleikha says will not be true:
" The way of truth then she does not pursue."
When the child's words had reached the Vazír's ear,
The vest's condition he made haste to clear.

The vest was torn behind: this he could see,
And blamed that woman for her treachery.
"I knew that this deceit had come from thee,
"That innocent he should imprisoned be.
"What fraud is this that thou hast done at last?
"What evil this that to thyself has passed?
"Thou takest off of honour's road thy stand,
"And of thy own slave love didst thou demand.
"Approving that which thou shouldst evil know,
"Of this didst thou the blame upon him throw.
"Man's heart in two a woman's fraud will rend—
"Of woman's treachery there is no end.
"Through woman's fraud the pure man falls and lies;
"To woman's fraud the learned is a prize.
"From woman's fraud may none despairing be!
"And may deceitful women never be!
"Seek in humility God's pardoning grace:
"For very shame turn to the wall thy face.
"Go: this disorder with thy tears allay,
"And wash this ill word from thy book away.
"Thou, Joseph, in this matter bind thy tongue,
"By none this secret from thy lips be wrung.
"This in thy converse be enough for thee,
"That thy own innocence is clear to me.
"Backbiter's path to walk on do thou loathe:
"Better than rending veils is it to clothe."
Thus spoke the Vazír as he turned away,
Well known for easy temper in his day.
Patience attracts the heart, yet not as this:
Good temper pleases, too, not such as this.
To ease his wife a man himself may lend,—
In cuckoldom (231) will such good nature end.
In a wife's matter not so lenient be:
'Twill break what is a bar to jealousy.

## Letting loose the Tongue of Reproach against Zuleikha by the Women of Egypt with Regard to Joseph's Love.

Now safety's corner suits not love in pace:
It loves the street of blame and its disgrace.
The pain of love in blame becomes more proud,
And in a tumult is its voice more loud.
Love's markets' guardian will blame ever be,
The polisher of rust to make it free.
The blame from all sides that on love is spent
But serves as whip-thong to the indolent.
When the steed of the road is heavy in pace,
The whip makes it sharp and keen for the race.
Zuleikha's secret's rose to bloom has sprung:
The world in blame's a nightingale in tongue—
And this when the Egyptian women knew,
To keen reproach they all receptive grew.
For good or bad they all upon her fell,
And in reproach their tongues were loosed as well.
" All shame and honour has she cast aside:
" Her mad heart to this Hebrew slave is tied.
" So has he grasped the marrow of her soul,
" Of faith and sense her hand has lost control.
" From the right path so strangely has she erred
" That in her sight her own slave is preferred:
" And stranger still, that slave from her must fly,
" And shun her friendship and her company.
" Nowhere he casts a look upon her face,
" Nor on the same road moves his foot one pace.
" When she moves on his wish is to stand still;—
" When she would stand to move on is his will.
" When from her cheek she would remove the veil,
" His eyelash shuts his eye as with a nail.

" At every grief he laughs where she would weep;
" All doors she opens he fast closed would keep.
" It may be in his eye she is not good,
" And thence towards her never bends his mood.
" If ever that charmer sat by our side,
" In no place else would he ever abide.
" On road of despair he would never move thus;
" Our wish would he give and gain his from us.
" Acceptance can not every one acquire,
" To be accepted nor can all aspire.
" Many fair cheeked and virtuous though we find,
" Yet towards them men's hearts may not be inclined.
" Full many a Leila, of caressing mood,
" Must pour as from a fountain springs of blood."
And now, Zuleikha having heard the case,
Determined these unjust ones to disgrace.
Without delay she bade a feast prepare,
And the women of Egypt summoned there.
What a feast in a royal banquet hall!
A thousand luxurious things at call!
What sweetmeats pure of each colour and hue,
Like a light reflected the darkness through!
And in crystal cups whose lip overflows
Is mingled rose-water with *attar* of rose.
Its ground was decked as with the sun's golden bars:
The silver cups a galaxy of stars.
Flavour and perfume from table and bowl,
Food for the body and strength for the soul.
Things there for eating whatever you wish,
Of bird they had brought together and fish.
Borrowed in place of sweets the fair, and drew
Sugar from lips and from teeth almonds, too,
Sweetmeats on boards of every hue and shade;
*Shirín* (232) foundations for that feast had laid.
In place of carpet spread upon the ground
Many gold bricks with candy laid around.

There sugar-eating lips with mouths of grace
Left for *luzinah* (233) in the mouth no place.
When to seek lozenges their palates came,
Their tongues of gardens never named the name.
None seeking wonders could have ever thought
Such baskets out of water could be brought
Of fruit as fresh, as juicy and as rare,
As gardeners with water could prepare.
Handmaids and waiting-boys on every side
In service stood as peacocks in their pride.
Of Egypt there the *Pari*-faced ones found,
On golden cushions seated all around,
From every table ate what they desired;
And did such things as the right way required.
When from before them all the cloths were raised,
Them all in sugared speech Zuleikha praised.
And for each woman laid with cunning art
A knife and orange by her side apart.
One hand the knife held, sharp its work to do,
Orange the other, gladness to renew.
The orange deepest yellow, yet the while
A famous medicine for curing bile.
Then said she to them: "All ye fair and sweet,
" At beauty's banquet ye who lofty sit,
" Why do ye my desire so bitter taste,
" This Hebrew slave's love that to blame ye haste?
" If full of light his eye ye could but see,
" Ye would in seeing make excuse for me.
" Here will I bring him if ye so decide,
" And for this purpose I will be his guide."
All cried at once: " In every word we speak,
" This only is the aim that we all seek. (235)
" Bid that in stately grace he here be led,
" Softly to spread his skirt about our head.
" With heart and soul do we his presence seek,
" Lovers of him, though yet unseen his cheek.

"Thy orange hold we in our hands awhile,
"For us, the bilious, as a cure for bile;
"To cut, his cheek unseen, would not be right,
"And none will cut it till he come in sight."
Zuleikha sent her nurse to bring him there,
And say: "Come to us here, thou cypress fair.
"Put forth thy foot, that I beneath may fall:
"Before thy beauteous stature I may fall.
"Thy tranquil home shall be my sorrowing breast,
"My eye the carpet on thy road to rest."
Joseph would at the nurse's word not come,
Nor would the rose with idle talking bloom.
On her own feet, then, thither where he dwelt,
Zuleikha went and down before him knelt.
Weeping she said: "O light of my two eyes,
"Longing in my pained heart for thee must rise—
"At first didst thou thyself inspire me hope;
"For longing now there is no farther scope.
"Disgraced among men have I been through thee,
"And of men's tongues the topic shall I be.
"I take it I am all mean in thy eye,
"And that on me thou never canst rely.
"Though unreliable and base, to shame
"Bring me of Egypt not before each dame—
"To eat thy lip's salt longs my wounded heart;
"To sprinkle salt upon it thy lip's part.
"Oh! of my faithfulness conceive no doubt;
"The rights of that salt do thou carry out."
Of her enchantments with the fire aflame,
Pliant to come thus Joseph's heart became.
To deck him out she rose up as the wind,
Like cypress garb of green on him to bind.
She hung the ringlets of his perfumed hair
Before his cloak like amber fresh and fair.
Thou wouldst have thought it was of musk a snake,
That wreathed itself around a verdant brake.

## Yusuf and Zuleikha.

Upon his hair-like waist she tightly bound
A golden girdle with gems studded round—
Those jewels' weight, those heavy rubies' pain,
I wonder such a waist could bear the strain.
Upon his head a jewelled diadem,
Delight was beaming forth from every gem.
Shoes on his feet of pearls and rubies full,
A string of pearls the latchets, too, to pull.
A girdle of brocade as chaplet hung,
A hundred hearts and souls on each thread strung.
She placed a golden ewer in his hand,
A gold-wreathed handmaid to before him stand.
A silver dish upon her hand she bore,
And step by step, as shadow walked before.
Thus bright and fresh whoever saw him stand
Of his dear life at once would wash his hand—
Of his look more than this I could not say,—
Beyond my praise he would be far away.
That hidden treasure from the private room
Came out like rosebud in its fullest bloom.
Saw Egypt's dames that rose-bed of delight,
And from that rose-bed plucked one rose of sight.
With that one sight their senses them forsook,
And from their hands the reins of power shook.
At that fair form of his were all amazed,
And, wond'ring, all like lifeless bodies gazed.
By that fair vision as was each inspired,
At once to cut her orange she desired.
From her own hand her orange no one knew,
And thus across her hand the knife she drew.
A pen made one her fingers with her sword,
Upon her heat devotion to record;
A reed, which if the sword should strike a blow,
Vermilion from each joint would quickly flow:
Out of her palm a silver page one made,
Where, as in calendars, red lines were laid:

From every line there flowed a stream of blood,
Beyond its banks o'erflowing in a flood—
And when they saw him of such high degree,
They cried aloud: "No mortal man is he,
" Not formed, like Adam, of water and clay:
" An angel pure below has found his way."
Zuleikha said : " This is that peerless one,
" For whom reproaches I have undergone.
" Your blame through which my very soul was torn,
" All for the love of this fair form was borne.
" Yet was his head not bowed down to my will,
" The hope of all my days he 'd not fulfil.
" My hope in soul and body him I called,—
" To union with myself him even called—
" If towards my aim he will not move his foot,
" Him in the prison's corner must I put.
" If in disgrace in jail he still delays,
" And would consume in trouble all his days,
" Let his rebellion in the jail reform,
" And in good habits yet his heart grow warm.
" Nothing the free wild bird will ever tame
" Like that case in a cage which he can claim."
As then his face the Egyptian dames beheld,
Their hands cut many with the knives they held.
And of those dames whose hands were cut, a part
Lost wisdom, patience, and all sense and heart.
From his love's sword their souls they could not save,
In that assembly still their lives they gave.
Another part from reason were estranged,
And from that *Pari's* love became deranged.
Bare both in head and foot they ran around,
Nor e'er again the light of reason found.
And yet a part to reason came at last,
But pained at heart for love their days they passed,
And, like Zuleikha, drunk from Joseph's bowl,
Caught in his snare were those birds of their soul.

Of wine was Joseph's beauty as a pot,
Where each found gain according to his lot.
From inebriety one profit gained;
From thoughts of being one release obtained;
One for his beauty gave her soul for nought:
One dumb remained, absorbed but in his thought.
By her alone should pardon be obtained,
Who from that wine no sort of profit gained.

## THE HOLDING EXCUSED OF ZULEIKHA BY THE WOMEN OF EGYPT AFTER HAVING SEEN JOSEPH'S BEAUTY.

When there search for goods men of every kind,
The buyer's heart tow'rds them is more inclined.
One maddening lover by one mistress blessed,
Perchance in love may comfort find and rest,
But with him when another lover vies,
A fire to scorch his heart will there arise.
The state of those whom Joseph rendered dumb,
Witness to Joseph's beauty had become.
Zuleikha's heart grew still the more inflamed,
And her soul greater love to Joseph claimed.
" When ye saw Joseph," to the dames she said :
" Your hands of love were wounded with the blade.
" If now his love ye hold excused in me,
" Let me from your reproach be ever free
" Enter the door of friendship as my friends,
" Give me your aid until the matter ends."
Then all upon the harp of friendship played,
And in their song for her excuses made :
" Joseph the lord in thy soul's realm would seem,
" And in that realm his orders are supreme.
" Him having seen, though as a stone he were,
" Refuse his heart to Joseph who would dare?

" For him although thy love distress thy mind,
" Excuse in his perfection mayst thou find.
" Was any ever born beneath heav'n's sphere,
" Who saw his face, and did not mad appear?
" If thou art in love, reproach is not thine;
" Thou in this traffic incurrest no fine.
" Though often round this earth has heaven been,
" But seldom has it such a loved one seen.
" May his stony heart grow soft with thy love;
" And shame his want of affection remove."
After this they turned towards Joseph round,
And these words of warning for him they found.
" O precious life!" thus him they addressed;
" In the cause of good name is rent thy vest.
" In this garden, where roses with thorns are born,
" Like thee never bloomed a rose without thorn.
" In this sea, of nine spheres each is a shell,
" Four elements, pearls, in thy honour dwell.
" Insist not ever on thy glorious base:
" Descend a little from thy lofty place.
" Pure one, Zuleikha's dust is at thy feet:
" Thy skirt draw thou at times along her street.
" To thee, pure-skirted one, what loss in this,
" Her dust that sometimes that pure skirt should kiss?
" Oh! strive no longer to defeat her aim,
" Permit with thee what is her only claim.
" On freedom from desire tak'st thou thy stand,
" Withdraw not from the needy now thy hand.
" What is thy service due has reached her ear;
" Forget not the dues of her service here.
" Regard her prayer: Do not too much coquet,
" O lofty cypress, this I fear as yet,
" Since thou but to rebellion dost incline,
" But fruit unpleasant will at last be thine.
" She from her heart will wash thy love away:
" Thee at her feet her hand of power will lay.

" A friend in anger, oh! of this beware,
" From his friend's head the skin will basely tear.
" When the floods of fear pass over her face,
" Her child a mother 'neath her feet will place.
" A threat of jail she holds before thy face,
" But for the ill-disposed of ease a place—
" Grave, dark and narrow where oppressed men lie,
" Whence far and away will the living fly.
" The living there can hardly draw their breath ;
" 'Tis a place for those who await their death.
" The hand of the builder has not made there
" A way that is light or a hole for air.
" With desperation's lock its door they close :
" There in pale pride the morning never rose.
" Its air the source of every plague would yield,
" Of all misfortune is its soil the field :
" Narrow and darksome as of pitch a jar,
" Chains, fetters, the goods of its people are.
" At boards without water and bread they lie,
" Yet sitting there are content to die.
" Jailors of hard face are there them among,
" Neighbours with bitter words upon their tongue.
" Folds to oppress men in their brows you find ;
" A hundred knots in each to plague mankind.
" Their tempers as with fire a world provoke,—
" Their faces all are black with that fire's smoke.
" Can such place of sorrow be ever fit,
" For such a charmer as thou art to sit ?
" For God's sake, on thyself bestow thy grace ;
" Ope her aim's door before Zuleikha's face.
" Pen-like, her head to comfort's line bring near ;
" From her heart's tablet wash the point of fear.
" Should discontent with her perchance there be,
" Or shouldst thou in her no great beauty see,
" When thou art free of her, be thou our friend,
" Towards us thy secret inclination bend.

" In beauty none with us can ever vie,
" Moons shining are we all in beauty's sky.
" When we our sugar-eating lips unclose,
" Her mouth from pure shame must Zuleikha close.
" So sweet and sugar-eating as we are,
" Above Zuleikha's is our station far."
When Joseph heard that this their treach'rous talk
Was merely meant Zuleikha's aim to balk—
Faith to forsake, in folly's ways to dwell,
Was not for him but for themselves as well.
At this their converse he was in despair.
His face then turning from their faces there,
To God he lifted supplication's hand:
" Thou, Who dost ever by the needy stand,
" Refuge of those who solitude observe,
" Friend of all those who chastity preserve,—
" The lamp of fortune of all innocence,
" From ev'ry ill a fortress of defence,—
" They in this thing have strangely wearied me;
" 'Twere well to be in jail them not to see.
" In jail I'd best a hundred years remain,
" So never on their face to look again.
" To look on the forbidden blinds the heart,
" And from God's presence throws us far apart.
" If Thou the crafty fraud turn not away
" Of those from wisdom's road and Faith's who stray,
" My place through them becomes too tight for me.
" Oh! turn them back: if not, oh! woe is me!"
When for a prison Joseph God besought,
God at his own prayer him to prison brought.
But had he asked for freedom from His grace,
Towards the prison He had never turned his face,—
From their calamity had him released,
And all the pains of prison would have ceased.

## The Preparing of Zuleikha by the Women of Egypt to send Joseph to Prison.

When of those hand-cut women by the guile,
Conceited, idols worshipping the while,
From chastity was not turned Joseph's will,
He clung to chastity the firmer still.
They, like the bats that from the sun take flight,
Became all hopeless at his nearer light.
Into Zuleikha's eyes they then threw dust,
And urged her Joseph into jail to thrust.
They said: "O poor wretch in oppression held,
"Thou art not worthy to be thus repelled.
"Although with Joseph, *Huris* cannot vie,
"Thou hast with him no hope of unity.
"In giving him advice we strove awhile,
"We made our tongue as rough as any file.
"But on his iron will the file not bite;—
"In hardness only is his craft aright.
"Make hot the jail for him, as furnace-glow;
"In that forge softer will his iron grow.
"And when the steel becomes soft in the fire,
"The master can work it at his desire.
"If thou canst not make it softer with heat,
"What wilt thou gain if cold iron thou beat?"
Now when Zuleikha on their magic tongue
In hope of union through the prison hung,
For her own comfort she desired his pain,
His treasure in that ruined house to gain.
If one to perfect love does not attain,
But his own purpose he desires to gain,
He would his love should follow his behest,
And suits his own affairs as he thinks best.
For one rose's scent of love from the mead,
Her soul from many a thorn of grief may bleed.

Zuleikha with the Vazír talked one night,
And of her heart the passion brought to light.
" In Egypt through this boy I've lost my name,—
" In Egypt's people's eyes have come to shame.
" And in this men and women all agree,
" That I am deep in love as I can be.
" His arrow's victim in this plain, they say,
" In blood and dust I am his trembling prey.
" So have the arrows pierced my very heart,
" That one dart lies upon another dart.
" Of his love is void no point of my hair:
" In his love of myself I am not aware.
" I think that this suspicion to repel,
" To send to jail the young man would be well,
" And that in ev'ry street we should proclaim
" His hopeless failure and his helpless shame.
" Thus is that sinner punished who would dare
" His master's property with him to share:
" Of his soul-tearing rage who will not think,
" Whose foot from his lust's carpets will not shrink.
" When all mankind this rage of mine shall see,
" They will dismiss their evil thoughts of me."
The Vazír's fancy by her counsel moved,
He smiled upon her, and her plan approved.
" I gave to the question," he said, " much thought,
" And to this matter much reflection brought.
" No better pearl than that which thou hast thread ;
" Naught better to my heart than thou hast said.
" To treat him as thou wilt thou hast thy way,
" Or else his dust upon thy path to lay."
When Zuleikha had thus obtained his leave,
She turned to Joseph again to deceive.
" O aim of my soul, desire of my heart,
" In life I have no wish from thee apart.
" Above thee the Vazír has placed me still,
" Thy head in my pow'r to do as I will.

"At will I place thee in the prison here,
"Or raise thy foot up to the heavenly sphere.
"Lay down thy head: how long wilt thou rebel?
"How long with me wilt thou unhappy dwell?
"Proceed with me upon the road of peace;
"Thyself from shame and me from pain release.
"Oh! grant my desire,—I will give thee thine:
"Thy name in the height of glory shall shine.
"Else, a hundred doors of pain open wide:
"Thy foot in torment in jail shall abide.
"Thus happy to sit and on me to smile,
"Were better than living in jail awhile."
Joseph allowed in blame his speech to flow,
And loosened his tongue in the way you know.
In Zuleikha's breast then passion awoke;
And to the guard without delay she spoke.
Then his golden crown on the ground they threw:
An old woollen coat on his form they drew:
His silver leg, with iron chain they deck,
With endurance collar around his neck.
As Jesus was, he was placed on an ass;
Through the streets of Egypt they made it pass,
And a crier aloud this warning gave:
"Ev'ry rebellious and impudent slave,
"Whoever, taking the way of disgrace,
"On his master's carpet his foot shall place,
"Should thus with the bad be ever disgraced,
"And with all contempt in the prison placed."
But there came to see him running the crowd,
And "May God forbid it!" all cried aloud.
"From such a good face can there evil spring?
"On men can such a charmer mischief bring?
"For this is an angel, perfectly pure,
"Who the works of Satan could not endure.
"From ill Fair-face will aye his foot withhold;
"He of good counsel well the tale has told

"For he upon the earth whose face is good,
"Far better than his face will be his mood,
"And he whose countenance is seeming ill,
"Than his bad ways his face more hideous still.
"Just as in evil good you never see,
"So in the good bad moods can never be."
Thus to the prison they took him away,
And to the jailors gave him up that day.
That living heart within its walls they knew,
And the prisoners there gained life anew.
Excitement rose in that abode of pain ;
The shouts of captives rent the air again.
At the approach of that king of the fair
The captives all to beat their chains prepare.
The fetters on their feet were chains of will,
And their neck-collars yokes of blessing still.
In gladness there their sorrow found relief,
Lighter than blade of grass their hill of grief.
Wherever those of *Huri's* nature dwell,
To paradise they ever turn a Hell ;
And where the rosy-cheeked belovèd goes,
A furnace even is a bed of rose.
The agitated jail again had rest,
The jailor then Zuleikha thus addressed :
"Upon his heart inflict no greater pain ;
"Loose from his neck the yoke, from foot his chain.
"His silver body be with wool not warm ;
"That palm tree with a golden cloak (236) adorn.
"The dust of sadness wash thou from his head :
"Exalt it with a crown of pomp instead.
"Prepare a chamber freshly for his sake ;
"Apart from all the rest his dwelling make.
"For him do thou both wall and door perfume :
"Adorn the roof and window of his room.
"Lay of brocade the richest carpet there ;
"And an enticing couch of silk prepare."

Then Joseph to that chamber when they led,
Carpet of prayer upon the ground he spread.
And in that place, as he was wont each day,
His face turned to the *Mêhráb* there to pray.
Manly, of patience sitting in abode,
Thankful, and saved of women's wiles from load.
To none misfortune happens on the earth,
To hope of favour that does not give birth.
To captives of misfortune in affright
The hope of favour makes their burden light.

## THE REPENTANCE OF ZULEIKHA FOR HAVING SENT JOSEPH TO PRISON.

Beneath this azure vault of ancient base
Are strangely careless those of Adam's race.
Favours with gratitude they never view,
And want of thankfulness their habit, too.
Although their lives are in all favour passed,
Their blessings are not known until the last.
Many a lover, who departs in pride,
And thinks that with his love he's satisfied,
When separating fire fate lights one day,
He melts like candle and consumes away.
As to the captives in the jail awhile
It was a rosebud from that rose's smile,
And to Zulcikha from that cypress fair
Her house was a rosebud whilst it was there;
So when that cypress from her mead withdrew,
More dark than prison that fair garden grew.
A hundred times his absence hard to bear—
Her heart lived in that prison in despair.
No trial worse can a lover bemoan
That her place his love should no longer own!
What ease can there be in that garden, bereft
Of its rose that has gone, when but thorns are left?

In a roseless garden by piercing thorn
The nightingale's foot will ever be torn.
That rose in her garden no more to view,
Like a bud her garment she tore in two.
From grief up to the lip when life is pressed,
What matter if the lover rend his breast?
She to his bosom opens up a way,
For grief to quit and leave his heart more gay.
Her cheek of roses with her nails she'd tear;
As spikenard root out amber-tinted hair.
Her face and hair were thus to all a sign
How in her lover's absence she must pine.
She beat her bosom's stone upon her heart,
And struck the war-drum's signal to depart.
Although of beauty's army she was queen,
In the beat of that drum defeat was seen.
She poured dust with her hand upon her crown;
From her moist eyes the tears came running down.
Of dust and water she made such cement
As in her heart to close her parting's rent.
The rent from parting in her heart that lay
Could be closed hardly with a lump of clay.
Her pomegranate lip with her teeth she ground,—
With a string of pearls that cornelian bound,—
But in this she desired the blood to stay
From her too heated heart that flowed away.
All blue she dyed her cheek of rosy hue,
Like a lily struck when the flood breaks through.
The days of our gladness agree with red,—
Naught suits but blue when we mourn for the dead—
From a bleeding heart on her cheek she wrote,
And in grief her knee with her hand she smote.
"Who has done ever such a deed as I?
"Who has drunk such a cup of poison dry?
"What lover e'er struck in this world of woe
"On his foot with axe such a fearful blow?

"I tore my eye out with my hand, my own,
"And thus blind, myself in a well have thrown.
"On my own back a hill of pain I bound;—
"Beneath that hill has now my back been ground.
"My heart became blood in the days I passed,
"Ere that beauteous picture I gained at last.
"Through treacherous fortune are my fortunes low.
"My hand allowed his skirt for naught to go.
"With my soul I went from my heart astray,
"And know no remedy to find my way."
Thus with heart-burning lamentation sore,
Her nights of sorrow into days she wore.
From everything his perfume where she knew,
In hope of him a heart-felt sigh she drew.
At times she even seized upon his vest,
Since it had one day rubbed against his breast.
Her palate she turned into attar of rose,
And soothed her heart's scar for its many woes.
At times, her face upon his collar placed,
Sadly she kissed the fringe the collar graced—
"This is the yoke of that neck's glory. Nay;
"The cord to bind my spirit;" she would say.
At times within his sleeve her hand would be,
She through its fortune gave herself the victory.
Then as with honour there her eyes she placed,
Filled them with silver as his arm had graced,
Or on her eyelid caused his hem to rest,
Since sometime on his instep it had pressed.
As she was hopeless now to kiss his feet,
That skirt she would with adulation greet.
She saw his head's crown lying on the ground,
And scattered pearls and rubies all around.
This had at times to that head given shade,
At whose feet had a world its forehead laid.
The belt that brought his waist to mind she viewed,
And of his service thought with gratitude.

In memory of that deer that was her prey
Upon her neck as noose the girdle lay.
Of his golden cloak as she the folds undid
Of her two eyes would moisture fill the lid.
She washed his skirt with the tears of prayer,
And formed of ruby tears its fringes there.
When she saw lying of his shoes a pair, (237)
She tried to kiss them in her soul's despair.
To be a pair to him passed through her heart,
And patience left her when from him apart.
Its latchets she made for her heart a tie,
Which she dyed in red from her bleeding eye.
Thus every moment a new grief was born,
And from every thing a new cause to mourn.
As she knew the bliss of seeing, each day
In pain of absence she melted away.
She from repentance thus no profit gained,
And in nought but patience a gain remained.
In such a case how could there patience be
And when could her heart from his love be free?
Woe to the lover from his love apart,
The more to him who has once known her heart.
When there is loosed the tie of sympathy,
Absence is torment for eternity.
Where lies no bond of sympathy between,
The grief from parting is not half so keen.
Now in despair was she herself beside,
When good availed not she with evil tried.
She smote with her own head the wall and door;
A bloody dagger to her bosom bore;
She watched on the palace terrace at night,
Herself to cast down headlong from the height.
Then she made a rope of her night-hued hair,
To block up the road of the outer air.
From the world's cruelty release she sought :
From her cup-bearer poisoned bowl she brought.

Of all things scarce and rare she some obtained,
And thus wha suited her for death she gained.
Her nurse her hands and feet kissed more and more ;
And from her inmost heart would blessings pour.
" Be by thy love thy wishes all fulfilled ;
" With his red wine thy cup be ever filled.
" From parting so mayst thou obtain release,
" That thought of parting may for ever cease.
" Come to thyself. In madness live not long.
" Folly forsake, in wisdom be thou strong.
" With grief into my heart thou blood dost pour,
" As thou now doest, who e'er did before ?
" Listen to me. Of old I tried this thing ;
" Success to thee can only patience bring.
" There's fever through impatience in thy vein :
" From patience' cloud on this fire water rain.
" Should *Sarsar's* blast with force begin to blow,
" Like weakly grass do not thou fall too low.
" 'Twere best thy foot within thy skirt to hold,
" And with firm step be like a mountain bold.
" Patience is aye the source of victory,
" And fortune's base of power will give to thee.
" Through patience thy hope's fruit shalt thou obtain ;
" In patience wealth eternal shalt thou gain.
" From rain through patience pearls bear oysters still ;
" Patience the mine with precious stones will fill.
" Through patience to an ear will grow a grain
" Provision whence the traveller may obtain.
" And in the womb one drop in patience sown
" Will in nine months a shining moon have grown."
Zuleikha, much distressed in heart and soul,
Must in some wise her nurse's words console.
Though to the hem her collar rent in two,
Her patient foot within her skirt she drew.
Patience those lovers who aye keep in view,
Will base their faith on wise men's counsel too,

Yet when the counsellor shall speak no more,
Out of their memory his words they score.

### THE IMPATIENCE OF ZULEIKHA AT SEPARATION FROM JOSEPH, AND HER GOING WITH HER NURSE TO THE JAIL AT NIGHT.

When in the jail set Joseph's sun of grace,
Hid to Zuleikha was the heaven's face.
As from Zuleikha's sky he disappears,
For Joseph's love the heav'ns weep starry tears.
The twilight with these blood tears was red,
And the sphere's skirt became as if it bled.
From Joseph's grief Zuleikha so was found,
That her tears' twilight scattered blood around.
Weeping she uttered a heart-burning cry,
Just as by day she heaved the bitter sigh.
Whenc'er a lover's day is turned to night,
Far greater then becomes his passion's might.
Dimmed is in parting of his day the light,
And still more darksome is his dreary night.
Although his day become from sorrow black,
His night increases further black on black.
The night bears ever in its dark'ning womb,
That hour for lovers that increases gloom:
Out of its membrane as the child comes, then
It sucks no milk, but blood from hearts of men.
Of such a mother who would eat the fruit,
Whose offspring such a food as blood would suit?
In her impatience then Zuleikha knew,
A night in which destruction (238) came to view.
Her charmer absent and her lover far (239),
No light at home, at night nor moon nor star.
When one loved face gives not the house its light,
A thousand torches cannot make it bright.

From grief of heart no slumber closed her eye,
The heart shed blood-tears, and she raised the cry
" What Joseph's state this night I cannot tell,
" Nor who is pledged to do him service well ;
" Beneath his foot who may have spread the bed,
" Or on the pillow who arranged his head ;
" Who lights the candle by his pillow side,
" What hand to smooth it may so gently glide ;
" Who from his waist the girdle may have loosed,
" Or told the stories that his sleep induced—
" Does the air of the prison suit him yet ?
" Like a bird is he tamed down in the net ?
" Is his rose as fresh as it was of old ?
" Do his spikenard locks still retain their fold ?
" Has the air robbed his fair rose of its bloom ?
" Is the spikenard dead and without perfume ?
" Does his heart, like the rosebud, tightly close,
" Or smiles wreath his lip as the opening rose ?"
Thus in every form her anguish she told,
Until the first watch of the night was old.
Then to wait no strength in her heart remained :
Her stream of patience no water retained.
Sharp fire of longing fell on her.  With eyes
Full of blood to her nurse she cried : " Arise !
" Let us now at once to the prison go ;
" Let us secretly enter that house of woe.
" In the jail's corner concealed let me be,
" That thence that moon of the jail I may see.
" In a jail where abides that glorious cheek,
" No jail, but a bright new spring we shall seek.
" In gardens opes the lover's heart with glee,
" And in the jail this rosebud blooms for me."
Like a graceful cypress her way did she find,—
Limping, her nurse, like a shadow, behind.
Like night-wandering moon to the jail she came,
And secretly called the jailer by name.

The door she beckoned him open ajar;
Thence he showed her that shining moon afar.
She saw from afar his carpet of prayer:
A sun overwhelmed with light, he was there.
At times as a candle he stood erect—
In his face the pris'ners a light detect.
Sometimes his body, like the new moon bent,
A ray of brilliance to his pallet lent.
At times to ask for pardon bending low,
As the fresh rose-branch nightly breezes blow.
Now in humiliation on his breast,
He sat like violet with head depressed—
Far from herself, yet was she near to him,
She sat concealed within a corner dim.
Wailing in heart and soul with sorrow new,
Her eye her jess'mine changed to tulip's hue.
With pearly teeth she bit her ruby lip,
And from her verdant palm the dates would strip.
With eyes that shed blood till her tears were red,
Burst from her heart her secret, as she said:
"O thou of all fair ones the lamp and eye,
" Their hearts' wish to all who in sorrow lie,
" Thy love has lit a fierce fire in my soul:
" Thy love my being is consuming whole.
" Thy union on my fire no water throws:
" Thy water quenches not my heart that glows.
" Thy sword, with cruelty my breast that tears,
" Brings to thy heart no anguish and no cares.
" For me oppressed dost thou no pity know:
" Alas thy mercy! my repulsion woe!
" Each moment by new sorrow am I torn:
" Would that my mother me had never borne!
" And when my mother bore me, on my head
" Would that my nurse her shadow had not laid!
" Or of pure milk had given not enough,
" Or savage, mixed it with some pois'nous stuff!"

Of her own state these words Zuleikha said:
From self-possession was not Joseph led.
He never moved by the breadth of a hair,
Or else no sign of his feeling was there.
Like the morn rising, as the night passed by,
In tears dissolved became Zuleikha's sky.
The royal drum's sound echoed through the air:
Muazzins (241) called aloud to morning prayer.
The dog wound his tail round his own neck tight,
His breath released from his barking at night.
The cock arose from his sleep, and, head high,
Gave out from his throat his resounding cry.
Gath'ring her skirt, Zuleikha passed away—
In reverence kissed the threshold as it lay.
And whilst that moon was hidden in the jail,
Her coming to the jail would never fail.
For the food of her soul she would come and go,
And no other road would her spirit know.
No garden to any attraction lent,
As that jail tow'rds which her sore heart was bent.
Yes, he whose love is in prison confined,
Except in that jail no comfort can find.

### The Going up of Zuleikha on to the Terrace of the Palace, and Looking at the Jail and Weeping at Separation from Joseph.

Night came when lovers' secrets hidden dwell;
Night came the hopeless' sorrow to expel.
Much is it possible to do at night,
Impossible to do, when it is light.
Zuleikha's nightly sorrow passed away,
No grief, but nightly mourning passed away.
Evil and trouble with the day came on;
Sorrow that burns the heart away came on.

No mind towards the jail to find her way,
Nor patience not in jail to spend her day.
Each moment now some costly gift she made,
And in the hand placed of some trusty maid.
Her she would send to Joseph in the jail,
In her own stead to see him, and not fail.
When from the jail that trusted one came back,
To her in caresses she would not lack.
At times upon her foot her head would lie,
Or she would kiss a hundred times her eye.
"This foot has walked in the same place as he,
"And with this eye his fair cheek didst thou see.
"Can I not press a kiss upon his eye,
"Oft on his foot's sole may my cheek not lie,
"That eye yet let me for one moment kiss,
"That sees at times that beauteous face of his.
"Let me for once my face that foot lay on,
"That where he sojourns to the place has gone."
Then would she question her about his state,
His handsome features, his propitious fate.
"From sorrow has his cheek no furrow seen?
"In his affairs has no knot fastened been?
"In that air does his rose not fade away?
"Or with that form the soil no mischief play?
"Of my dainties sent does he eat or drink?
"Of her who loves him does he ever think?"
With many questions her would she thus ply,
Then rise from her place with blood-streaming eye.
There stood a window on the terrace high,
From which the prison terrace caught the eye.
There would she take her solitary seat,
The window closed of people to the feet.
Her eye-lash threading the pearl in her eye,
Aye at the jail would she look and would cry:
"Ah! who am I his rosy face to see?
"To see his terrace hence enough for me!

## *Yusuf and Zuleikha.*

" To see his face unworthy though I be,
" To see his door or wall is joy for me.
" My moon wherever he his place may take
" Will mead of Paradise his prison make.
" From Fortune capital that roof has won,
" For in its shade lies of the world the sun.
" My back does that wall ruin with despair,
" That leant against its back my moon is there.
  Fortune with head erect may pass that gate,
  'Neath which my cypress bows his head of late.
  And oh! how prosperous must that threshold be,
" Kissing the feet of charmers such as he!
" Oh! happy 'twould be if his sun's sword-ray
" Of my form made atoms to float away!
" Down from his window I headlong would fall,
" Before his bright sun so glorious all!
" A thousand envies bear I 'gainst that ground,
" Where in such grace he ever moves around.
" From his skirt's dust upon it perfume lies;
" From amber-shedding locks there amber flies."
In short, till night there nothing else occurred,
Her occupation was this only word.
In such talk to her life her spirit rose;
Her day passed on to night in these her woes.
And she bethought herself, when next night came,
As on the previous night to do the same.
Such was her night, and such as well her day,
So long as in the jail her heart's light lay.
At night to the jail she planned to repair:
By day she would gaze from her window there.
And at no time could aught else there befall,
But looking on himself or on his wall.
Thus Joseph so she in her heart enshrined,
That life or world she never bore in mind.
In her deep thought of him herself she lost;
Out of mind's tablet good and bad she crossed.

In spite of handmaid's oft repeated call,
She to her right sense never came at all,
But told those handmaids in the self-same strain
"I never to myself shall come again."
She said: "In words attention do not seek:
"First shake me well, and then begin to speak.
"By shaking ye bring me to reason near;
"To listen then may I open my ear.
"My heart is aye with my prisoner there,
"And from him it comes that I thus despair,
"And in whosever heart that moon may dwell,
"How of another tale can she tell?"
One day her state of health so changed indeed,
That of the lancet's wound there came a need.
And to no one's eye on the ground there came,
But of Joseph, Joseph, in blood the name.
The light-handed expert her vein that smote
With lancet pen but this letter wrote.
So full of her friend were her skin and vein,
That friend's name from her skin they could but gain.
Oh! happy he who from himself obtains
Release, and knowledge of himself regains!
In his heart his charmer he has so enshrined
That no one else an entrance there may find.
Each vein of his life she so enters there,
That unfilled of her one may see no hair.
Neither scent is left of himself nor hue:
Peace or war with none ever comes to view.
Nor crown nor throne does he ever require:
From his street departs all evil desire.
Of aught but love he ne'er conceives a thought,
And to account himself is never brought.
If he speaks a word, with his love he speaks:
All hope he may have from his love he seeks.
From what is raw to ripe he turns his face:
This being in his thought ne'er finds a place,

*Jámi*, from self, too, do thou pass away:
To the eternal mansion find thy way.
I know the way there thou dost know indeed:
The wealth of being is not worth thy heed.
Out of this weary life thy foot remove:
The wealthy home of non-existence prove.
Once wast thou not, and didst no loss sustain:
Be not to-day, for all that thou canst gain.
Seek not in self well-being any more;
From such desire no profit is in store.


SETTING FORTH THE BENEFITS CONFERRED BY JOSEPH ON THE PEOPLE IN THE JAIL, AND HIS INTERPRETATION OF THE DREAM OF THE SERVANTS OF THE KING OF EGYPT, AND THEIR RECOMMENDATION TO RECALL HIM TO THE KING'S MEMORY.

He who is born upon a happy day,
This beaming light sweeps darkness all away.
He seeks the thorn-brake: 'tis a bed of rose:
The rose for him to Tartar musk-bag grows.
Like cloud if he a thirsty field pass by,
A Paradise beneath his feet will lie.
Like breeze if he across a garden flit,
A bright lamp on each flower's cheek is lit.
If a prison he enters happily,
The prisoners there of their grief are free.
The prison thus to each imprisoned wight
Became a smiling mead at Joseph's sight.
When Joseph arrived there, great was their glee;
From the bond of pain and grief they were free;
The yoke on their necks a collar of gain,—
A ring of joy on their foot was the chain.

If sick became any prisoner there,
Or became a captive to toil and care,
He girt his loins to sick men to give heed,
Till from all care and sickness they were freed.
And if a captive's heart were in despair,
Some means to set him right would he prepare.
With open face he sought his love to gain,
And from his strait conveyed him to the plain.
If a poor man's joy turned to bitterness,
And waned his poverty's moon to grow less,
From the wealthy he seized a golden key,—
With joy broke the lock of his misery.
And if some good man dreamed a dream of woe,
His goods in thought's whirlpool swam to and fro,—
To him the dream's meaning would he declare,—
And his goods reach land from the vortex of care.
Two trusty men of the king of that land
Had been driven away from near his hand.
On equal terms these in the prison spoke,
And in that mourning house bore equal yoke.
Each of these two men dreamed a dream one night;
The souls of both were troubled in affright.
His dream gave one the good news of release,
The other the sad tidings of decease.
To neither of them was the meaning known,
And both a heavy load of care must own.
Each of his dream to Joseph told the word,
And of his own dream each the answer heard.
One then they punished on the gallows-tree;
One in the king's court was again set free.
Towards the king this young man turned his face,
Of honour and of dignity the place;
Towards the king upon his throne he went,
And by his mouth a message Joseph sent.
" When access to the king thou shalt obtain,
" A chance of speaking to him must thou gain.

" In the assembly bring me to his mind,
" And thou an ample recompense shalt find.
" ' A stranger in the prison lies,' declare,
" Of grace from thee, just king, denied all share.
" Keep not the guiltless thus in misery :
" For this from justice' road to stray would be."
By fortune favoured, when the man drank up
The wine of nearness from the royal cup,
So passed that message from his mind away,
And came not back again for many a day.
The plant of his promise brought forth despair,
And kept tightly bound the prisoner there.
He of all others whom God may think fit,
Beloved on the seat of honour shall sit.
The road of causes for him will He close,
Nor on security of man repose.
His face will he turn to His own alone ;
Aside for others must his love be thrown.
In others' hands He will not leave him prey :
To others He desires not he should pray—
Him in His snare alone that He may see,
His hand on others' skirts laid must not be.

### THE SENDING FOR JOSEPH BY THE KING OF EGYPT FOR THE INTERPRETATION OF HIS OWN DREAM.

Many the lock for which there is no key
To open which a road there may not be,
When in spite of endeavour, care, and thought,
The wise man's devices may come to nought.
Though an artist's hand should not intervene,
Though no creator appear on the scene,
From mystery's world a sudden door will ope,
Reveal the deposit and grant our hope.
When Joseph thus abandoned all his plan,
He of his stratagem cut through the span ;

Except in God no refuge there remained
By which in evil he might be sustained.
By his own wisdom when he could not stand,
God, in His mercy, took him by the hand.
To Egypt's ruler wise and king one night,
In dreams seven cattle there appeared in sight;
These all were very good and full in hide,
And with each other in their beauty vied.
Seven other cattle were behind them seen,
Equal in size, but all dried up and lean.
Upon the seven first these seven lean ones set,
And as grass in the field completely ate.
Seven green, fat corn-ears in the self-same wise,
Food for the heart, provision for the eyes,
Arose. Seven other dry ears, by-and-bye,
Behind them coming, made them also dry.
Next morning, when the king from dreams arose,
He asked the wise their meaning to disclose.
All said: "This dream's impossible to tell;
"Fancy and doubt there may be here as well.
"Its meaning wisdom never can explain:
"From all attempts 'twere better to refrain."
Then that young stripling who of Joseph knew,
From face of his affair the veil withdrew.
"In jail of royal beauty one there lies
"In solving subtleties accounted wise;
"Quick to interpret dreams and subtle, he
"A diver for this sea of pearls will be.
"This secret will I at thy word explain,
"And thy dream's meaning bring to thee again."
He said: "From me leave why dost thou require?
"More than clear eye the blind can not desire.
"Blind from that moment is my wisdom's eye,
"Since from that secret's knowledge far I lie."
Then straightway went the young man to the jail,
Of the king's dream to Joseph told the tale.

He said : " In ears and kine ye years may see,
" Descriptive each of its own quality.
" When the kine are fat and the ears are green,
" In this way a prosperous year may be seen.
" When ears are dry, and cattle lean appear,
" A sorry tale they tell thee of the year.
" In those seven years that ye may see at first,
" For rain the field and grain will never thirst ;
" Men full of Grace these seven years will see ;
" But afterwards seven other years will be ;
" Consumed the former bounties that are giv'n,
" To wretchedness will people's lives be driven.
" No cloud of bounty o'er the sky shall pass ;
" The ground shall not produce a blade of grass.
" The pleasures of the wealthy all will cease,
" The poor in misery will all decease.
" On Time's board will there be so little bread,
" ' Bread !' will men cry, and give their lives instead."
The young man heard the word and turned him back ;
Nor did the king's boon comrade justice lack.
As Joseph's tale and the dream's sense were told,
Did as a rosebud the king's heart unfold.
He said : " Arise, and Joseph hither bring,
" That I may trust him in this subtle thing.
" When one the charmer's voice itself may hear,
" Through other's mouth why bring it to the ear ?
" As sugar sweet thou bring'st this friendly word
" Far sweeter were it from himself when heard."
Back to the jail once more his way he made,
And to that precious one the news conveyed.
" Thou of the garden cypress pure, proceed,
" And plant thy footsteps in the royal mead ;
" Walk on in beauty with thy charming face,
" And with thy roses that fair garden grace."
He said : " To such a king why should I go,
" Who wretched me, though guiltless, long ago

"Has to the jail in years gone by conveyed,
"And hopeless of his mercy's tokens made.
"If he desire my foot without should stand,
"Out of this sorrow-house let him command
"That those who on my face when first they gazed,
"And cut their hands before me, all amazed,
"As Pleiads may altogether appear,
"And the veil lift up my affair to clear;
"What was my fault, and what they saw in me
"That to thy prison brought my goods should be.
"Then for the king will the secret be sure,
"That from this sin my skirt is clean and pure.
"Myself to wickedness I never brought,
"Nor of such sin has ever been my thought.
"Evil of mine in that house none might see,
"But truth and purity was found in me.
"Better as burglar treasure bear away,
"Than of the house the honour to betray."
When the young man told these words to the king,
He bade them those women of Egypt bring.
Towards him together they all took their flight,
As the moths aye flutter towards the light.
When that assembly all together came,
Like a candle he loosed his tongue of flame:
"What in that holy light had come to view
"That ye on him the sword of scandal drew?
"Ye were through his face in a bright spring mead:
"Why did ye him towards the prison lead?
"An idol who too heavy feels a rose,
"Who wise on such a neck would chains impose?
"The rose of night winds that bears not the pain,
"Why binds its foot with more than water's chain?"
"O thou of happy fate!" the women said,
"Prosper still more thy throne and crownèd head!
"In Joseph saw we only purity,
"But perfect honour and pure dignity.

"No pearl in oyster-shell can purer be
"Than he from accusation's stain is free."
Zuleikha also then was sitting near,
Her soul from fraud, and tongue from falsehood clear.
Behind a veil her treachery would she hide,
And the promptings of love were laid aside.
Truth's flag was by her spirit held aloft :
And like truth's morn her breath was pure and soft.
Fully her own transgression she confessed :
"The truth is clear!" a voice came from her breast
"In Joseph is no kind of fault," she said :
"'Tis I who in his love astray am led.
"His union with me first did I require,
"He drove me off, ungranted my desire.
"Through my oppression he in prison fell :
"And to his grief my sorrows led as well.
"And when my grief was more than I could bear,
"I that contagion called on him to share.
"And as from me that cruelty he knew,
"To him from me is compensation due.
"Whatever favours to bestow the good king please,
"Joseph deserves a hundred such as these."
These well-weighed words the monarch heard disclose :
He smiled as rosebud, blossomed as the rose.
He bade them Joseph, from the prison freed,
Into that garden of enjoyment lead—
Of pleasure's garden him, a smiling rose,
Best in a garden, not a jail, enclose.
In the soul's realm a prosperous king is known :
No seat becomes him better than a throne.

## The Coming of Joseph out of the Prison, and the Honouring of him by the King, and the Death of the Vazir.

The custom in this ancient cell is this ;
Without pains bitter there is no sweet bliss.
A child for nine months eating blood must lie,
But with its moon-like face comes by-and-bye.
In rock the ruby hardship much goes through
Before the bright sun gives it proper hue.
When Joseph's night turned from its weary way,
A remedy appeared with rising day.
When as a mountain heavy was his woe,
Rose from behind the hill the sun in glow.
To pay him all respect and honour due,
The courtiers soon their monarch's message knew.
From the king's hall that aped the sun in pride,
Beyond the plain two *farsangs* (244) on each side,
On to the jail two rows there stood arrayed,
And his own retinue each there displayed.
There saucy slaves with golden girdles wait,
In robes of golden cloth, of graceful gait.
Of sun-like forms the singers thither throng,
With strains of Hebrew and of Syrian song.
There of rough-riders a whole army ride,
On Arab steeds, exulting in their pride,
With lords of Egypt reck'ning that defied,
Who scattered offerings on ev'ry side.
The poor around, in hope of reaping them,
One stretched his robe, the next his garment's hem.
As Joseph came towards the royal seat,
With robe of honour for a monarch meet,
Upon a charger, which, from foot to crown,
With gold and jewels thou wouldst say would drown

Of musk and amber trays stood everywhere ;
And purses full of pearls and jewels rare
Men scattered freely on the horses' road.
Beggars became free of their beggar's load.
When came the royal palace into sight,
Did Joseph from his swift-paced steed alight.
Beneath his feet were silk and satin spread ;
To cast beneath his feet they raised the head.
He walked over satin and fine brocade,
As the moon in the sky, over satin laid.
Of his approaching when the monarch knew,
To meet him fortune-like he forward flew.
Tight to his own bosom him he drew,
As rose-cheeked cypress, box of rosy hue.
On his own throne he placed him by his side,
And to sweet questionings himself applied.
First of his dream he asked him the intent ;
His sweet lip Joseph to explain then bent.
Of ev'rything he asked him after this,
Nor did he circumstance or action miss.
With pleasant and sweet answers he replied,
And the king's wonder grew and multiplied.
At last he said : " This dream that I have seen,
" And which by thee interpreted has been,
" For this what remedy can I provide,
" The sorrow of the world to set aside ?"
He answered : " Now of plenty in the day,
" When cloud and dew to fall do not delay,
" Thou shouldst by crier in each realm enjoin
" To tillage people should themselves confine :
" With their own nails the hardest rock should tear,
" With sweat of face to sow the seed prepare.
" And when the ear the swelling grain shall fill,
" Lay it aside for future eating still :
" From the corn's body growing thus the spike
" Upon the face of foes a spear to strike.

"Those ears when in the house they thus shall store,
"Or famine or want shall be seen no more.
"Let each one take for his mournful desire,
"All from those treasures that he may require.
"In all things caution let them exercise,
"And prove in management that they are wise;
"That he to do the work who has the skill,
"That work may yet be able to fulfil.
"In aught that in the world thou mayest try,
"More learned pledge thou wilt not find than I.
"The matter's management confide to me,
"No one more suited to it canst thou see."
And when the king saw his ability,
In Egypt's realm he raised his dignity.
He placed the army under his command,
To his authority gave up the land;
He placed him in his seat on golden throne,
With many honours Egypt's Vazír known.
When with his foot the golden throne he graced,
Beneath his feet the whole world's head was placed.
When from the hall upon the plain he went,
The voice of heralds the high heaven rent.
On ev'ry side when he to ride was wont,
A thousand grooms would move along in front.
When through a province he his course would hold,
A countless army there one might behold.
When God had Joseph thus exalted high,
And given with his rank nobility,
Fortune from Egypt's Vazír turned away,
Reversed of dignity his standard lay.
He took this injury so much to heart
That he became the target to Death's dart.
Zulcikha turned her tow'rds the wall of woe;
Parted from Joseph, was her back a bow,
Backed no more by the Vazír's dignity,
Nor was her heart from grief for Joseph free.

To be aye slow to love, and quick to hate,
In this abode of woe 's the work of Fate.
One like the sun it raises to the sky,
One like a shadow on the ground may lie.
Happy that wise man who in ev'ry thing
To his own work no confidence may bring.
Not through good fortune is his head raised high,
Nor his soul melts in ruin's misery.


SETTING FORTH THE CONDITION OF ZULEIKHA THROUGH THE DEATH OF THE VAZIR OF EGYPT, AND HER BEING OVERPOWERED BY THE LOVE OF JOSEPH.

The heart that by its charmer may be grieved,
Is both of gladness and of woe relieved.
Nor to his skirt another's love is bound,
Nor any gladness hovers him around.
Thus had the world become a sea of woes,
And waves of sorrow like the mountains rose.
Their moisture on his skirt were never known,
Nor by their grief would he be overthrown.
Of joy a banquet if Fate should prepare,
And should eternal pleasure show him there,
He looks not on that feast of loveliness,
Nor wishes his sorrow one hair the less.
Zuleikha, that bird of a plaintive tone,
To her the world's birdcage had narrow grown.
In those days when Fortune to her was good,
And her private house as a garden stood,
The Vazír for her head a shadow made ;
And to her loveliness his plant gave shade.
All things collected for her pleasure there,
Her cheek was lit up as a candle fair.

Yet grief for Joseph never left her heart,
Nor would from off her tongue his tale depart.
Of the Vazír when she was then bereft,
And of the goods of wealth was nothing left,
The thought of Joseph's face was still her friend,
And to her wounded heart would comfort lend.
In deserts in his memory would she roam,
And now in sorrow's corner make her home.
In separation she could neither eat nor sleep,
And from her eyes the blood-red tears would weep.
" Happy when I the fruit of Fortune ate,
" And in one house was with my lover set ;
" Or, when through trusty eyes still him I saw,
" A hundred times his form might fancy draw ;
" When of that wealth my fortune me deprived,
" In jail to shut him wretched I contrived.
" In the dark night I made my way there soon,
" And used to look upon that shining moon.
" The rust I rubbed off from my heart by day,
" And gazed at door and wall wherein he lay.
" To-day from these far distant I remain,
" Apart in body, with my soul in pain.
" I only hold his image in my heart,
" Nor from that image am I e'er apart.
" That image gone, to me what would life be?
" That image in my heart is life to me."
This tale she told, and mingled it with sighs ;
And fire struck sun and moon both in the skies ;
Like Aleph's Madd (245), the smoke was of her sigh,
Upon her head a black tent spread on high.
From evils of the sun at any place
Of refuge save that tent there was no trace.
Above her head it stood not as a tent,
But to guard heaven from her arrows meant.
Against those darts had heaven no defence,
That vault they would have passed through so immense.

She from her eye-lash blood-red tears (246) would shed—
Not tears, but drops of blood (246) I should have said.
When from burnt heart the fever burning grew,
Upon her lip her eyelash water threw.
She washed not from her cheek the tears she shed,
And from her tears her cheek was tinged with red.
From bloody tears her cheek grew crimson hued,
And in her heart the bond of love renewed,—
For that affair as ready cash was brought,
For marriage dowry heart's blood only sought.
With nail she sometimes tore her cheek of rose,
And her eye blood's fountain would disclose.
Each was an inkstand of vermilion bright,
For grief's divorce with which a deed to write.
At times her breast, at times her heart, she tore ;
Nought but love's image on her soul she wore.
She struck upon her knee of wild-rose hue,
And brought the water-lily's colour blue.
"Worthy," she said, "of my friend's love I prove ;
"If he's the sun, yet I as lotus move.
"And since the sun is friendly to the West,
"To act as lotus will for me be best."
Her cone-like heart she struck once and again,
And bit her fingers as 'twere sugar cane.
Her hand, of every gaze that was so shy,
From wounded fingers had a crimson dye.
A pen she of her bleeding fingers made :
Her camphor-palm like book she open laid,
And in that book a word of grief she wrote ;
Of any other thing she made no note.
Yet in that book the story that she told,
Unwritten might her lover ne'er behold.
For many wretched years such was her state
At separation, aye disconsolate.
Ageing her troubled youth from Heaven knew,
Her pitch-like hair assumed a milk-white hue.

O

The morning came: its crew night gathered up,
And poured in camphor to its musky cup.
From Fate's fell arrow had the raven fled,
And in its nest the owl had made its bed.
(No ancient man could this e'er bring to mind,
That in a raven's house an owl you'd find.)
Tears from her eye washed out the dark'ning hue,
In that narcissus bud the jess'mine grew.
When glad beneath this vault of crooked track,
Her eye that saw the world was clothed in black;
When it, then, turned to mourning through despair,
Why turned the blackness into whiteness there?
From India came the pattern of the thing,
That Hindoos love the hue of falcon's wing (247).
On her fresh rosy face a trembling fell,
On her wild rose were wrinkles seen as well.
Upon her brow that fold which stood in grace
Fell through old ages's sickness on her face.
In this old hermitage none ever knew
The water rippling when no breezes blew.
Now with no wind, or blew the breezes keen,
Rippling like water both her cheeks were seen.
Her cypress crooked must love's burden own;
Ring-like towards her foot her head had grown.
From head to foot her destiny was marred,
And like a ring, of union's feast debarred.
Here where is wet with blood of men the clay,
And vision's capital has passed away,
Her head fell forwards as her back was bent,
As if to find her capital intent.
Thus in that desert months and years passed down,
No anklets wore her feet, her head no crown.
No satin robes upon her back she wore,
And in her ears no drops of pearl she bore;
Upon her neck no jewelled collar borne,
Upon her cheek no gold-wrought veil was worn.

Beneath her side an earthen cushion lay;
Her tender cheek its pillow made on clay.
With Joseph's love yet were her couch on clay
Better than silk bed on which *Huris* lay.
The brick beneath her face, at thought of him,
A pillow gemmed from Paradise would seem.
To this sad pain, but part of which I've sung,
And to describe a hundred pearls have strung,
No name but Joseph's on her tongue there passed,
And none brought comfort to her soul at last.
Silver and gold stores whilst she yet possessed,
A thousand caskets full of gems the best,
Her Joseph's tale would any then repeat,
She cast her gold and silver at his feet;
Like a casket of gems, his mouth for him
She filled all full of pearls up to the brim:
Thus spending all in her liberal way,
Her gold and silver had all passed away.
With a woollen garment was she content,
The belt a fibre from the palm tree rent.
Those who spoke of Joseph, no more would tell,
But down on the knee of silence they fell.
Passed the time when from the wise she could hear
Of Joseph, and draw soul's food through her ear,
It came to this, that losing all her strength,
A reed house on his road she built at length;
That when his army passed by in its course,
Her soul might from their voice derive fresh force.
Alas! that wretched one no more might stand,
The reins of power fallen from her hand,
From her love's union's board debarred so long,
Unpleasing, out of tune her pleasure's song.
Union with him she loved no power lent;
No strength'ning message from his country sent.
At times to winds would she his secret speak,
And from the birds at times his traces seek.

When on the road she saw that trav'lers passed,
The dust of exile on their faces cast ;
She kissed their feet as those of men of name,
And washed those feet that from his province came.
When on that road his course her Sultan took,
On him she had no pow'r to cast a look.
By his road's dust her heart was ever eased,
With his army's voices she sat well pleased.


### The Coming of Zuleikha on to Joseph's Road, and her Building a House of Reeds, that she might enjoy the Sound of him and his Army passing.

Zuleikha, lonely, of her life despaired ;
A reed house she on Joseph's road prepared,
And this with plaited reeds was fenced around,
That gave forth music with a plaintive sound.
Of separation when she made lament
Was from each reed a plaintive murmur sent.
When separation's fire began to blaze,
Flame in each separate reed her sighs would raise.
Wounded and fallen in that brake she lay,
While arrows pierced her like a hunted prey ;
But as she suffered yet from love's sweet pain,
Each arrow was to her as sugar-cane.
In Joseph's stable was a steed *Div*-bred,
That threw down spheres and raised the heaven's head.
This courser, piebald as the sphere of light,
To-day a thousand segments joined from night.
One could in him both light and darkness see ;
As old Time's nights and days combined was he.
In heav'nly Virgo from his tail a cup,
The moon's bowl by his hoof was wrinkled up.

Upon each hoof a golden crescent bound,
And as its nails the stars were fastened round.
As his hoof's wound upon the hard rock rang,
From each of his new moons a planet sprang,
And if there in his course flew off a shoe,
Appeared a moon in heaven that was new.
In the hunting field he aye outstripped the prey
And flew like arrow from its side away.
If there had been a plain from East to West,
Like lightning he'd have crossed without a rest.
The dust around if he raised in his race,
When would the wind of *Sarsar* reach his face?
On the road though full of his drops of sweat,
On him had no one seen a drop as yet.
His temper such that he would gently go,
Like flood from drops that may begin to flow.
With his own pluck he like a treasure flew,
Nor of a whip's lash the misfortune knew.
Tame had he stayed in stable and content,
The spheres their neck had in his service bent.
If he had so desired, he might have won
In the moon's kettle water from the sun;—
For him had they prepared by night and day
Barley from Virgo, grass from the Milky Way (248).
Of silken hair they had prepared a sieve,
Barley by night for moons and years to give.
He chose the *Sidrah* birds that sing at morn
To come and pick stones for his barley corn.
The "Twins" hung from his saddle down a pair,
His stirrups on each side a crescent fair.
His foot when in the stirrup Joseph placed,
As in the "Twins" the moon, his seat he graced.
When that *Canopus* (249) 'neath his thigh he drew,
Tow'rds ev'ry side the courser keener grew.
In ev'ry place whoever heard him neigh
Needed no drum as summons for the way.

Around that monarch all assembled soon,
Like a group of planets around the moon.
Zuleikha, also, when she heard the neigh,
Ran from her hut of reeds upon his way.
In grief she sat of the road by the side,
Lamenting so wildly, where he would ride.
And when without Joseph appeared the crowd,
The boys would call to her in jesting aloud:
"Lo! on the road is Joseph coming on,
"Joseph the envy of the moon and sun."
Zuleikha said: "Of this Joseph of mine,
"Ye delicate ones, I perceive no sign.
"To my heart with these jests give no more pain,
"For no scent of Joseph comes to my brain.
"On every stage where that charmer goes
"The land full of musk of Tartary grows.
"In any company where he may be
"The breeze of his presence must come to me."
And with the crowd when Joseph drew more nigh,
And his might moved their hearts, they then would cry,
And say to her: "Oh! Joseph is not here;
"No traces in this crowd of him appear."
"Strive not to cozen me with this," she cried;
"And of my friend the coming do not hide.
"That idol to whom souls their kingdom yield,
"How may his coming be from me concealed?
"This breeze to my soul's garden vigour gives,
"Not that alone, but every soul that lives.
"When on the road revived the spirit goes,
"The news of that reviving soul it knows."
When that distracted, lonely one could hear
The heralds shouting out the road to clear,
"Distant an age!" her cry would rend the air;
"A hundred woes I in this absence bear.
"To bear more absence I have not the pow'r;
"Except by force I will not wait an hour.

" How long must I be absent from my love?
" Now from myself 'twere better I should move."
Thus saying, often would she senseless fall,
Forgetful even of herself and all.
Oblivion's cup would not then leave her hand,
In her reed hut unconscious she would stand.
Among those reeds when breathed her sadden'd soul,
Cries and complaints arose beyond control.
After this manner passed her ev'ry day,
And of employment gave no other way.


THE TAKING HOLD OF JOSEPH BY ZULEIKHA AND FINDING FAVOUR WITH HIM, AND HER BEING CONVERTED.

Hopeless lovers are ne'er content: the pow'r
Of longing increases from hour to hour.
Never long (250) at rest in the same desire,
And ever looking for something that's high'r.
Smelling the rose, he would have it in view,
And when he has seen he would pluck it, too.
Zuleikha, who sat by the road at first,
For the luck to see him was now athirst.
One night before that idol she lay,
To worship which had been ever her way.
" O thou tow'rds whose beauty I pray," she said:
" And in whose worship I lay down my head;
" Long with my soul to worship thee I stand.
" The jewel of my sight has left my hand.
" Look with thy own eye on my sore disgrace;
" Light to my eye again give in thy grace.
" Apart from Joseph how long must I be?
" Give me my eye that I his face may see.
" I have at any time, in any place,
" But one desire, and that to see his face.

"As thou art able, grant me my behest;
"Give me my wish: do what to thee seems best.
"Such hardship on my soul impose not still:
"My life with such ill fortune do not fill.
"What life is this that not to be is best?
"To tread annihilation's road is best."
Dust on her head she strewed, as thus she said,
And moistened the dust with the tears she shed.
Mounted his Eastern throne the sun one day,
And rose the sound of Joseph's piebald's neigh.
Zuleikha, as a beggar clad, appeared,
And on a narrow place stood as he neared,
After the mode of beggars, with her cry
In lamentation raised her voice on high.
On every side to the heavens there rise
"Stand out of the road," the heralds' cries.
There falls on the ear from many a place
The neighing of horses the road that pace.
In that confusion no one saw her state.
(How she then was may no one contemplate!)
Her hopeless heart in many fragments torn,
From street of pleasure wandering forlorn,
She walked, and from her pained heart uttered cries,
And scattered round the hot fire of her sighs:
Back to her house of trouble when she came,
For each reed-handful she brought many a flame.
Out of its place then that stone idol brought,
She with tongue loosened consolation sought.
"O stone, thou of my dignity the cup,
"With stone my ev'ry road that blockest up,
"Thou to my heart dost narrow fortune's road;
"'Twere best if on that heart I stones should load.
"In worship when I fall before thy face,
"Upon a painful road myself I place.
"Each wish with weeping I from thee demand,
"And of the hope of both worlds wash my hand.

" Far from thy shame, O stone, then would I fly:
" Broken with stones thy power, thou shalt lie."
With the hard stone she wounded, as she spoke,
And like the friend of God the idol broke.
She broke the idol in her active mood,
And in good order thence her matters stood.
And when in breaking she had done her part,
With tears and blood she purified her heart.
Upon the ground she humbly rubbed her face,
And wept and wailed before the throne of Grace.
" O, thou with love who dost the wretched view,
" Idols, their worshippers and makers, too,
" Did not the image Thy own face reflect,
" Who to an idol would e'er show respect?
" With love dost Thou the idol-maker move,
" And thus his idol carving dost approve.
" Before an idol he who falls in prayer
" Will say that in the idol God is there.
" O God, to idols when I turn my face,
" 'Tis on myself, O God, I bring disgrace.
" That wrong with Thy own favour pardon Thou:
" The sin that I have done oh! pardon now.
" On sin's road grievously I went astray,
" And Thou my gem of sight didst take away.
" Off me hast Thou the dust of error swept;
" Oh! now restore me that which Thou hast kept.
" Be my heart healed of the scar of regret,
" I may pluck flow'rs from Joseph's garden yet."
And when that king of Egypt turned and went,
Once more upon his road she made lament.
" All pure is He a slave Who makes a king,
" And round his head shame's shadow, too, can bring;
" Who on the slave's head, poor and broken down,
" Of royal pomp and honour sets the crown."
And when this found a place in Joseph's ear,
Joseph became beside himself with fear—

He told his chamberlain : " In these her prayers
" She from my soul all strength and power bears.
" Of audience bring her to my private hall,
" My friends alone where I together call,
" That I may ask a little of her woes,
" Ask of her fortune 'midst her ruin's throes.
" Since of that rosary the sound I heard,
" My heart within me wondrously is stirred.
" If to her skirt there cling not grievous pain,
" Why should her saying such influence gain ? "
Two hundred souls I offer to that king,
Men's sighs or looks who can to judgment bring—
To know pure justice-seekers does not fail,
Of erring ones discerns the lying tale—
Who, as the prelude to the dawn is true,
Gives to the liar the reward that's due.
Who, of the modern days unlike the king,
In hope of gold will not excuses bring ;
No tyrant looking for a piece of gold,
Who hundreds' hands beneath a stone would hold,
With gold who hundreds would to honour bring,
To whom oppression is a futile thing.

### The Coming of Zuleikha to the House of Joseph, and regaining her Sight, Beauty, and Youth through his Prayer.

What for a lover can there be more sweet
Than that his love with due return should meet ?
Entrance when to her secret's place he gains,
When does her bosom from his load feel pains ?
Tells in her ear of former days the tale,
And of her secret sits and lifts the veil.
Of his army's bustle beyond the call,
Joseph sat down in his audience hall.

The chamberlain entered: "O thou alone
"In the world's tale who art for goodness known,
"There now stands at the door that aged dame,
"To seize thy reins upon the road that came,
"Thou didst command me: 'Be her escort here
"'And at the palace gate with her appear.'"
"Fulfil her wishes," Joseph then replied;
"Be she heart-sore, a remedy provide."
He said: "No woman of short sight is she,
"That all her wishes she should tell to me."
"Permit her here to enter," he replied:
"And to raise the veil that her state may hide.
Like Venus in dance, as she leave obtained,
Thus to his private room she entrance gained.
Like a smiling rosebud or blooming rose
Her smiling mouth with blessings overflows.
At her smiles as Joseph astonished gazed,
He asked her name and condition, amazed.
She said: "I am she who once saw thy face,
"And chose thee out of all the human race,
"Gems, treasures to thee devoted my whole,
"And gave for thy love my heart and my soul.
"In grief for thee I squandered youth as well,
"And into old age, as thou seest, fell.
"In thy arms that beauty, the State, has bloomed,
"And I am here to forgetfulness doomed."
Thus who she was her words to Joseph bore,
And in compassion he lamented sore.
He said: "Zuleikha! Ah! what is thy state?
"Ah! what has come to thee through cruel Fate?"
Oblivion's wine now so inflames her heart,
Her very senses at his voice depart.
When to her senses she returned again,
This was of Joseph's questioning the strain:
"Where are thy beauty and thy youth?" he said.
"Far from thy union," answered she, "it fled."

"Why bent thy delicate cypress?" he asked—
"By parting's load," she said, "'twas overtasked."
"Why is thy eye of brightness void?" he cried.
"'Twas drowned in blood without thee," she replied.
He asked: "Where is thy silver, where thy gold,
"The chaplet for thy head and crown of old?"
"Whoe'er of thy beauty told me," she said,
"Poured pearls of thy praises upon my head;
"Head and gold offered at his feet I poured,
"The jewels I gave were his due reward.
"My crown of glory I placed on his head,
"And his gate's dust wore as my crown instead.
"No gold or silver is left in my hand:
"My heart is love's treasure, and here I stand."
He said: "To-day what dost thou ask for? say,
"Who for thy needs will be surety to-day?"
"At my needs," she said, "is troubled thy soul,
"But thou for those needs art the surety sole.
"With an oath if thou my surety wilt be,
"I will loosen my tongue and speak to thee.
"But if not, my lip on the tale shall close,
"And I must suffer yet more grief and woes."
Generosity's mine he then swore by,
That pillar architect of prophecy (251).
For whom bloomed tulips and sweet herbs from flame,
To whom from God the robe of friendship came;
"Whatever wish thou show to me to-day,
"I will fulfil with speed, if so I may."
She answered: "First my beauty and my youth,
"As thou hast seen and knowest is the truth;
"To see thee next my eyesight would I seek,
"And pluck a rose from garden of thy cheek."
At once then Joseph moved his lip in prayer,
And from his lips poured out life's water there.
On her dead charms the breath of life he breathed,
And round her cheek auspicious fortune wreathed.

Her water gone he to its river led,
And thus refreshed of youth her roses' bed.
Her camphor musk became of Tartar deer,
And her dark night through her morn's dawn grew clear.
From her musk locks then disappeared the white,
Her dark Narcissus beamed again with light.
From her rose-cypress the bend disappeared,
And from her pure silver the wrinkles cleared.
A halo round her age her youth was seen,
From forty years old she became eighteen.
Her beauty changed to a loveliness rare,
Than in former days she became more fair.
Joseph-again said: "Thou of nature sweet,
"What more may be thy wish to me repeat."
She said: "I have no other wish than this,
"That I may rest me in thy union's bliss:
"That thou shouldst be aye in my sight by day,
"At night on thy foot my head I may lay;
"Of thy cypress tall in the shade may lean,
"From thy smiling lip I may sugar glean;
"May lay a plaster on my heart of pain,
"And in all matters my desire may gain;
"Whilst over my field, now withered and dead,
"From thy friendship's fountain may water spread."
When Joseph had heard the hope she expressed,
In silence awhile with head on his breast,
He answered her with neither "yes" nor "no",
Its purpose that the unseen world might show.
Will, no-will between he was wavering,
Till he heard the sound of Gabriel's wing.
This message he spoke: "O reverend king,
"From the pure God to thee I greeting bring.
"I have seen Zuleikha's humility,
"I have heard her piteous prayer to thee.
"From her wave-exciting weakness and toil
"Has my forgiveness' sea begun to boil.

"Unwounded with sword of despair her mind,
"Upon the throne thy knot with hers I bind.
"Tie thou her knot that may for aye endure;
"Unloose those knots that now her way obscure.
"That thou in pure regard with her mayst be,
"And from this union pearls of offspring see."

### The Marriage of Zuleikha with Joseph by the Command of God the Most High (Glory be to Him), and the Wedding Night.

When God's commandment Joseph knew aright
That with Zuleikha he should now unite,
Foundation for a royal feast he laid,
And for the banquet preparation made.
The king of Egypt with his nobles all,
Seated on honour's seat, came at his call.
By Abram's law and faith that Jacob knew,
In perfect manner and mode fair to view (253),
He bound Zuleikha with his marriage knot,
That precious jewel into union brought.
From crescent to full moon were offerings laid,
Congratulations king and army made.
Short-comings to excuse did Joseph rise,
And to those present made apologies.
Zuleikha, at his questionings content,
Forthwith was to his private chamber sent.
Then ran before her every serving maid,
Both coronet and head before her laid.
Exulting ever in her beauty rare
Gold robes for her adornment they prepare (254).
And when men's bustle gave to quiet place,
Tow'rds their own home when all had turned their face,
The moon bride on her face a dark veil bound,
And spread a golden curtain on the ground.

For victory upon the azure height
The earth lit up with stars a shining light.
Heav'n in the sky the Pleiads' cluster hung;
Rubies and pearls together twilight strung.
For the world's secret veil night's hair provides;
Within that screen a world its secrets hides.
Consorts together then their secret place,
Closed with an amber veil to others' face.
In her own veil Zuleikha sitting waits,
Her heart within her body palpitates.
" This thirsty one with tears whose eyelids gleam,
" Is she awake, O God, or in a dream?
" Will water ever, then, this thirst allay?
" Will from this heart the fever pass away?"
At times there filled her eye the joyous tear,
At times 'twas blood from disappointment's fear.
At times she said: "I can not yet be sure
" That days of gladness will for me endure."
At times she said: "God's grace belongs to all,
" From God's grace hopeless it were wrong to fall."
Her heart in tumult with such thoughts as these
Happy at times, at times but ill at ease.
Sudden before the door the curtain rose,
A veil-less moon within it to disclose.
As fell Zuleikha's eye upon that sight,
She saw it ever with increased delight.
Unconscious she became when rose that day,
In sunlight darkness' shadow passed away.
That faith and lovingness when Joseph knew,
That madness that to him alone was due.
Her to the throne of gold he kindly led,
And made his breast a pillow for her head.
With his own scent did he her sense redeem,
And brought her back awake from her sweet dream.
If on that face which erst had shunned his eye,
His heart for long had passed with loathing by,

When on her face again his glance he threw,
As Chinese pictures on brocade to view,
Sweet as a *Huris'* face to loving heart,
With cheek unadorned by tire-woman's art,
Then when his eye found its rest on her face,
The reins drew him on to kiss and embrace.

\* \* \* \* \* \*

[*Thirty-two couplets, up to the end of the chapter, are here omitted as unsuited to European ideas.*]

## Concerning the Communication of Zuleikha's Love to Joseph, and his Running after her and Tearing her Robe, and the Founding of a House of Worship.

Lovers the road of love who purely tread
At last will earn the name of "loved" instead.
With the pure flame of love who ever burned,
From lover into loved that was not turned?
Zuleikha, who in love was pure as day,
And in love equally life passed away,
When in her infancy with dolls she played,
Herself their friend in love affairs she made.
When she engaged herself in any game,
"The game of love," it always was the same.
And when to play two dolls she might prepare,
One was the lover, one the loved one there.
Her right hand from her left when first she knew,
And to sit down or rise more forward grew,
In that sweet dream her wakeful fortune brought,
In Joseph's love snare she at once was caught.
From her own country she withdrew her heart,
And to the land of Egypt would depart.
Not for her own, but only Joseph's sake,
From her own town to his her way she'd take.

In thought of him her precious youth she passed,
In hope his union she might gain at last.
In age into desire for him she fell,
And into blindness for his love as well.
And when in age her sight and youth returned,
With love of that fair face her soul still burned.
Thenceforward in his love would she abide,
And in his faith's bond aye she lived and died.
Since her sincerity all limits passed,
To Joseph its contagion spread at last.
And Joseph's heart affection so inflamed,
That of such love his heart became ashamed.
Over his heart that charmer gained such pow'r
He could not be without her for an hour.
To please her so her heart he wandered round,
That the two ever face to face were found.
He watered so her field of joy indeed,
Of water every moment there was need.
When thus through him Zuleikha's veil was rent,
The sun of truth his ray towards her bent.
That sun upon her with such fury smote,
That Joseph vanished in it as a mote.
And in that crucible of love profane
Her days were ever passed in melting's pain.
But when the sun of righteousness arose
There was before her nothing to oppose.
Of truth the blandishment upon her lay,
From all that was not right she fled away.
One night from Joseph's hand in haste she fled,
And limping to obtain release she sped.
Behind he seized her garment as she flew,
And by his hand her robe was rent in two.
Zuleikha said to him : " In days of yore
" Thy robe from off thy body once I tore.
" Thou hast my garment now from off me torn,
" And I my crime's just punishment have borne.

"Of right and wrong I now no longer fear ;
"In tearing robes we both stand equal here."
Tow'rds piety when Joseph saw her bent,
And towards that purpose her heart fully leant,
Of gold he built for her a palace there,
No house of pleasure, but a house of prayer.
Like heaven's azure vault its bricks in glow,
Through art its ground as Paradise below.
From floor to roof this handsome paintings fill ;
Geometricians spend there all their skill.
Out of its windows shone forth fortune's light,
And from its doors wealth's herald took his flight.
Far from its terrace evil eye he sent !
Like *Huri's* eyebrows were its arches bent.
The sun its source in its light's image made,
The house in it impervious to shade.
From painters' happy brush there came to view
In the walls' date-groves many trees that grew.
And on each branch there many a bird reposed,
But to melodious song their beaks were closed.
Within that house a glorious throne was laid,
A part of gold, a part of rubies made.
Two hundred pictures rare were in it hung,
And thousands of fair pearls were in it strung.
He took her hand, and as the throne he graced
Her, too, with heart's affection on it placed.
He said : "O thou endowed with many a grace,
"Till Judgment Day thou bringest me disgrace,
"For in the day thou calledst me a slave,
"Thy favour even then a dwelling gave.
"Of rubies made, of red and yellow gold,
"Full of all beauty that a house might hold.
"And now, reward for all thy favours rare,
"I built at thy advice this house of prayer.
"In thankfulness to God sit ever there ;—
"Thou owest thanks to God in ev'ry hair.

" He gave thee riches after poverty,
" And after old age gave he youth to thee.
" The eye that had gone He gave light once more,
" Before thy face He opened mercy's door.
" The age when sorrow He has made thee taste
" With union's antidote has He replaced."
Zuleikha also through the Heavenly Grace,
Upon the royal throne thus took her place.
In that seclusion made her glad abode,
Through Joseph's union and the Grace of God.


### THE SEEING BY JOSEPH OF HIS FATHER AND MOTHER IN A DREAM, AND ASKING FOR HIS OWN DEATH FROM GOD.

Well done for whom his mournful state
Changes to union's hall propitious Fate.
His arms round fortune's beauteous idol close;
He parting's grief into oblivion throws,—
And when grief's dust his heart no longer sees,
Passes his days in happiness and ease.
Sudden the wind of ruin he may know,
And the *Simoom* of separation blow:
Its way to union's garden then it makes,
And of the tree of hope the branches breaks.
Her hope Zuleikha had from Joseph gained,
And in his union lasting ease obtained.
In joy of heart and mind she lived indeed,
And from the griefs of this world had been freed.
Thus did for many days her union last,
And in that bliss full forty years had passed,
That fruitful palm its fruit would aye renew
In children, nay, in children's children, too
There was no earthly wish within her heart,
To her hope's table that would not impart.

Joseph one night towards the *Mehráb* lay;
Sleep's robber stopped of wakefulness the way.
He saw his father with his mother sit:
Their sunny face with veil of light was lit.
They cried to him: "Be thou aware, O son,—
"The days of absence hasten to be done.
"Thy feet on earthly clay and water place,
"To the soul's goal and home thy way to trace."
From the *Mehráb* then Joseph took his way,
From dream awoke, to where Zuleikha lay.
His dream's full tale he told into her ear,
And to her quickly made his purpose clear.
The dream-like thought of absence he instilled;
Her soul with fire of separation filled.
From his own way the heart of Joseph ceased,
His longing for the eternal realms increased.
Out of the straits of lust his steps he bent,
And tow'rds the amplitude of myst'ries leant.
From earth he bore his mortal goods away,
And to th' eternal *Mehráb* turned to pray.
"O Thou who grantest the poor man's desire,
"And makest with a crown the lofty high'r,
"Who fortune's crown upon my head hast placed,
"The fortunate with which were never graced;—
"My heart is raised up from this transient land:
"The reins of government gives up my hand.
"Freed from myself, thy own road to me show,
"A mandate for th' eternal world bestow.
"The righteous who the road of faith pursued,
"To them near Thee high station has accrued.
"Among the common count me not below;
"At Thy high table nearness may I know!"
And when Zuleikha heard this secret word,
With smarting wound her inmost heart was stirred.
She surely knew that to his prayer from heaven,
A clear and speedy answer would be given.

No arrow from that bow e'er went away
To reach its aim, that ever knew delay.
To narrow hut she entered void of light,
Spread out her ringlets of the hue of night;
From grief of parting wreathed her head with dust,
Whilst on the ground her bleeding face she thrust.
Her joy and grief at odds and evens played,
And as the tears rained from her eyes, she said:
" O medicine of grief for those who mourn,
" Mender of robes for all whose hearts are torn,
" The aim of those themselves who hopeless find,
" Opening a way for those the 'six doors' bind;
" The key by which closed doors asunder part,
" The bandage-tier of the broken heart,
" Saver of those whom sorrow casts away,
" Light'ner of woes as hills that heavy weigh;
" A captive to my wounded heart, I bleed,
" And am much straitened in my every deed.
" In Joseph's absence must I ever pine.
" Oh! with his life take from my body mine!
" Without his beauty life to me no gain,
" In realm of being would I not remain.
" My life without him is a leafless tree;
" Eternal life without him death to me.
" Right by the laws of faith 'twould not appear,
" If I were still on earth and he not here.
" If his companion here I may not stay,
" Oh! first take me and then bear him away.
" Apart from him I do not wish to sit,
" Or see a world not by his beauty lit."
Weeping in grief her time thus passed away,
Nor night to her was night, nor day was day.
Whosever heart may be with sorrow tight,
To him of one hue are both day and night.

## The Death of Joseph and the Destruction of Zuleikha through Separation from Him.

Next day, when Joseph in the early morn,
When from day's grace to all hearts joy is borne,
Arrayed himself in robes of royal pride,
And came outside with the intent to ride,
When in the stirrup one foot he had placed,
Said Gabriel to him: "Make no further haste.
"From deadly fate no surety canst thou gain,
"In other stirrup that thy foot remain.
"From hope and safety now draw back thy rein,
"And from life's stirrup now thy foot restrain."
When Joseph's ear now these good tidings knew,
Glad from this being he his heart withdrew.
His skirt of courage gladly he spread wide,
And of his realm's heirs called one to his side.
King of that land in his own stead he willed,
Into his heart all excellence instilled.
Again he said, "Call ye Zuleikha here:
"To bid me now farewell let her appear."
They said: "In sorrow's hand is she a prize;
"In blood and dust now overwhelmed she lies.
"Her grieving soul this load could never bear.
"Leave her alone in thy great pity there."
He said: "I fear the scar of this great debt
"Till Judgment Day will lie upon her yet."
They said to him: "God give her joy at length;
"In resignation ever be her strength!"
In Gabriel's hand there was an apple borne,
That Eden's grove with beauty would adorn.
In Joseph's hand as he the apple placed,
He smelt it and gave up his soul in haste.
Of life's fair garden as he knew the scent,
He with that perfume to life's garden went.

As Joseph yielded to that scent his soul
Burst from those present cries beyond control.
And as the voice of weeping went on high,
The sound rose upwards to the azure sky.
Zuleikha said: "What is this noise and cry,
"Resounding loud throughout the earth and sky?"
"That king of prosp'rous fortune," then they said:
"From throne towards the bier has turned his head.
"To this world's narrow house he bids good bye,
"And makes his new abode above the sky."
She heard these words and was of sense bereft,
And the bright light of sense her body left.
That active cypress at this dismal tale
Fell on the ground three days a shadow pale.
On the fourth day awoke from dreams at last,
Hearing, into unconsciousness she passed.
Three times three days she all unconscious lay,
With burning heart passed from her sense away.
On the fourth day when she returned to sense,
To ask for Joseph she would first commence.
Upon the pillow he no more reclined,
Nor on the earth his coffin could she find.
And she of him these tidings only found:
As treasure they had laid him in the ground.
At first as cruel fate her onwards bore,
As the pure dawn her collar then she tore.
Then with that fire at heart that hidden lay,
From that torn collar opened out a way.
Thus in her soul that fire would never cease,
But every moment farther would increase.
Holes in her fair cheeks with her nails she tore,
And made a river for her fount of gore,
That from that fountain flowed each stream within:
*Arghwán's* bride-chamber made the jessamine.
With nail on rosy cheek she drew a line,
As vein through brilliant eyeballs coursing fine.

Upon her breast with stone she struck a blow;
And her fair cheek with many a slap would glow.
On silver there the fresh cornelian grew;
From this the tulip took the lotus' hue.
To her own head she raised her hand again,
And on that tender head inflicted pain.
The garden cypress of its green bereft,
The spikenard plucked, the grove was empty left.
Moaning in soul and with a heartfelt cry
From a sad breast she raised her voice on high:
"Oh! where is Joseph who adorned the throne,
"Who ever to the poor has mercy shown?
"When he on narrow steed the saddle tied, (255)
"And to the everlasting realm would ride;
"Such eager haste did he display in this,
"That even I his stirrup could not kiss.
"When from this vault of grief he went away,
"I was not present 'Why dost go?' to say.
"I saw no head that on his couch he threw,
"Nor gathered from his wild-rose face the dew.
"When that fierce wound upon his breast was seen,
"His back upon my breast he could not lean.
"From throne when on the bier he lay at rest,
"That bier by fortune as the throne was blessed.
"Rose-water from my eye I did not seek,
"Nor with that water did I wash his cheek.
"When on his body they the shroud had tied,
"And in his burial were occupied,
"Ropes I had never learnt the art to reeve,
"That sewn on him my thin form I might leave.
"When in my heart they broke of grief the thorn,
"And from this earthly stage his load was borne,
"So full of tuneless melody my tongue
"As bell upon his litter was not hung.
"When in the earth his place of sleep they found,
"And laid him as a rare pearl in the ground,

"The ground above, below, I did not sweep,
"Nor in his arms, as I desired, could sleep.
"Alas for this sad injury! Alas!
"Alas for this terrific grief! Alas!
"Come, my heart's wish: my disappointment see!
"On me oppress'd of heav'n the tyranny!
"Cut off from thee, nor in thy memory had,
"Thou didst not with thy presence make me glad.
"O faithful one, was this good faith in thee?
"Tow'rds friends should this the form of friendship be?
"Why, then, didst thou reject me from thy heart?
"In dust and blood why throw me and depart?
"Thou brokest in my heart a wondrous thorn,
"Which from my clay alone can forth be borne.
"Thou didst prepare to travel to a place,
"Whence backwards no one ever turns his face.
"It would be better now to spread my wing,
"And in one flight myself to thee to bring."
She spoke, and called her litter-bearers there,
And bade her litter for herself prepare,
And with one movement from that grief's abode,
To Joseph's halting-stage on earth she rode.
There of her jewel pure no sign she found,
Only a heap of moist earth on the ground.
That sunny foot, her face upon the mound,
Threw down herself like shadow on the ground—
A golden shade from her pale cheek she threw,
And tinged it with her tears with ruby's hue.
At times the foot she kissed, at times the head;
"Oh! and alas is me!" she cried and said.
"Thou hast gone down, as in the earth the rain,
"Whilst I as thorns and rubbish here remain.
"Like rose's root thou hidest in the mud,
"Whilst I as rose-branch am above and bud.
"Thou hast in earth as treasure found thy place,
"And I, gem-weighing cloud, am on its face.

"Upon my dust blood-waves thy image throws,—
"Through parting fire upon my rubbish glows.
"On my life's rubbish hast thou cast a flame:
"My smoke, thence curling, up to heaven came.
"None ever opened eye upon my smoke,
"That water from his eye did not evoke."
Thus did she wail, and aye her wounded breast
With hundred griefs upon the earth she pressed.
And when her grief beyond all limit went,
To kiss the earth her head she lowly bent;
Up to her eyes her finger then she bore,
And her two eye-balls from their sockets tore.
From her head's cup these in his dust she pressed,
And said: "To sow narcissus were it best.
"When thy rose-face my eyes no more may see,
"Of what use in this world are eyes to me?"
Of those o'erwhelmed with grief it is the way
Upon the coffin almonds black to lay,
But as that wretch his coffin could not view,
But two black almonds on his grave she threw.
She laid her blood-stained face upon the grave;
Kissed the dust humbly and her spirit gave.
Happy that lover is who when he dies,
In hope of union with his loved one lies!
Then when her state her own companions knew,
Out of their hearts the loud lament they drew.
For ev'ry sigh that she on Joseph spent,
Two hundred times for her did they lament.
They made lament as hired mourners cry,
For that fair silver form, exceedingly.
Now as the sound of mourning grows more cold,
Their sleeves together they to wash her fold.
They wash her with the tear-flood of their eyes,
As wash the rose-leaves clouds in summer skies.
Like bud that from a branch of jess'mine grows,
In shroud of verdure they her form enclose.

They clean the dust of parting from her face,
And in the earth by Joseph's side they place.
None in his death such bliss may ever gain,
That his love's company he should obtain.

### STORY.

But the wise man who this sweet tale relates,
Which he has heard from ancient people, states.
That on the bank of Nile, he will attest,
Wherever Joseph's pure form lay to rest,
Famine and plague there opposite arose,
In place of favours evil's many blows.
One counsel when at last they all embraced,
In a stone coffin they his body placed.
With pitch they closed up of the stone each chink,
And in Nile's bottom let the coffin sink.
Behold the trick performed by faithless Fate,
Her dead from Joseph thus to separate.
What spite it bore to them I cannot say,
Thus to disturb their rest beneath the clay.
The one of them in friendship's sea was drowned,
On separation's land one thirsting found.
How well said he whose feet in love were sore,
Who gain and loss from love no longer bore :
Love at what place its market brisk may be,
It can from unrest never once be free.
A lover's shroud at length it rends away,
Though he himself be sleeping 'neath the clay.
Happy the lover who in absence dead,
To his love's bridal-room his soul has led.
No one can say that with such courage high,
Men in their shrouds can as Zuleikha (256) lie.
All but one love she from her eye withdrew,
And then life's cash upon his dust she threw,

A thousand graces on her soul and body be,
And by her love her soul enlightened be!


REBUKE OF HEAVEN, WHICH HAVING TWISTED ITS FOLDS LIKE A SNAKE ROUND THE WORLD, AND HAVING BROUGHT ALL WITHIN THE CIRCLE OF ITS DOMINION, INFLICTS A WOUND ON ONE AND GIVES POISON TO ANOTHER.

The heaven's a dragon on itself that turns,
In plaguing us to prove its strength that burns.
All captive in its curling folds are we:
How from its tail shall we be ever free?
Thou seest no one that it does not wound,
And out of hundreds none has mercy (257) found.
For its oppression no one may avoid,
What breast has this oppressor not annoyed?
In the bright lamp that shines in every star,
On the free heart it aye inflicts a scar.
A thousand scars and not a plaster there,
Yet for this want of salve it has no care.
And there are seen in every gloomy night
A thousand windows in the world of light;
What profit, since on us there falls no gleam,
And on our minds contentment does not beam?
Like lions, it is single-hued by day,
At night a tiger's colours 'twill display,
Except to be oppressed what is our plight
When the day-lion tiger grows at night?
'Tis fit that at our bitter joy I should be grieved,
With lion and with tiger that I am deceived.
From any one who now may be thy friend
In parting surely thy affair must end.
Constant revolved this (258) vault of heaven green,
In movement moon and sun and stars were seen,

Till all the elements together mixed,
And in a net the soul's bird was fixed.
But this unhappy bird had not as yet
The grain of its desire picked from the net,
When broke the elements each other's chain,
And to its prime source each returned again.
Then must the bird, with bleeding heart, remain
Far from its nest, no water and no grain.
Look on the circling sphere and ardent sun ;
For malice they display they shame have none.
Few to their love (259) like morn their hearts have bound
As twilight red with blood that are not found.
He its banquet who awhile no grief has borne,
For ages long through it occasion had to mourn.
Tread for awhile in spring the garden's bound,
And look upon the streams that flow around :—
Why has the bud its vest asunder thrust ?
Why does the green herb basely lie in dust ?
Why is the rose's garment torn apart,
Flames in its mouth and full of sparks its heart ?
The graceful cypress who, then, has thrown down ?
And who the *Arghaván* in blood would drown ?
Why is the fading spikenard sad to view ?
Why filled Narcissus' eye with tears of dew ?
The mourning violet is clad in blue (260) ;
The tulip washed has scars of bloody hue.
The fir, with heart in many pieces split,
In holes the sun's sword has its body slit.
The rose-bush, back and face, by roses is full scarred,—
Torn by its cruel nail the jess'mine cheek is marred.
Trees in the breeze are mournful dancing still ;
The birds' pathetic chant from hill to hill.
The turtle-dove coos ev'rywhere away,
" Where in the world is rest ?" as if 'twould say.
" Happy is he," the nightingales in thousands mourn,
" Who from this garden has but little sorrow borne."

And by its collar is the dove's neck chained,
Whence freedom ever no head has obtained.
The world and its fair spring thus dost thou see;
Now of its autumn warning take from me.
See of the autumn wind the breath so cold,
Of its vine-leaves the yellow face behold.
Of parting's anguish is this bitter air
That severs friend from friend and pair from pair.
With parting's grief that cheek is pale to see,
For after nearness distance must there be.
Of loveliness and hue the garden shorn,
The black clothed crow has thither come to mourn.
The nakedness of ev'ry branch must show
Beneath the peacock's tail the foot of crow.
From the wild rose's head the veil has fallen down;
The elm has lost its tent-like covering and crown.
Pomegranates their heads' crown have cast below,
From which the garden old fresh youth may know.
Its heart although thou see with laughter thrill,
Blood with a hundred sparks it aye will fill.
Fairer the garden's maiden bare to view,
Than when her beauty's clothed in yellow hue,
Than when her paling cheek's begrimed with dust,
And from her lovers she afar is thrust,
When the keen frost the water's face with harshness
    binds,
Cuirass to weave the wind the way no longer finds.
Ravished by frost's cold hand thou seest the plane;
The grove thou hearest of the cold complain.
From fear of cold thyself dost thou not dare
From the bough's sleeve thy hand to render bare.
Such is earth's autumn, aye, and such its spring,
One than the other a more grievous thing.
In grief's abode can one live free of grief,
And can a withered heart ere find relief?
Upon the earth a trace of joy is not,

Or should there be, it is in no man's lot.
Fill not thy head with blandishments of friends,
For all men's fortune in misfortune ends.
No hope of gladness let thy heart retain,
No thought of freedom linger in thy brain.
With unfulfilled hope's scar contented be ;
Beneath the yoke of service still be free.
From all with pleasure that thy heart may bind,
Or with its love that may attract thy mind,
Thou wilt be severed full of grief at last,
And thou must taste its parting's pain at last.
Loosen thy hand ; break from thy foot the chain ;
Undo the bond of what can bring no gain.
For if thou loose it not, He who has bound
With open hand to break it will be found.
Thou sleep'st the sleep of carelessness, and He
Sudden will take what He bestowed on thee,—
With harshness bring thy foot against a stone,—
In longing's plain will leave the lame alone.
In longing's place seize thou thy staff in hand,
To thee when lame as courser it may stand.
Branch from its root when a fresh wind shall tear,
Not with dry sticks can one its ties repair.
With force it loosed the power of thy grasp,
Seized that desire's cash that thy hand did clasp.
Tow'rds all thou stretchest out thy hand of greed,
But in thy hand will nothing e'er succeed.
When leaves thy hand the power of its strength,
With that hand's force pain not thyself at length.
The coin of brightness from thy eye is gone ;
Why blindly *Surma* dost thou still rub on ?
Thy eye has not the quality of sight :
Rub *Surma* only on the eye that's light.
To blindness' utter straits reduced the eye,
In glasses (261) canst thou find a remedy ?
With silver *Sins* as thy mouth's *Mim* is fair to view.

As *Lab* with *Lám* and *Bá* they number thirty-two. (262)
But in that string has such a breach occurred,
That of a greater none has ever heard.
Silent art thou or dost in folly speak,
In lips a cov'ring for it dost thou seek.
As thou art harsh sometimes and sometimes weak,
In this a hundred failures are to seek.
Thou see'st thy failures from a single place ;
In one event thou findest out their trace.
What in thy body or thy soul may lack,
On doubt of earthly things thou fallest back.
This of thyself thou wouldest never say,
That He who gave can also take away.
In this world thou art far too tightly pent :
To reach another hast thou no intent ?
Another world than this dost thou not know,
Whence benefit or loss must surely flow ?
I fear that when thy death comes on the scene,
Thou wilt not care thy heart from earth to wean.
With spirit full of many kinds of doubt,
Thou from the world wilt pass ignobly out.
When fate's cup-bearer hands death's cup to thee,
Still tow'rds this desert will thy liking be.

\*       \*       \*       \*       \*

[*The next four Couplets, which are not translated here, contain an anecdote of the physician Galen, omitted in Rosenzweig's edition, which are untranslatable for their obscenity, and quite incomprehensible to Europeans.*]

To that heart-cheering dome prepare a way ;
To-morrow's pleasure shalt thou see to-day.
Does it, then, never come into thy mind
To see the state thou in the world mayst find ?
Earth's leather's ever a foot-pinching shoe,
With many sand-like hardships in it, too.

From off thy foot 'twere best it to remove,
Else with hurt foot the road thou mayest prove.
Lift up heav'n's curtain from before thy face ;
Henceforth be not forbid the holy place.
Beyond the veil there is unbounded light,
Each beam of which is sun-like in delight.
In that beam let thy ev'ry hope be lost ;
And like an atom in the sun be tossed.
Once lost in it, thou then shalt find release ;
And parting's pain and absence' grief shall cease.


GIVING ADVICE AND IMPOSING BONDS ON HIS BELOVED SON THAT HE SHOULD BE ZEALOUS IN ACQUIRING PERFECTION.

May God, my noble son, thy refuge be !
The Lord from evil thy protection be !
From all advice may He such gain bestow,
That in need's time to use it thou mayst know—
Thy years are sev'n, while sev'nty is my score :
Thy fortune is approaching, mine's no more.
I grieve for what has vanished of my day,
Mourn years, moons, weeks, that all have passed away.
To any profit now I cannot till,
And only thorns my rose produces still.
The thing has left my hand : what profit now remains ?
Out of my hand have slipped of my free-will the reins.
Thou hast the means ; an effort should be made,
That fortune on thy head may make a shade.
Do thou such things as may of lasting profit be,
That rain of generosity may rain on thee.
First make thy gain all wisdom to acquire ;
From folly's careless town do thou retire.
For it is known to all, both slave and free,
Whilst the fool dies, the wise will living be.

To excellence he who a claim may make,
How with the dead will he his dwelling take?
Plant thou thy foot of wisdom in the way;
Knowledge endureth long, while life's a day.
When thou hast knowledge gained, thyself to deeds devote;
Wisdom without deed's poison without antidote.
What gain from alchemy that thou mayst learn,
To gold thy copper if thou canst not turn?
When through thy deeds the robe thou mayst assume
Of honour, this with purity perfume.
For ev'ry act of purity that's bare,
But crude work those who are mature declare;
And from crude actions none can profit gain,
As uncooked sweetmeats can bring only pain.
Though thou art true and pure, beware thou yet:
A hundred dangers may truth's road beset.
For back and belly ease do not prepare,
Nor for good food or clothing practise care.
To ward off heat and cold is raiment worn:
A man cares not himself much to adorn.
And if to clothing coarse thou shouldst resort,
Like hedgehog's thorn, 'gainst evil 'tis thy fort.
In mildness fox-like if thou takest pride,
Those of dogs' nature will tear off thy hide.
Do not, like flies, seek after what is sweet,
For in the end the honey clogs thy feet.
Drink thou the bitter of this cruel sea,
Till, oyster-like, with pearls filled thou shalt be.
Thy fingers at whose board thou mayest stain,
Make of thy hand no fist to give him pain.
When for thy food thou hast made use of salt,
With the salt-cellar do not thou find fault.
With bounteous hand on friends thy favours lay;
Set not thy foot on miser's narrow way.

Take no half *habbah* (263), nor to any lend;
Debt is a scissors that will cut a friend.
With presents do thou aye their burdens bear,
Nor drive them with their debts into despair.
Yet in bestowing gifts thy foot so set
That on thy own neck fall no load of debt.
Life as an offering for thy friends bestow,
But do thou well discern thy friend from foe.
That friend of God alone should be thy friend,
To whose heart friendship a clear light may lend.
Thy load he'll bear when thou oppressed shalt be,
And be thy aid when mischief threatens thee;
Who in bad times himself thy hand will meet;
With counsel's water who will quench thy heat.
When from defilement he shall make thee free,
Pure as a hair from leaven render thee:
In ev'ry good work thee with aid provide,
And to the street of good name be thy guide.
Win thou his dust, if such a friend thou find,
Thyself a captive to his saddle bind.
Or else towards the wall thy own face bend;
Leave strangers; of the cave (264) be thy own friend.
Let not time's sorrows ever trouble thee,
And in the world's griefs sit thou calm and free.
Make not of many occupations much;
In worldly business keep with One in touch.
Be it by day or in night's darkness dim,
At ev'ry house still stay thy heart on Him.
Though this good fortune never to thee came,
Of idleness incur thou not the shame.
Thy face tow'rds books be from this workshop brought,
And practise ever upon books thy thought.
This subtle thought is well known of the wise:
"Books hold the learnèd in his grave who lies."
A book in a lone corner's aye a friend:
To wisdom's dawn a book will brightness lend.

A book 's a master without thanks or pay;
To thee it ever opens learning's way.
A pithy friend, who will thy faults conceal,
Who tells thee secrets, yet will ne'er reveal.
As bud its inside is with leaves replete,
Whose price would with a plate of pearls compete.
Its litter is of coloured leather made,
In which as vest two hundred flow'rs are laid.
All cheeks of musk, each fold in gold's embrace,
And delicately laid there face to face.
All of one hue, of equal back and face,
On their lip finger when can any place?
To utter jests their lips they open wide,
Shed thousand gems of mystery beside.
The Koran's mysteries at times they tell,
And of the Prophet's sayings speak as well.
At times as those whose hearts are pure, are they
With lights of truth aye pointing out the way;
And when at times in current phrase they speak,
Point to the lore and science of the Greek.
At times they tell the story of the past,
Or what will henceforth be before thee cast.
At times they pour from the poetic sea
In wisdom's breast their pearls of mystery.
Towards whatever aim thy ear thou set,
Never the aim thou hadst at first forget.
Towards this if fully thou turn not thy face,
Thy foot at least no other road should trace.
Ere of thy heart the secret thou shalt tell,
First of its good and evil ponder well.
When from its cage the bird has taken wing
To bring it back is not an easy thing.
With thy heart black through love of pinchbeck gold,
Be wisdom's praises by thy tongue untold.
Though wisdom be as slender as a hair,
With the heart black what does it profit there?

Make not a *Sufi* immature thy friend ;
Crude is the work of crude men in the end.
The way of perfect work they do not know,
Crudely thy fruit upon the ground they throw ;
And from its stem this fruit, when cut away,
Remains unripe until the Judgment Day.
Thy hand devoid of silver and of gold,
Let one of kindly feeling only hold.
When in his hand thy willing hand is placed,
With blessing's treasure it will soon be graced.
Canst thou, like *Isa*, sleep without a mate,
Surrender not for naught thy single state.
Far from thy eye the dream of rest to keep
Were better than in *Huris'* arms to sleep,—
Better on furnace ashes hot to lie
Than on soft pillow with a woman by.
If suddenly thou fear the sense of lust,
Thy foot on to the plain of sin may thrust,
'Gainst marrying place on thy foot a chain,
So that it move not from its place again.
With this end if thou strike a woman's door,
See not her beauty, but her virtue more.
She who from chastity is red of cheek
Need for her face no other colour seek.
In that adornment she has *Huris'* grace,
That from forbidden things she hides her face.
Nearness to monarchs is a flaming fire,
Before it, like the smoke, do thou retire.
When once the fire the torch's flame has lit,
But from afar do thou make use of it.
If thou too near approach, I greatly fear
The light of thy own life will disappear.
Place not thy feet 'mongst those of high degree,
To raise or lower lest a mark thou be.
To rest upon that couch be not unwise,
Lest some one seize thy hand and bid thee rise.

From place to want of office turn thy face:
Than office better far is want of place.
Be ev'ry thought of thine devoid of pride,
Tow'rds ev'ry one humility should be thy guide.
From pride does not preserve itself the ear,
And thus its head the scythe will quickly shear.
A humble place the grain in dust will seek,
And from the dust the bird will raise it in its beak.
After the seat of worth do thou aspire,
Than lofty head esteem thou honour high'r.
See how the masses lose their fortune high,
As ciphers more they add to reckon by.
No promise make, but if thou promise, pay;
Avoid thou of unfaithfulness the way.
From that God being's favour who bestows,
The call "Perform your promises" arose.
Like fools, rest thou not in thy father's bond:
Be merit's son;—thy father pass beyond.
Since light the smoke can from the flame not be,
What profits it the son of fire to be?
Except in private mention not his name,
He is well pleased to hear thy virtue's fame.
Should counsel a wise counsellor impart,
Wisely make room for it within thy heart;—
Not like the fool who hears but with one ear,
And through the other lets it disappear.
The corn sprouts from the dust but with delay;
No drop becomes a jewel in a day.
By no one has this proverb not been heard:
"If one is in the house, enough's one word."
Its mighty movement should the sea provoke,
What matters of the senseless frog the croak?
Of this false world 'twere best within the cell
To work, within thee that God's grace should dwell,

## A Talk with Regard to Himself, and Advancing Him from the Low Ground of Selfishness to the Summit of Magnanimity.

Turn, *Jámi*, to the work of ripened men :
Never hereafter do crude work again.
What is it to be ripe ? But to be free,
In non-existence' dust to fallen be.
In this rust-coloured vault dost thou not see,
Whilst it is green the fruit clings to the tree?
To ripeness when is turned its face, 'twill fall,
Nor the boys' cruel stone require at all.
Do thou from right men's board thy food provide,—
And stand from the crude slingers' stones aside.
Tear with content up avarice's root ;
With resignation break of thy desire the shoot.
Build thee a house of courage in the town ;
In *Anká's* solitude thy rest lay down.
Let loose no tongue to glorify the base ;
Incur not for a loaf (265) the viles' disgrace.
From heads of kingdoms do thou ever flee,
And turn thy back on all the pow'rs that be.
The seasons four in order due behold,
In which the course of time is onwards rolled.
Last year's and this year's spring both equal see,
And how both autumns in their hue agree.
Summer and winter both will intervene,
And thou canst see no difference between.
I know not why in this recurring state,
At such revolving thou shouldst be elate.
In repetition though thou magic find,
It must bring melancholy to the mind.
Pass by the loss and look towards the gain ;
To non-existence turn from life again.

Thy mind from works of busy men make free ;
From demons' business also loosened be.
Teach not love's magic to the base (266) of mind,
Nor kindle thou a night-lamp for the blind.
From folly aye do thou thy sense preserve :
Control of sense the traveller (267) should observe.
The soul that in intelligence may fail,
The lengthening of a life will not avail.
If sighs' smoke (268) should the brain of wisdom flout,
The lamp of life will with a puff go out.
Youth from thy realm will darkness bear away,
And by old age illumined is thy day.
Of blindness and of distance gone the night,
The fringe of grey hair now has brought thee light.
Since from that darkness thou hast gained no fruit,
Plant in the ray of this light now thy foot.
Perchance thus to a road thou mayst attain,
The scent of faith thy nostrils whence may gain.
From thy white hair what dost thou gain of grace,
If it bestow not whiteness on thy face?
Is thy heart not ashamed of such a hue,
Give it no dye, as would black-dyers do.
Old age is on thy head as glorious snow ;
From ice as water should thy grief's tears flow.
Proceed thou, weeping, on contrition's track,
Wash with ice-water from thy heart the black.
Black from thy heart canst thou not wash again,
Of all this blackening I know not the gain.
Since thy hand trembles, cast away thy pen :
Tear up the leaf : thy care is all in vain.
Devoid of light, thy lamp of thought has paled,
And in thy poet's garden water failed :
In this auspicious garden now I see
A raven's foot alone is left to thee.
On peacock's road with such foot wilt thou go
From captives' jail release how wilt thou know ?

To cease from doubt and pride is to be free,
From making lines and stringing poetry.
Where is *Nizámi?* where his pleasing verse,
His subtle nature's troubles to rehearse?
A place within the veil himself he gained,
And all without the veil but he remained.
No profit 's gained since hidden there he lay,
Except that secret which he bore away.
Coming to God, that secret has not he,
Whose heart of all but God may not be free. (269)
When from this narrow corner he then took the road
Towards the ample space of holiness' abode,
Escaped from those entangled in this snare,
Beneath the skirt of God's throne he lies there.
His heart, of form of Multitude washed free,
Has found the mystery of Unity.
This heart if thou shouldst not find in thy side,
How would it be to turn from self aside,
On one in business skilled thy trust to lay,
An athlete among those who know the way?
That heart replete with wisdom well has said:
"He who is fasting is acquiring bread!"
No woman old knows rightly how to pray, (270)
Weakness and failure ever are her way.
If thou a man art, on this road proceed;
This with the knowing is the way indeed.
A heart like that which I to thee have sung,
And in describing pearls of mystery strung,
Seek in the side of some old, perfect man,
For this a heart to capture is the plan.

## Conclusion in Thankfulness for Completion, and the Date of Finishing, and Prayer to God the Most High for Favour in the World to Come.

Praise be to God that now, against Time's will,
This heart-alluring tale is ended still.
My heart, in making verse, that trouble knew,
With care of finding rhymes full weary grew,
Throws from its hand the scales of thought away,
And has from stringing rhymes an idle day,—
Has found a firm support in leisure's wall,
Into the road of ease from work to fall,—
My heavy head has lifted from my knee :
Of secret load my mind is light for me.
My rider-pen, that inky-fingered one,
From Abyssinia that to Roum has gone,
Has of his coming left in Roum a trace,
And tells the present news of future grace,
Alights from off his horse in search of rest,
Lies at full length upon a couch with zest.
His head no longer by scribe's hand is bent,
Nor with reproach his hand on pen-knife leant.
The inkstand is of Tartar musk a tray,
And with the pen's aid musk around will lay.
There is upon its mouth of wax a seal,
'Twere better thus the tray's mouth to conceal.
The leaves that are no longer scattered wide,
Feet drawn within their skirt, are side by side.
Rose-like, two hundred leaves one skin within
Until the heavens may tear off their skin.
Like roses, may they be in good demand,
And may their binding firm for ever stand !

Behold a book, writ with the pen of truth
In name of sweetheart and her well-loved youth.
I like a sugar-eating parrot came,
And coupled Joseph's with Zuleikha's name.
How fair in God's name is this fresh spring grove,
That *Iram's* garden will to envy (271) move!
Each tale in it is as a garden fair ;
A sign of fair ones in each garden there.
A thousand roses blooming from it peep ;
Narcissuses two hundred, soft in sleep.
Mysterious groves where branches interfold ;
Their words are singers who in song are bold.
Its lines of musk upon a camphor sheet,
Like light and shade of trees upon the feet.
Each letter in it that you looped may count
Of hidden sense a wave-exciting fount.
On all sides rills their course from fountains trace,
With running streams of water, full of grace.
Happy the trav'ler who, with fortune's aid,
Upon their banks a resting-place has made!
Their waters' look will free his heart of pain,
And cleanse the dust off from his mind again.
Forth from his soul faith's mystery will stand,
And from his breast pluck out of prayer the hand.
From waves of sea of grace at Allah's hand,
For thirsty lip he will a drop demand.
Fresh roses to his breast he gathers, yet
Him never will the gardener forget.
The author's pen of this so precious thing,
Did with the year it to an ending bring.
The couplets of it, too, I took to count,
A thousand four times told was their amount.
And when there shall have passed one new year more,
Eight hundred ninety-nine the year will score.
On love's road, God, for men their way who trace.
And at love's halting-ground their burdens place,

Of mystery's chamber may this new bride be
From ev'ry failing skirt and bosom free!

  \*  \*  \*  \*  \*

[*Here follow thirteen couplets of blessing on the Sultan Hussein Mirza Baihasa, his Vazirs, and others. The book thus concludes:*]

With blessing now that thou thy song hast sung,
*Jámi*, in absolution loose thy tongue.
In black deeds, like thy pen, do not engage;
Now purify with bleeding eyes thy page.
Turn from this desert back thy courser-pen,
With this aim traverse thy black book again.
With punishment of silence curb thy tongue;
Silence prefer to all that thou hast sung.

# NOTES.

1. *Behruz* also means a kind of spear. Hence the idea of fighting conveyed in the word *firuzi*, or "victory", in the next line.

2. Musk is obtained by cutting it open from a bag attached to the navel of the Tartar musk-deer.

3. "Káf to Káf"—the fabulous mountains supposed to be the boundaries of the world.

4. The poet is here supposed to be looking forward to a time when his verse will have been forgotten—when the exhilaration arising from its perusal will have passed off, and when, deprived of all renown and enjoyment from his yet unwritten composition, he will be left to mourn alone. Finally, however, he exhorts himself to be timid no more, but plunge into his venture, and write what he has to write, be it good or bad, clear wine or dregs.

5. "Whose praise on men's tongues is as the sheen or lustre on swords."

6. There is a play here on the words *kám* and *gám*, the former meaning "desire", or an object wished for; and the latter the "jaw", or palate. "'The tongue in the mouth" is the literal translation.

7. A play on the words *anjuman* and *anjum*—"host" and "stars".

8. These two couplets are reversed, as in Rosenzweig's edition.

9. Literally, "Search on His road is without hand or foot."

10. *Azrak Tailisán*, the blue ends, or fringes, of the head-cloth allowed by priests to hang down on the shoulder, to give an appearance of dignity. The commentators explain

that reference is here made to the stars, on whose back lies, as it were, the blue mantle of the sky—the mantle which, according to the next couplet, scatters light on the world. This explains the following couplets.

11. These refer to the movements of the moon and sun respectively, the former moving more and more eastward from the new to the full, and the latter always sinking in the west, like a bark in the ocean. This is shown in the next couplet.

12. Those referred to in the former are said to be the propitious planets, Jupiter, Venus, and Mercury, and those in the latter line Saturn and Mars, which are of bad omen.

13. That is, the stars do not presume to act of their own free will, but all look to God.

14. *Háthá rabi* (Arabic), "This is my God."

15. The friend of God was Abraham.

16. *Lá ahab al afálina* (Arabic), "I love not those who go down." It is related of Abraham in the 6th Sura of the Korán that, after he had watched the moon and sun in their rising and setting, he would no longer worship them as his gods, but turned to Him who had created them, and worshipped Him only.

17. Literally, "When thou readest this on the tablet of the brick, thou remainest not ignorant of the state of the brickmaker."

18. "Surma" is antimony rubbed on the eyelids to make the eyes appear bright.

19. *Hazkar* in the text is a misprint for *bezikr*.

20. *Gul* and *gil* are here played upon.

21. Rosenzweig's edition has *khandán*, "smiling," in place of *chandán*, "so much," in the former line; and *dandán*, "tooth," in place of *sindán*, "anvil," in the latter. It is preferable in line 200, but not in 199. The *pastah* is the pistachio-nut.

22. "Pigh" also means the beard of wheat or barley.

23. There is a play on the words *saudá* and *sudí*.

24. An allusion to the ring-formed shape of the letter *Mim*, the first letter in Mahomed's name.

25. Difficult to understand, but said by Rosenzweig to refer to the saying attributed to Allah in the *Hadis-i-kuds*, "If it had not been for thee (Mahomed), I would not have created the heavens." *Mulk* and *malak*, "kingdom" and "angel", are brought into the latter line because both commence in *Mim*.

26. *Hâ*, the second letter in Mahomed's name, is also the first in *Hâsh*, and the expression, "Hâsh Allah!" (God forbid!). It is also one of those mysterious letters placed before many Suras of the Korán, of which Allah alone is believed to know the meaning.

27. The six-sided sphere is the earth, its directions being above, below, forwards, backwards, right and left. The eight-sided grove is the regions of Paradise, of which there are eight. The Mussulmans have only seven hells, to show that Allah's anger is less than his mercy.

28. *Dâl* is the last letter in the Prophet's name. His foot, or end, is thus said to be adorned with it as with an anklet. The second line is literally, "The head of the Faithful was laid under his feet."

29. "Jud" is the mount of Ararat.

30. That is, the fire into which, according to tradition, Abraham was thrown, by order of Nimrod, became, by God's breath, as cool as a rose-garden.

31. "Kalím," the speaker of God, or Moses.

32. Saleh was a prophet, and the father of Heber. He was sent to preach to the inhabitants of Petra, and, to convince them that he was commissioned by God, is said to have caused a rock to open, and a female camel, with its foal, to come out of it. The people clung to their unbelief, and killed the camel; but the young one escaped into the rock, which closed over it. Caravans passing through the valley even now utter loud cries to drown the noise of the camel, which is said still to lament.

33. *Mahmil* may mean the rope by which a camel's load is fastened, or the cloth that is sent annually to the Kaaba at Mecca. What it signifies here is not known. Rosenzweig does not translate the word.

34. The "Chutter" is the umbrella held over royal heads in the East in token of majesty.

35. *Sipar*, the shield or orb of the moon. When the people of Mecca demanded a sign of Mahomed, he is said to have split the moon in two. This miracle is described in the next couplet as the dividing of the *Mim*, the first letter of *Mah*, into two *Nuns*, or half-moons. *Mim*, in numerals, also represents 40, and *Nun* 50. Thus, forty is said to have been made into two fifties, by his thumb, *shast* (spelt with *sin*, and not *swad*, as in the text), which also means 60.

36. *Injil*, the gospel, is a corruption of ευαγγελιον, or Evangelium.

37. Mahomed was wounded in the lip by a stone in the battle of Bedr, but is said to have blinded his enemies by throwing at them a handful of sand, given him by the angel Gabriel.

38. The four friends were Abubakr, Umar, Usmán, and Ali.

39. The night of Power or Destiny, the 27th night of the month of Ramzán, on which the Korán is said to have been revealed. On this night Mussulmans believe that the water of the sea becomes sweet, many wonders happen, and the destiny of men for the coming year is decided.

40. That is, its darkness surpasses that of the ebon locks of the Huris of Paradise.

41. The lamp; that is, Mahomed.

42. Mumeháni was the daughter of Abu Tálib, and sister of Ali Murtuza.

43. Námus, the angel Gabriel.

44. The green peacock: that is, the earth.

45. Burák, the miraculous steed on which Mahomed took his flight to Paradise.

46. The Humá, or phœnix, the fabulous bird of fortune.

47. A quotation from the 17th Sura of the Korán.

48. The "Aksa" was the temple at Jerusalem. The hoof-marks of Burák were as round as coins or dirams.

49. The legend says the Prophet tied his steed to the door-ring of the Temple, as the old prophets used to do.

50. Imám, a high or chief priest.

51. A play on *Atárid*, Mercury, and *Atá ríz*, "gift-shedding."

52. *Zuhrah*, Venus, had the *chang*, or lute, devoted to her, and the same word, under the meaning of "claw", is embraced in the words "seized upon", or "seized with her claw".

53. The word *Aftábah*, "an ewer," is used here as a play on *Aftáb*, the sun, the ruler of the fourth heaven.

54. There is a play here on *musht*, "a handful," and *Mushtari*, Jupiter, who presided over the sixth heaven.

55. A similar play on *Zuhal*, Saturn, and *hal*, a loosing or solving.

56. The Sídrah was a tree in Paradise, on which the angel Gabriel was said to sit.

57. "The daughters of the bier" was the name given by the Arabs to the constellations of Ursa, Major and Minor.

58. "Nasr-i-Táir," the constellation of the Eagle.

59. "Nasr-i-Wáka," the falling eagle, or the Lyre.

60. The Atlas was the ninth, or highest heaven.

61. Saráfíl, the angel of death.

62. "Rafraf" is a kind of green cloth of which counterpanes and other bed-furniture are made.

63. "Arsh," the throne of God.

R

64. The "khirkah" was the tattered dress common to the Dervish, or religious mendicants.

65. This translation is doubtful.

66. Mystic utterances which the commentators do not explain.

67. This probably means that, beyond this, God alone remained.

68. "Mahrumán," literally, "those who are excluded," as from God's presence.

69. "Burd-i-Zamáni." Striped cloth, made in Zaman, is used for shrouds.

70. Táif is a town in Arabia Petræa, whence water is taken to Mecca when the latter is overcrowded with pilgrims.

71. That is, "from off our faces that had become of the colour of gold through grief."

72. The "Mehráb" is the arch in mosques towards which the Faithful turn in prayer, as towards Mecca.

73. Ubeidullah was a Coptic slave of Mahomed. Ali converted him to Islam, and the Prophet gave him his freedom.

74. Contrasting the ragged *khirkah* of the Dervish with the *kabá* or tunic of the well-to-do man.

75. *Keh*, "which," appears required after *khák*.

76. "Faghfur," Emperor of China.

77. That is, earth would be raised to heaven by the spiritual gifts he could bestow.

78. An obscure passage. Rosenzweig renders it: "If thou knowest how to plough his clean field, it is as if thou shouldst say, 'O Greatest Spirit!'" He explains the sense to be that the practice of good works is as praiseworthy as prayer.

79. From the full to the new moon, or from the moon to the fish; that is, when the moon is a crescent in the shape of a fish.

80. It is difficult to determine whether, in some of these verses, God or Mahomed is meant.

81. Conjectural translation, as no nominative case to the verbs is apparent.

82. This would appear to apply to Ubeidullah's sons.

83. Rosenzweig's edition here has *bulbul*, "the nightingale," in place of *sanbul*, "spikenard."

84. Presumably by way of divination, to ascertain who her lover would be.

85. "'Z behar-i-áïnah," in the text, should read "'z har áïnah".

86. Rosenzweig's edition has *juyán* in place of *guyán*, and *vice versâ* in line 576. These readings seem to conform better to the sense.

87. That is, those who dive for pearls.

88. Arabic, *Subhána zi 'l malak*.

89. Alluding to the habit of moths flying towards lights, and being burnt in their flames.

90. It would be better if the position of these two couplets were reversed, as in Rosenzweig's edition.

91. Here the love of God is referred to.

92. That is, the tale of the moth's love for the light, and the nightingale's for the rose.

93. That is, on the schoolmaster's black-board.

94. "Pír," or spiritual teacher.

95. That is, "when thou hast not enjoyed the love which thou canst see, thou canst not appreciate the love of God, which is still hidden from thee."

96. The form, or what is here visible to thee.

97. The "cell", or monastery of the world.

98. "Istikbál," the ceremonial meeting of anyone with honour, on his arrival at a place.

99. The Arabic words descriptive of creation, *Kun fa kána*, "Be, and it was."

100. The same letter, *Káf*, is the first letter of *kalam*, "a pen."

101. *Díbá* and *zíbá* are here played upon. A dot over one letter (*Dál*) is the only difference between them.

102. Rosenzweig's edition has *dar*, "gate," in place of *durj*, "casket". The whole passage is a very difficult one. *Suls* means the third part, and refers to the one-third of beauty left to the fair after Joseph had taken the two-thirds noted in the preceding couplet. It also means a heavy kind of writing, differing from *naskh*, and used chiefly for inscriptions on coins, etc. *Khat* means a "line" of beauty, as well as a line of writing, and *naskh* the usual type or writing, as well as destroying or obliterating. *But* is a "beauty", and, as such, an idol to worship. The whole couplet is thus a play on different words, of which the meaning cannot be conveyed in a foreign language. The general idea is that Joseph's beauty may be made supreme. The order adopted for these last three couplets is that of Rosenzweig's edition. In Rosenzweig's edition, this, and the preceding chapter, are inverted.

103. *Ruz*, "day," has been substituted for *daur*, "revolution," as in Rosenzweig's edition.

104. "Mehráb-gáh," mosque or place for the Mehrab, the world. "Rakht bast," tied on his goods, in order to march.

105. Idrís is the Enoch of the Old Testament.

106. This world is the house of fraud.

107. The play on *Idrís* and *tadrís* will be observed.

108. That is, when Noah died. The flood of destruction is used in contrast with his own flood of water.

109. The friend of God, or Abraham.

110. Literally, "his table of invitation," an allusion to Abraham's legendary hospitality.

111. Literally, "when from this plain he beat the road of non-existence"; that is, died.

112. Literally, "Joseph had the road to his soul."

113. Joseph is here compared to a rosebud, closely enfolded in its calyx.

114. Literally, "she washed his sugar (mouth) with her milk."

115. That is, he made his sister's breast take the place of the oyster that had nourished the pearl.

116. Kiblah, the place towards which the face is turned in prayer, as Christians' towards the East and Jerusalem, and Mussulmans' towards Mecca.

117. Graceful women in the East are compared with the box-tree.

118. "Inverted Nûns"; that is, eyebrows.

119. The pair of "Swáds" were the eyes, that are supposed to resemble that letter.

120. The *Mim's* ring was the mouth, and the *Aliph* the nose.

121. *Sifar*, "the cipher," or round circle of the mouth.

122. *Sin*, the teeth serrated like that letter.

123. Alluding to the tithe of property, which all the Faithful should give to the poor.

124. This line should commence with *bedu*, "with two."

125. *Kafur*, a well in Paradise, mentioned in Sura 76 of the Korán.

126. A literal translation. Rosenzweig gives the meaning that her round fist overcame the moon with its superior beauty.

127. The kings of Persia, of the Sassanide dynasty, are said to have been possessed of a golden ball so soft that it could be squeezed together in the hand. This is presumably the meaning of *dast-afshír*, the golden ball being the upper part of Zuleikha's body, just spoken of, and the silver the lower part, about to be described. It is said to have had the property of enabling its holder to read the thoughts of anyone present.

128. Rosenzweig's edition has for this line: "Like her in grace (*lutf*) none is lord of the foot;" that is, no one is possessed of stability. The present translation is conjectural.

129. That is, was not active.

130. *Bustán-sará*, the garden-house of the world.

131. The mouth, under the figure of a pistachio-nut.

132. Literally, "she rubbed a dry clod on her lip."

133. Literally, "makes a wink," *i.e.*, shows its presence.

134. Literally, "sprouting and appearance."

135. *Khisáb*, "dyeing the nails or hair," should be substituted for *khitáb*.

136. Genii and spirits, when tamed, were shut up in bottles.

137. The abode of the Anká, or phœnix, is unknown.

138. *Salámat* is substituted for *malámat*, as in Rosenzweig's edition.

139. Here "Pari" is used for "Div", an evil spirit.

140. For *dush*, read *dud-ash*.

141. That is, the rivulets from which the cypress is irrigated.

142. The Arghaván, or *Syringa Persica*, bears red flowers.

143. That is, from my leg like silver.

144. "Azíz" was also the official title of the Vazír of Egypt.

145. For *ju*, read *cheh*.

146. The alternative reading of *Shám* for *Roum* is preferable, as giving a play on *shám*, "evening," in line 1,750.

147. Literally, "was turned upside down."

148. *Khwísh* is a kind of cotton-cloth.

149. With wind in hand, *i.e.*, with nothing to grasp.

150. Literally, "those who were near."

151. It is the custom in the East to give orders on certain villages or provinces to provide for the maintenance of royal or other favoured personages.

152. Rosenzweig's edition preferably has the verb in the second person plural, as it is translated here.

153. Rosenzweig's has *khila'at*, "robe of honour," for *khilwat*.

154. "Tatár," Tartary.

155. "Kamár," Comorin.

156. Surma and six other things were considered requisite for a beauty's toilet.

157. Rosenzweig has the preferable reading, "zin dar zar giriftah."

158. Conjectural. Rosenzweig translates this: "The drum calls in friendship's tone: 'Strike, for see, the skin was already asleep'."

159. That is, the stars and night marched off together.

160. *Hudá*, the noise made by camel-drivers in urging on their beasts.

161. Descriptive of the marks left by horses' hoofs, sometimes crescent-shaped, and sometimes round, like the full moon.

162. By the rampant deer are probably meant the soldiers, attracted to the female attendants.

163. Rosenzweig's edition has an extra couplet here:
"Both king and army many a jewel threw,
And from full moon to crescent praised her, too."

164. *Diram*, a silver coin.

165. *Nárustah*, as in Rosenzweig, has been adopted here, in place of *burushtah*, "roasted," or "broiled."

166. There is a play on the word *lakht*, "torn," and *lakht*, "a moment."

167. *Haram*, "the Harem," or women's apartments.

168. *Safah-i-bár* is explained to be a house where the people have permission to come.

169. *Dar giro*, in thrall or pledge.

170. That is, upwards, downwards, forwards, backwards, right and left.

171. *Duzdídah* should be read *dar dídah*.

172. The Sidra was a tree in Paradise, on which sat Gabriel.

173. Literally, "security for our affairs and fields."

174. Literally, "their backs were broken."

175. Literally, "we are not Mussulmans."

176. The Ihrám is a garment put on by pilgrims on entering Mecca.

177. This line is Arabic.

178. *Attar*, "attar (commonly called 'otto') of roses."

179. Rizván was the porter of Paradise.

180. "The Faithful Spirit," *i.e.*, Gabriel.

181. A well at a town of that name in Transoxiana, from which Hakim bin Hasham made a false moon appear, to prove his divine mission.

182. Khisr, the guardian of the water of life.

183. The word in the original is *drahma*.

184. Literally, "twisted round upon himself."

185. The translation is conjectural.

186. Literally, "from the sign of the litter."

187. An alternate reading would be, "from which she fell unconscious."

188. Literally, "though I be wanting in merchandise."

189. A free translation, but expressive of the meaning.

190. A play on the words *duri* and *burj*.

191. Literally, "her casket of cornelian."

192. Conjectural translation. Rosenzweig's is unintelligible.

193. Literally, "without defilement of water and mud."

194. *Makna*, a woman's coif.

195. The two deer were her two eyes.

196. *Shunídastam* is a poetical form of the first person singular of the past tense indicative of *shunídan*, "to hear."

197. Here Rosenzweig's reading of "his" is adopted, in place of "thine".

198. Referring to the ripples on water from wind.

199. Literally, "behold my distress from grief, and console me".

200. *Dáná*, "wise," may be read here for *dánah*, "grain."

201. Literally, "business and seed."

202. Literally, "thou hast brought my soul to my lip."

203. Iram, the garden of Paradise.

204. A play on the word *sur*, "a wall," and *sur*, a kind of bright red rose.

205. The Zanár was a belt worn round the waist by Persian fire-worshippers to distinguish them from Mussulmans.

206. "Majasti" was the name of an old philosopher, and an astronomical work. This probably means that he drew astronomical charts and solved astronomical problems.

207. "Aklidas," Euclid.

208. For *kazá*, read *fazá*, and for *karhá*, *khánahá*, as in Rosenzweig's edition.

209. Not a literal translation.

210. *Riváj* literally means, "anything that is easily vendible."

211. Alluding to the appearance of the new moon after the fast of Ramzán.

212. The *míl* here played upon is an iron bodkin with which collyrium is applied to the eyes.

213. The meaning is very obscure.

214. The filberts here mean her finger-tips.

215. The crescents at the finger-ends above the full moon at the base of the nails. The similes are very far-fetched.

216. That is, through the transparency of the chemise.

217. The fish were the hands.

S

218. Her head was the harvest of musk.

219. The Sarsar was the hurricane mentioned in the 69th Sura of the Korán.

220. The six gates were the last six points in the game of backgammon.

221. Harem, in the sense of a sacred, secluded place.

222. By rosebud, the mouth is, of course, meant.

223. Literally, "by the Incomparable One whose form are those who are comparable."

224. Rosenzweig's reading of *masti* for *hasti* is adopted.

225. The rest of this line is purposely omitted. Similarly, a whole couplet after line 4,860.

226. That is, "I have no copper coin to change such silver."

227. That is, "tore away the Aleph from the combined letters, *lám-aleph*," or himself from her embrace.

228. Literally, "with thy people."

229. *Rást* means both the right side, and morally right.

230. Literally, "a witness without witnesses."

231. *Dayusí* is adopted for *bad-khui*, as in Rosenzweig.

232. A play on the word *Shírín*, which may mean "sweet", or may be taken as the name of the Queen of Khusro Parvíz, who built a celebrated castle for him.

233. *Luzínah*, or *luzanj*, "a sweetmeat," whence is derived our word lozenge.

234. A line of obscure meaning. *Ba Hashush* may be the plural of *hash*, "gardens," with the preposition *bah*. Or the word may be *hasho*, said by the commentators to mean a profitless word. The couplet is translated by Rosenzweig: "Yet, when they sweetened their palates like lozenges, they filled their mouths with them." The translation here given is quite conjectural.

235. This strange couplet does not appear in some MSS.

236. The first word should be *be zar-kash*.

237. The play upon the word *juft*, in these couplets, is so complicated that it is difficult to understand what is meant.

238. *Khunkh 'áragi* is, literally, "blood-drinking."

239. For *duz*, read *dur*.

240. Different postures adopted by Mussulmans in prayer.

241. The Muazzin is the crier who, from his minaret, calls the Faithful to prayer.

242. Literally, "in season and out of season."

243. By "the carpet" is metaphorically meant the wife of the house.

244. The *farsang* is a Persian land-measure.

245. The *Madd* is a kind of circumflex accent placed over *Ah*, the Persian word for "sigh". It is here likened to smoke, or a black tent, or a sunshade.

246. A play on the words *khun-áb* and *khun-i-náb*.

247. This is a literal translation, but the meaning is obscure. Rosenzweig seems to have considered it an allusion to the Hindoos using white as a sign of mourning, in place of black.

248. The word for "Virgo", in Persian, means "ears of corn"; and that for "the Milky Way", the "thief", or "drawer of straw".

249. There is a play here on *Suhail*, "Canopus," and *suhail*, "a horse's neigh."

250. Literally, "two moments not at rest."

251. That is, Abraham.

252. For *mará kh'ákhi*, in this line, Rosenzweig has *'z ná khákhi*. The former may mean, "If thou desire (to come to) me," and the latter, "In place of absence of will." Neither has been taken in the translation.

253. This is a doubtful translation.

254. Rosenzweig's reading is adopted as preferable.

255. The saddle of the bier.

256. In the original, "that lion-like woman."

257. *Rahmi*, as in Rosenzweig, is preferable to *Zakhmi* here.

258. *Tábish* is preferable to *nábish*.

259. *Mehr*, meaning "sun", as well as "love". There is a play on the words.

260. Blue is the mourning colour among Mussulmans.

261. Literally, "the Frank eye."

262. By *Sin* is meant the teeth, and, by *Mim*, the mouth, as already shown. *Lub* is "narrow", as well as *lab*, "lip"; and *lim* and *be* represent respectively 30 and 2, the number of the teeth.

263. The Habbah is a small coin. The meaning of the passage is, "Neither borrow nor lend." The quotation in the second line is Arabic.

264. A friend of the cave, an intimate friend. A name of Abubakr, stepfather of Mahomet, who hid with him in a cave in flight from his enemies.

265. A play on *nán*, "one loaf," and *du nán*, "two loaves," or "the vile".

266. *Dunán*, as in Rosenzweig, is preferable to *durán*.

267. The traveller on God's road.

268. *Paf*, in place of *taf*, as in Rosenzweig, is preferable.

269. The quotation is Arabic.

270. The negative, as in Rosenzweig, is preferable to the affirmative in this line.

271. Literally, "is thorns on thorns."

272. That is, in round numbers only.

www.ingramcontent.com/pod-product-compliance
Lightning Source LLC
Chambersburg PA
CBHW032144230426
43672CB00011B/2445